Designing with JavaScript
Creating Dynamic Web Pages

Designing with JavaScript
Creating Dynamic Web Pages

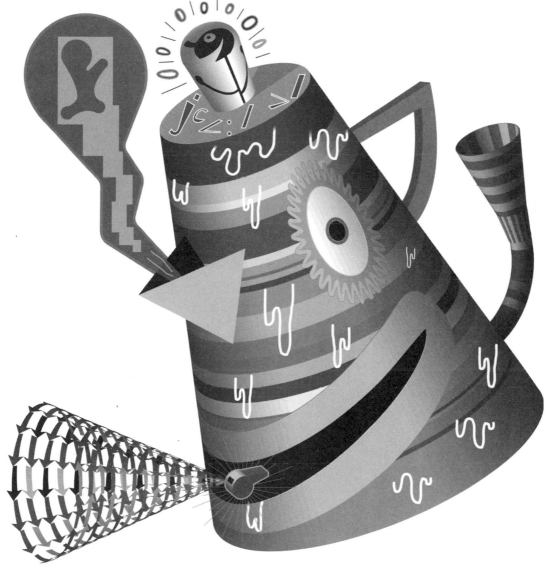

Nick Heinle

W e b   R e v i e w   S t u d i o   S e r i e s

Designing with JavaScript: Creating Dynamic Web Pages
First Edition
By Nick Heinle

Published by Songline Studios, Inc. and O'Reilly & Associates, Inc.
101 Morris Street, Sebastopol, CA 95472

Printing History: September 1997: First Edition.
October 1997: Second Printing.
December 1997: Third Printing.

Edited by Richard Koman

Cover Illustration by John Hersey

ISBN: 1-56592-300-6

Contents

Foreword

By David Siegel, Studio Verso

The fact that you are reading this book says you're a member of the avant garde — the people who push the Web and lead the way into the future. Documents are becoming applications. To others, this may come as a surprise, but you know it to be true. Since the day someone put the first "submit" button on the first Web page, the nature of Web was not "electronic paper," but something much more. In the hands of the unimaginative, Web sites are brochure-ware. In the hands of a skilled designer working with a technologist, a Web site comes alive, offering to do much more than static paper can.

This book is a power tool. Use it well, and you will be part of the next generation of digital designers to harness the power of the Web and bring it to users around the world. Use it for its own sake, and you will be among the embossed-lozenge rotators, happily spinning logos, ringing bells, and tooting your own horn, much to the dismay of overwhelmed visitors. Use it subtly and people will feel like they are in a special, magical place where things seem to respond naturally to their every movement. Use it to bring out your content, not to overshadow what you are trying to say.

This book is remarkable not just because Nick Heinle is a good writer and knows as much about JavaScript as anyone on the planet, but also because Nick Heinle is 17 years old. At my studio, where we pride ourselves on producing some of the best HTML in the world, we use Nick's scripts all the time.

Nick is a member of what I call the digerini — the kids sucking the digital world down so fast it makes my Stanford education look like a HyperCard stack on a Mac Plus. He doesn't know anything about convergence — for him, everything has already naturally converged. This is why we should read what he has to say, not just for what he says but how he says it. Nick knows how to make Web pages do things.

Perhaps the most important lesson we can learn is his attitude — he won't settle for what he's given. He constantly tries to invent new ways to get what he wants. Read between the lines and you'll learn about Nick Heinle, the person, the problem-solver, the kid whose future is so bright, he has to wear shades. Maybe some will rub off on you.

David Siegel is principal of Studio Verso (http://www.verso.com) *and author of* Creating Killer Web Sites *(1996, Hayden).*

Preface

In the beginning there was HTML, and it was good. HTML
allowed Web authors to create structured, laid out pages, with
images, text, and the like. HTML was — and is — a good tool for
displaying static information in a comprehensible and often visually
appealing manner. But Web authors soon realized that HTML was
not enough. As the Web grew in popularity, it needed interactivity
and instant feedback. Static HTML was not enough anymore.

A solution to some of the problems and limitations of static
HTML came in December 1995 from Netscape Communications
Corp., and its name was JavaScript (originally deemed LiveScript,
but changed for marketing reasons). JavaScript was designed to be
a simple, effective, scripting language for the Web, and it tied
closely with HTML. Unlike other programming languages at
that time — such as client-side Java and server-side C, C++ and
Perl — JavaScript was built directly into the browser and worked
alongside HTML.

Why JavaScript is important

HTML is a language with the sole purpose of laying out and
formatting text and images. The purpose of JavaScript is to add
some interactivity to HTML, to allow for user interaction and
feedback, multimedia and animation, and to link HTML to other
technologies such as Java, ActiveX, and even plug-ins.

Major aspects

Throughout this book, you'll become familiar with the different
parts of JavaScript, and you'll see why these parts are important
and how they can be used as a whole to create more interesting

and exciting Web sites. The following list of some of the major aspects of JavaScript explains why the language is so important to Web development:

- With *event handlers,* JavaScript can catch events that occur on a page, such as the clicking of a form button or the mouse moving over a link. JavaScript's event handlers can then execute code in response to these actions.
- With the *document object model,* JavaScript has the ability to control HTML-defined objects, such as forms, frames and layers of content. The document object model defines which objects on a Web page JavaScript can control, and how JavaScript can control them. As you'll discover, the document object model has progressed over several generations of JavaScript-enabled browsers (though this progression has caused some compatibility problems).

    With the advent of Dynamic HTML (Chapter 9), JavaScript's object model has complete control over every object on the page, allowing JavaScript to be used in the creation of powerful Web based multimedia applications.
- *Non-HTML objects* give JavaScript access to parts of the browser that are not related to the HTML in Web pages. With non-HTML objects, JavaScript can determine which browser is being used, which platform the browser is running on, and in Netscape Navigator, even which plugins are installed in the browser (Chapter 6). Non-HTML objects also give JavaScript access to browser cookies (Chapter 8), giving JavaScript the ability to store information, though with some limitations, over a long period of time.

Most importantly, JavaScript exists because it's a language for the people. And as you'll learn throughout this book, JavaScript doesn't require a computer science degree to master it; it allows designers as well as programmers to use the language in creating Web sites. *That's* why JavaScript is important.

Issues and problems

Even though it is widely used, JavaScript has its fair share of problems. The fact that it keeps evolving in form and function from one browser to the next creates compatibility problems. For example, the dynamic images discussed in Chapter 7 are not supported in the original version of JavaScript (version 1.0) that came with Navigator 2.0. Therefore, scripts like this that use newer features need to be written around older browsers.

Another ever-present issue with JavaScript is that scripts often behave differently in Internet Explorer than they do in Navigator (see Appendix C); this is, of course, because Microsoft had to reverse-engineer its implementation of JavaScript, called Jscript. More significantly, this problem occurred because there was no original JavaScript standard for anybody to follow.

In June 1997, however, the European Computer Manufacturers Association (ECMA) finally decided upon a standard for JavaScript. Unfortunately, it will be a while before both companies release browsers with JavaScript implementations that completely adhere to this standard.

What do I know about JavaScript?

Back in April of 1996 I launched a Web site called *JavaScript Tip of the Week* to help the denizens of the Web learn about this fledgling scripting language. I began with limited knowledge of the subject myself; when I began the tips and techniques that I talked about on the site were ones that I had only recently applied to my own creations. I was learning as I was teaching and because of this, I think I was able to give explanations about my code that made sense to just about everybody.

Back to my story. Little did I know how popular *JavaScript Tip of the Week* would become, and how interested Web developers would be in this new language and what it could accomplish. Clearly, Web developers recognized that it was an important part of their future. So for eight months, I faithfully put up weekly tips every Monday evening. Then, on a fateful day in late October of 1996, I received this email:

> From: Richard Koman <rkoman@webreview.com>
> Subject: write a book?
>
> Hi, I'm really impressed with this site. I'd like to talk to you about possibly writing a javascript book for o'reilly. Email if you're interested to: rkoman@webreview.com

Since you're reading this book, you can tell what my reply was.

JavaScript Tip of the Week

The demands of writing a book necessarily curtailed my ability to produce *JavaScript Tip of the Week*, although I have been producing a biweekly column called "WebCoder" for *Web Review* for some time. You can still read the JSTotW columns at *http://webcoder.com/tip/*. Now that I've finished writing the book, I'm actively building what I hope will be the definitive place for learning about JavaScript and other client-side scripting languages. It's called *webcoder.com* (that's also the URL).

I wrote this book in the hopes that it will give people what they want while teaching them what they need to know. More specifically, this book attempts to give useful, sought-after examples of JavaScript in action while teaching the concepts and syntax of JavaScript. This book is written for designers and programmers alike, though it may appeal to designers and non-programmers more than most JavaScript books because of its practical, real-world applications.

My real hope for this book is that it will make the Web more interesting. There are many talented Web authors out there, and the greater part of them have yet to discover JavaScript. But when they finally do, the results are always interesting. People who have only just discovered JavaScript often email me with great examples that they put together themselves — examples that I'd never thought of, examples that were just plain cool.

Email Nick

Nick's email address is
nick@webcoder.com

To my delight, many of them started their adventures with JavaScript on my site, JavaScript Tip of the Week. And that's why this book exists. It's a starting point for JavaScript; it's a place to begin, a place to learn, and a place to mature. Of course, it is only a book ….

Acknowledgments

I'd like to thank:

- All the JavaScripting denizens of the Web for visiting my site, reading my material, and giving me original and inspired ideas
- Andy King and Bob Peyser of webreference.com for giving me their server space and a special place on their site for those eight months JTotW was at its best.
- Richard Koman, my editor, for sending me that fateful email and taking a chance on me.
- My family — my mother, father, brother, and dog — for encouraging my interest in programming and writing and supporting (putting up with) me throughout this whole ordeal.

Nick Heinle
August 1997

1

Diving into JavaScript

If you've read other JavaScript books, you may have had to slog through pages and pages about functions, methods, operands, and so on, before you ever learned how to write even the simplest script. As you get into JavaScript, you'll need to understand those concepts and more, but you can start spiffing up your Web pages by just diving into JavaScript.

That's what this chapter is about. By the time you've finished with this chapter, you'll know two handy scripts. More importantly, you'll understand why the scripts do what they do and you'll be ready to wade into JavaScript a little deeper.

With these scripts you'll be able to:

- Add descriptive comments in the status bar;
- Use the time to serve custom pages.

The concepts we'll cover in this chapter include:

- event handlers;
- working with objects;
- writing to a document;
- *if* statements.

Adding descriptive links

Did you ever wish links could talk? In other words, wouldn't it be helpful to tell users what to expect if they click on a link? You can do this easily with JavaScript.

Figure 1-1 shows the table of contents for my Web site, *The Manhattan Project*, located at *http://www.gis.net/~carter/ manhttan/project.html*. Each graphic on the right-hand side of the page links to a different part of the site. The graphics themselves don't tell you much about the contents of each section. When the user moves the mouse over the link, however, a small description of the link is displayed in the browser's status bar. If the descriptions are well written, they'll add useful context to the site. Here, putting the mouse over the "Who's Who" graphic displays "biographies of important scientists involved in the Manhattan Project" in the status bar. (In addition, the "Who's Who" text turns

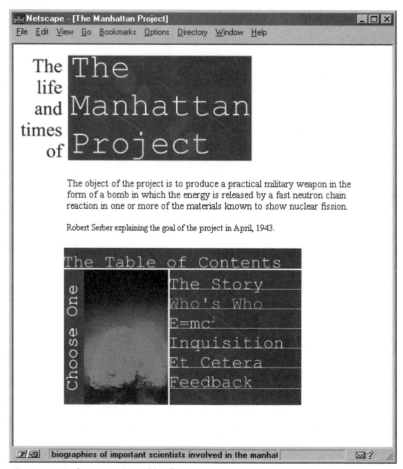

Figure 1-1. Manhattan Project Table of Contents
http://www.gis.net/~carter/manhattan/project.html

```
<A HREF = "thequiz.html" onMouseOver = "window.status = 'Biographies of important
scientists involved in the Manhattan Project'; return true;">
<IMG WIDTH = 167 HEIGHT = 25 BORDER = 0 SRC = "thequiz.gif"></A>
```

Figure 1-2. Code for adding status bar text to an HREF link.

yellow; that little trick makes use of JavaScript's dynamic images
function, described in depth in Chapter 6, *Dynamic Images*.)

This is really quite simple to do. Figure 1-2 shows the code
for the "Who's Who" link:

The event

This looks like a normal link, but it's obviously a little different.
Inside the *HREF* tag, there is a small piece of JavaScript code. The
code starts (and the HTML ends) with *onMouseOver*; this is one of
JavaScript's built-in *event handlers*. An event handler is code that
runs when an event occurs. What's an event? It's something that
happens, such as the user placing the mouse over a link or a page
loading. In this case, we're dealing with the *onMouseOver* event,
which occurs when the mouse moves over the link.

Table 1-1 shows some of the other common event handlers
supported by JavaScript.

The amazing event handlers

Event handlers can be used in many elements of the page, including links, form buttons,
and client-side image maps. This table lists some common event handlers, the tags where
they can be used, and what events they handle.

Event name	Where it goes	When it works
onMouseOver	Links, Image maps	When mouse moves over a link
onMouseOut	Links, Image maps	When mouse moves out of a link**
onChange	Select Menu	When an option is selected*
onLoad	Body, Frameset, Image	When the document is done loading
onUnload	Body, Frameset	When the document is exited

* In Netscape 2.x, you must first click outside the Select Menu for it to change.
** Only implemented in Netscape 3 and greater.

Table 1-1. Common event handlers supported by JavaScript.

The code that follows *onMouseOver* runs when the event occurs (here, when the mouse moves over the link). Combining the event handler with some useful code gives you a link that does something when the mouse moves over it. In this case, the code displays the description of the link in the browser's status bar.

It is important to note that *onMouseOver* is followed by an equal sign. The equal sign says, "When *onMouseOver* occurs, do the following ..." The code that follows must be surrounded by double quotes so the handler knows which code to run (all the code in quotes, and nothing else).

Applying it to your links

Now that you know how to use *onMouseOver*, it's time to learn about the code that follows it. This code is enclosed in quotes; in this example it starts with *window.status*.

This code tells the browser's status bar (*window.status*, as JavaScript knows it) to display the text " biographies of important scientists involved with the Manhattan Project."

```
"window.status = ' biographies of important scientists
involved in the Manhattan Project '; return true;"
```

There are a few things to notice here. First, the text to be displayed is enclosed in single quotes. That's because the description occurs inside of the quoted JavaScript string. If you used double quotes for the link description, the JavaScript interpreter would think that the JavaScript code ended with the second double-quote character. Whenever you're *nesting* a string inside another string, you must alternate between single and double quotes.

Next, note the semicolon after the description. Get used to this; virtually every line of JavaScript ends in a semicolon.

So far so good, but why are the words *return true* at the end of this code? For now, it's enough to know that it's required. If those words weren't there, the description wouldn't be displayed in the status bar. We'll discuss this *return* feature in a number of scripts later in the book.

Night and day

Now it's time to make your first real script; this involves learning some new concepts. If you're not familiar with programming (in

Pesky details

If you have an apostrophe inside single quotes, you must place a slash [\] directly before it. Again, this is to avoid confusion, since an apostrophe is the same character as a single quote. You wouldn't believe how many people make this mistake.

Designing with JavaScript

C, C++, VB, Pascal, or whatever), this script is for you. While the last example did incorporate JavaScript, it was more like an enhanced *HREF* tag than an actual script. This example is more involved.

If we assume that people's interests vary according to the time of day, your Web site might be well served by promoting different kinds of content depending on whether it's day or night. For instance, a March 1997 issue of *Web Review* had articles on repetitive stress injuries and the Hale-Bopp comet. Why not promote the work-oriented RSI article to daytime users and the fun comet article to nighttime users? Figures 1-3 and 1-4 show what these two pages might look like.

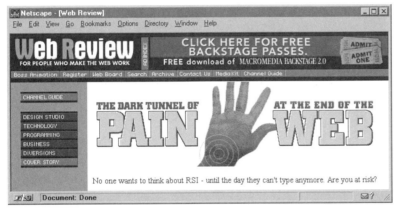

Figure 1-3. The "day" page.

Figure 1-4. The "night" page.

How is this done with JavaScript? Basically, the script checks the time and then delivers either the daytime or nighttime HTML. We're going to cover a number of concepts in this little script:

- the *Date* and *document* objects
- properties and methods
- variables
- *if* statements

Figure 1-5 shows the code for this temporally shifting page.

The amazing *SCRIPT* tag

All scripts start and end with one common element: the *SCRIPT* tag. The HTML document in Figure 1-5 is basically one big *SCRIPT* tag; there's no content in the body of the document other than the *SCRIPT* tag.

The browser considers everything within the *SCRIPT* tag to be pure JavaScript and nothing else. This is where most of your scripts will reside. The *SCRIPT* tags can be placed anywhere inside an HTML document: in the head or in the body. In this case, the *SCRIPT* tag is placed where the script does its work (printing out a page) — in the body. In other scripts, you'll see functions defined in the head of the document and called from *SCRIPT* tags placed all over the page.

You may be asking yourself, "Why is there a *LANGUAGE* option in the *SCRIPT* tag?" That's because JavaScript is not the only Web scripting language. VBScript, which is a scripting language based on the Visual Basic programming language, can also be used. But so far, VBScript is only supported in Internet Explorer, limiting its practical use.

The *Date* object

The first part of the Night and Day script detects the time of day, using your system clock. It does this using the *Date* object, which is built right into JavaScript.

In this script, the first line Ⓐ simply creates a new *Date* object and gives it the name *now*. From this point on, the current date and time can be referred to as *now*. Next Ⓑ the script says, "Take *now* (the current date and time), ask it for the current hour, and put the answer into a variable called *hour*."

Now that you have the current hour, you need to do something with it. This script's whole purpose is to use that

```
<HTML>
<HEAD>
<TITLE>Night and Day Script</TITLE>
</HEAD>
<BODY>
<SCRIPT LANGUAGE = "JavaScript">
<! --
(A) var now = new Date( );
(B) var hour = now.getHours( );
(C) if (hour > 4 && hour < 18) {
(D) document.bgColor = "#FFFFFF";
(E) document.fgColor = "#000000";
(F) document.write ("<CENTER><IMG HEIGHT = 150 WIDTH = 515
    SRC = '/97/03/07/feature/graphics/head-pain.gif'>");
(G) document.write ("<P>No one wants to think about RSI - until the day they
    can't type anymore.
    Are you at risk?</CENTER>");
    }
(H) else {
(I) document.bgColor = "#000000";
(J) document.fgColor = "#FFFFFF";
(K) document.write ("<CENTER><IMG HEIGHT = 144 WIDTH = 515
    SRC = '/97/03/07/hour/graphics/head-comet.jpg'>");
(L) document.write ("<P>Is it the End of the World or just a great light show?
    Find out online. </CENTER>");
    }
    // -->
</SCRIPT>
</BODY>
</HTML>
```

Figure 1-5. The Night and Day script.

information to display (or "print" in programmer's parlance)
a page accordingly.

Displaying the page

This brings us to one of the most useful applications of
JavaScript: the ability to "print" HTML directly onto a Web page.
This is done with a function called *document.write( )*. (F) (G)

```
document.write ("<P>No one wants to think about RSI -
until the day they can't type anymore. Are you at risk?");
```

Everything between the double quotes in *document.write( )* is printed onto the page. The above example starts a new paragraph and displays some text. You can display images (and any other HTML content) in the same way:

```
document.write ("<CENTER><IMG HEIGHT = 150 WIDTH =
515 SRC = '/97/03/07/feature/graphics/head-pain.gif'>");
```

This displays the image file *head-pain.gif* directly on the page.

Putting it all together: The *if* statement

You now have two pieces of knowledge: how to get the current time in hours and how to print out the page. But how do you combine the two? By using something called *if* statements. *If* statements use a very simple concept, one of the first concepts that human beings learn: *"If* this happens, then do that." In JavaScript, if statements look like this:

```
if ( this is the case ) { then run this code }
```

It looks like fractured English, but there is a method to this madness. All *if* statements consist of the word *if* followed by a statement in parentheses and a block of code in braces. The parentheses contain the condition that is being checked. The braces contain the code that will run if the condition is met.

In this script we're checking the hour and displaying the appropriate graphic and promotional text. If the hour is between 4 am and 6 pm (hours are specified with a 24-hour clock), we'll serve the RSI page; if it's between 6 pm and 4 am, we'll serve the comet page. Here is a simplified version of the code:

```
if (hour > 4 && hour < 18) {
document.write ('<P>RSI - Are you at risk?');
}

else {
document.write ('<P>Is it the End of the World?');
}
```

The first line says, if the value of the variable *hour* is greater than 4 and less than 18, then run the code in braces. You probably remember the greater than (>) and less than (<) signs from some basic math class; the double (*&&*) ampersands mean "and."

What happens if it's 7 pm? Since we weren't testing for this time, the *else* statement applies. With *else,* we're saying, "If the

Designing with JavaScript

condition isn't true, then do this instead." If it's 7 pm, then it's not between 4 am and 6 pm, so the script runs the code following the word *else*. In this example, the code simply prints out "Is it the End of the World?"

Now that we've conquered the logic of *if* and *else,* let's look at the actual code for these pages. Notice that not only the graphics and text are different, but also the background color and the text color.

If the hours are between 4 and 18, the script changes the background color **D** to white, the text color **E** to black, displays the graphic *head-pain.gif,* **F** and writes the text "No one wants to think about RSI ..." **G** If the hours are not between 4 and 18, the *else* statement **H** tells the script to change the background color **I** to black, the text color **J** to white, display the graphic *head-comet.jpg,* **K** and write the text "Is it the End of the World ..." **L**

Changing the colors involves two new properties. The background color is changed by assigning a hexadecimal color to a property called *document.bgColor*; the text color is changed with the *document.fgColor.* The background color can be changed on the fly, at any time during the document's existence. The property for the text color can only be changed when the document is initially displayed.

We'll learn how to change colors and appearances of text on the fly in Chapter 9, *Dynamic HTML.*

What else can you do with the date?

In the Night and Day script, you work with the time in hours. Of course JavaScript lets you access all the parts of the date and time. But the syntax isn't exactly plain English. Table 1-2 shows how to get the various parts of the date and the form in which they're returned.

Keep in mind that when you get times and dates from JavaScript they are returned as numbers, not words. This means that if you ask a *Date* object for the day of the week using *getDay( )*, you will get a number 0 through 6, not Sunday or Monday. Though numbers are useful for database applications and the like, you may want to put them in a more digestible form. For example, you can create a script that uses *if* statements (in combination with *getDay( )*) to translate the numeric values to their actual names as shown in Figure 1-6.

Getting the time from JavaScript

Unit of time	How to get it	How to use it
Second	*second = now.getSeconds();*	The time in seconds is returned as a number 0 through 59.
Minute	*minute = now.getMinutes();*	The time in minutes is returned as a number 0 through 59.
Hour	*hour = now.getHours()*	The time in hours is returned as a number 0 through 23.
Day	*day = now.getDay();*	The day of the week is returned as a number 0 (Sunday) through 6 (Saturday).
Month	*month = now.getMonth();*	The month of the year is returned as a number 0 (January) through 11 (December).
Year	*year = now.getYear();*	The year is returned as a number 0 through 99. This format stays the same until you reach the year 2000. When the year 2000 is reached, instead of being returned as a 2-digit number, the year is returned as a four-digit number, e.g. 2020.

Table 1-2.

```
A  var now = new Date( );
B  var day = now.getDay( );
C  var dayname;
D      if (day == 0) dayname = "Sunday";
E      if (day == 1) dayname = "Monday";
F      if (day == 2) dayname = "Tuesday";
G      if (day == 3) dayname = "Wednesday";
H      if (day == 4) dayname = "Thursday";
I      if (day == 5) dayname = "Friday";
J      if (day == 6) dayname = "Saturday";
K  document.write("Today is " + dayname + ". <BR>");
```

Figure 1-6. Connecting number values to day names.

So how does this work? First, a new *Date* object named *now* Ⓐ is created and the day of the week, which is in number form, is given to a variable named *day*. Ⓑ Then a series of *if* statements match up the number of the day with the day's full name and store the name in the variable *dayname*. Ⓒ For example, if *day* is 0 Ⓓ then it must be Sunday, if *day* is 1 Ⓔ then it must be Monday, etc. Finally, the day's full name, in variable *dayname*, is displayed on the page using *document.write( )*. Ⓚ

Hiding JavaScript from old browsers

The only problem with putting a script in a Web page is that older browsers (such as Mosaic, Lynx, etc.) will see all of the code that you include and display it in the Web page as normal text. But there is a simple way to get around this: good old HTML comments.

```
<SCRIPT LANGUAGE = "JavaScript">
<!-- hide me from antiquated technology
JavaScript Code
// stop hiding me -->
</SCRIPT>
```

Everything between HTML comments will be ignored by older browsers. These types of comments can only be used at the beginning and the end of the script. It's important to put these comments on their own lines. If you put them on the same line as code, that line will be commented out and the script won't work.

Notice the use of // at the end of the HTML comments; this is what's known as a *code comment*. Code comments hide text and other information from the script. They can be used to contain notes or other information about a line of code right in the script. There are two types of code comments: // (I like to call them one-liners) and /* */. One-liners, which originate from C++ comments, simply hide the rest of the line. The other type of comments, /* */, come from C, and can be used to hide whole blocks of text:

```
<SCRIPT LANGUAGE = "JavaScript">
<!-- hide me from antiquated technology
JavaScript Code
/* This is a block comment; the script
   will ignore all of this text */

More JavaScript Code     //Here is another comment, just a one-liner

// stop hiding me -->
```

Objects, properties and methods

There are millions of "objects" in the real world: trees, telephones, people... almost everything we deal with is an object. One could say that we live in an object-oriented world. Because of this, programming languages, such as Java and C++, are object-oriented as well. JavaScript is supposed to be an object-oriented language, but it lacks many principals of object-oriented programming as most programmers will tell you. Regardless, you should treat JavaScript as an object-oriented langauge.

In JavaScript, there are a large number of objects, the greater part of which will be discussed in this book. For example, the page is an object: *document*. The (browser) window is an object as well: *window*. Another one we encountered in this chapter is *Date,* which refers to the date and time showing on the user's computer.

In JavaScript we can do things not only to objects but to their properties. For instance, in our first script, the status bar is a property of the *window* object and this is referred to as *window.status.*

To understand how this works, it's helpful to relate it to real life. Let's be a little abstract and think of your car in terms of JavaScript. First of all, let's create a new *car* object, which we'll call *mycar.*

```
var mycar = new Car();
```

You saw this syntax in the "Night and Day" script, when we created a new *Date* object. Now we can begin to manipulate the *mycar* object, and in the process learn a few things about object-oriented programming.

The property concept

Your car has many different properties: color, brand, horsepower and price, to name a few. What if you want to paint your car red? In JavaScript terms, you would change the color property of your car to red, like so:

```
mycar.color = "red";
```

Your car object, *mycar*, is separated from its property, *color*, by a dot. This is the equivalent of saying, "the *color* of *mycar.*" After you have referred to your car's color property in this way, you can then do something with that property.

In this example, the *color* property of *mycar* is set to "red" using an equal sign. This is like finishing the sentence, "I want the *color* of *mycar*... to be *red.*"

To apply this to JavaScript, let's introduce a property of the *window* object: *location*. Simply put, the *location* property controls the location of the window, i.e. the file that is currently being displayed. The following code, for example, takes the (browser) window to a document located at *http://www.yahoo.com*:

```
window.location = "http://www.yahoo.com";
```

Just as color is a property of your car, *location* is a property of the browser window. To change the location of the window, use the same syntax as you did before, separating the *window* object from its *location* property with a dot (and setting the combination to a value).

Methods to the madness

With properties, you can change certain attributes of your objects, but to do more with JavaScript we have to use methods and functions. Methods, like functions, are used to "act" on JavaScript objects. The difference is that methods are directly associated with an object.

Think about it in terms of your car again: *mycar*. In addition to having properties, your car has actions that you can do to it, such as accelerate, brake, and honk. These actions, when associated with the car object, are referred to as methods. To accelerate your car object, you could run its accelerate method:

```
mycar.accelerate( );
```

This looks like a property but with one important difference; those parentheses indicate that this is a method. A more useful *accelerate( )* method would allow you to tell the car object by how much you want to accelerate. Perhaps you could pass it the speed in mph.

```
mycar.accelerate(15);
```

This would accelerate the car by 15 mph.

In the Night and Day script, we use the *document.write( )* method to display some HTML on the page. You always pass the *document.write( )* method a value, as you did with *mycar.accelerate( )*. The value that you pass *document.write( )*, most likely some text or HTML, is displayed on the page.

```
document.write ("<P>No one wants to think about RSI - until the day they can't type anymore. Are you at risk?</CENTER>");
```

There are a multitude of objects in JavaScript, and therefore a multitude of methods as well. Even variables can have methods, as you will see later on.

If you do this for each unit of time, day, month, date, and year (e.g. Friday, January 1, 1999), you can create a script that displays the fully formatted date on the page. The best way to do this involves arrays, something you'll learn more about later in the book. If you're curious, see "Doing the date right," in Chapter 5, *Getting in Line with Arrays*.

Time shifts

The *Date* object is not limited to the current time; you can also create a *Date* object for a specific date in the past or the future. For example, to create a new *Date* object for July 4, 1998, either of the following ways would be acceptable:

```
var then = new Date("July 4, 1998");
var then = new Date("July 4, 1998 00:00:00");
```

The JavaScript tree

The document and its *bgColor* property are separated by a period. Thus, *document.bgColor* refers to the background color property of the document. That seems simple enough, but what do you make of this?

```
document.mailform.address.value
```

That refers to the value of the address element of a form called *mailform,* which is in the document. It makes a little more sense if you think about it like a tree.

In general, JavaScript organizes all of the parts of the browser window and all of the elements (e.g. forms, images) on a page like a tree. First there's a main object (the trunk), then there are objects off of the main object (branches), and finally there are methods and properties off of those objects (leaves). Technically this is referred to as the "document object model," but this is an easier way to think about it.

The main object, the trunk, is always the current browser window, referred to as *window*. There are many branches off of the browser window: the page currently displayed in the

```
Ⓐ  var now = new Date( );
Ⓑ  var then = new Date("July 4, 1998");
Ⓒ  var gap = then.getTime( ) - now.getTime( );
Ⓓ  gap = Math.floor(gap / (1000 * 60 * 60 * 24));
Ⓔ  document.write ("Only " + gap + " days  \'till the Fourth of July");
```

Figure 1-7. How long until July 4?

Notice that you are passing your new *Date* object a specific date.
This feature is commonly used to create countdowns to times or
dates such as anniversaries, product launches, etc. So, if you
need a script that will display the number of days between now
and the Fourth of July, create a *Date* object for now, a *Date* object

window, called *document*, the current location of the window, called *location*, and the history
(all of the visited pages) of the window, *history*. Inside each of these branches, you'll find more
objects. For example, the *document* object contains all of the elements on a given page: forms,
images, applets, even plug-ins are reflected as objects. To illustrate this concept, here is a
small "slice" of the JavaScript tree.

As you can see, the tree begins with the browser window and branches off from there
(this is by no means the complete JavaScript tree, which would take up about 20 pages). So,
whenever you want to access something in the JavaScript tree, you have to "climb" up to it. To
better understand this, let's create our own example of "climbing the tree" using forms. Here's
the HTML document that we will be working with:

```
<HTML>
<BODY>
<FORM NAME = "branch">
<INPUT TYPE = "text" NAME = "leaf">
</FORM>
</BODY>
</HTML>
```

The names of the form and text input as defined in their HTML tags correspond to the names
used by JavaScript. Here we have a form named *branch* and a text input field named *leaf*. To
get the text entered by the user, you need to ask for the *value* of *leaf*. That's the *value* of *leaf* in
form *branch* in the document in the window:

```
window.document.branch.leaf.value;
```

for then, and subtract to find the difference. The 5-line script in Figure 1-7 shows you how to do it.

First the script creates a new *Date* object named **Ⓐ** *now* for the current time and one named **Ⓑ** *then* for the Fourth of July. The current date, *now.getTime( )*, is then subtracted from the Fourth of July's date, *then.getTime( )*, and the resulting value (the remaining time between the two dates) is given to variable **Ⓒ** *gap*. So we have the difference in time between now and the Fourth of July in variable *gap*, but there's a problem: it's in milliseconds. We need to convert milliseconds to days. This is accomplished **Ⓓ** by dividing *gap* by the number of milliseconds in a day (1000 milliseconds x 60 seconds x 60 minutes x 24 hours): *gap / (1000 * 60 * 60 * 24)*. After being rounded, the difference in time, which is now in days, is displayed on the page **Ⓔ** with *document.write( )*.

2 Doing Windows

In this chapter

- Changing a window's location and history
- Launching new windows
- Creating a remote control
- Writing functions

Everything that happens on a page takes place in a window. This chapter will teach you how to control, create, and communicate with windows. You can control their location and history as well as create new windows of various sizes and with various elements. And, most powerfully, your windows can talk to one another. Remote controls and floating toolbars — which you'll learn in this chapter — are just the beginning.

The basics

Let's start with some simple window controls. In this section, we'll change the URL the window displays and create links for moving back and forward in the user's history.

Changing the window's location

The simplest example of manipulating a window with JavaScript is to load a new page in the current window. Figure 2-1 shows the code for this.

Web surfers usually think in terms of going to a different page or moving from site to site. Of course this is metaphorical: Your browser isn't going anywhere; rather a different page is being

```
<SCRIPT LANGUAGE = "JavaScript">
<!--
window.location = "http://www.yahoo.com/";
//-->
</SCRIPT>
```

Figure 2-1. Script for loading a new page in the current window.

```
 Go to Page 

<FORM>
<INPUT TYPE = "BUTTON" VALUE = "Go to Page">
</FORM>
```

Figure 2-2. Code for creating a button in an HTML form.

loaded into the browser. Thus, in JavaScript, you can change the current URL by changing the *location* property of the current window. Just as *color* is a property of your car, *location* is a property of a window.

The name of the current window — the one where the script resides — goes by the name of *window*. (Actually, it doesn't need to be known as *window*; it can also be referred to as *self*.) When you say *window.location*, you are referring to the *location* property of the current window. This property determines which file the current window will display. Here the window will display Yahoo's home page.

Changing locations with forms

Let's make this a little more useful. How about creating a form button that loads a new page when you click on it? We haven't yet dealt with forms and JavaScript but, assuming you know the basics of creating forms in HTML, this should be a breeze. First create the form. Figure 2-2 shows the code for creating a simple button.

Now you have a simple form button, but how do you connect it to the script? In Chapter 1 you learned about event handlers: little statements that "catch" an event and then "handle" it. In this scenario, you want to load a different page when the form button

```
<FORM>
<INPUT
 TYPE = "BUTTON"
 VALUE = "Go to Page"
 onClick = "window.location = 'page.html';">
</FORM>
```

Figure 2-3. Code for loading a new page when the form button is clicked on.

Designing with JavaScript

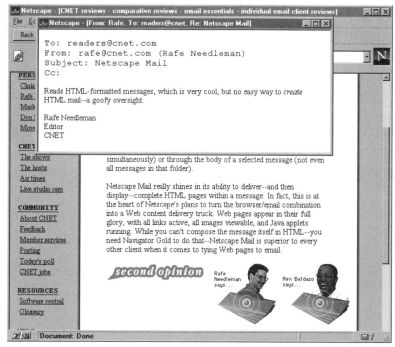

Figure 2-4. Clicking on the pictures of the editors brings up an email-like message.

is clicked. Would you use *onMouseOver*, as we did in Chapter 1? Not here. The event you want to handle is the clicking of the button. JavaScript's handler for that event is *onClick*. If you add the *onClick* event handler to the form button, the specified code will be executed when the user clicks on the button. Figure 2-3 shows a form that loads a file called *page.html* when the button is clicked. (When referring to a location, you can use either relative or absolute syntax.)

c|net: Launching new windows

JavaScript is not limited to controlling and working with only one browser window. It can create and manipulate multiple windows just as easily. Figure 2-4 shows a c|net article reviewing email clients. At the bottom of each review the two editors share an additional opinion of each product. Since the article is about email, why not have small email-like messages for each editor's opinion?

```
<A HREF="javascript:open_window('netscape1.html')">
<IMG ALIGN=top BORDER=0 SRC="Images/rafe.gif"
WIDTH=130 HEIGHT=110 ALT="Rafe Needleman says...">
</A>
```

Figure 2-5. *HREF* code for creating a link that opens a new window.

Open those windows

How did they do this? It's not terribly hard but to make much use of it you have to learn the basics. First, take a look at the code c|net used for the image of editor Rafe Needleman. Figure 2-5 shows the *HREF* tag used for that image.

As you can see, the only thing unusual about this *HREF* tag is the presence of *javascript:open_window('netscape1.html')* instead of a normal URL. To understand what that line does, we need to cover some basics first.

When you create a window using JavaScript, you are actually opening another browser window. You can set properties (or attributes) such as height, width, and whether or not the window will have a status bar or toolbar, as shown in Figure 2-6. This script is quite similar to the one used by c|net in the software review page.

Pesky details

When including the window opener code in a script, *do not* include any carriage returns (the thing that happens when you press Enter or Return) or spaces. All of the window code should be on one uninterrupted line; otherwise you are likely to get some very strange error messages.

```
<HTML>
<HEAD>
<TITLE>Windows</TITLE>
<SCRIPT LANGUAGE="JavaScript">
<!--

aWindow=window.open("page.html","thewindow",
"toolbar =no,width=350,height=400,status=no,
scrollbars=yes,resize=no,menubar=no");

// -->
</SCRIPT>
</HEAD>
<BODY>
</BODY>
</HTML>
```

Figure 2-6. This code creates a 350x400 window that contains scrollbars.

Designing with JavaScript

Unlike *window.location*, which is a property, *window.open( )* is a method of the current window. A method is similar to a function: you can run it, pass it values, and have it do something with those values; however, a method is attached to an object. In this scenario, that object is the current window. So, *window.open( )* is the method that opens a new window. The values we pass it are the properties for the window. Table 2-1 shows all the possible properties for the window.

Based on this table, you can see that the window displays *page.html*, has a target name *thewindow*, is 350-pixels wide and 400-pixels high, and has all the other properties turned off.

Notice in Figure 2-6 *aWindow* precedes all of the code. This is because whenever you open a window, you have the option of giving that window a name. In this case, the window's name is

Properties controlled with *window.open( )*

Properties	Value	What it controls
width	number	The width of the window in pixels.
height	number	The height of the window in pixels.
toolbar	yes/no	If the window will have the standard browser toolbar.
menubar	yes/no	If the window will have the application menus at the top of the window.
status	yes/no	If the window will include the small status bar, which often contains useful information, at the bottom of the window.
scrollbars	yes/no	If the window will display scrollbars.
resizable	yes/no	If the user will be able to resize the window.

Table 2-1.

aWindow. If you name a window you can manipulate it later: you can change the window's location, write dynamically to the window, and perform a great deal of other tasks dealing with that window. But if you don't give the window a name, you have little control over the window after it's initially created.

This window's target name is *thewindow*; and it can be used (with limited effect) to control the window when used in conjunction with an anchor's *TARGET* attribute. The *TARGET* attribute is generally used with frames. To make a link load a page in a separate frame, specify a target for that link. You can do the same with windows. If you want to load a different page in this window, simply add *TARGET = "thewindow"* to any of the links in the window's opener (the browser window that launches the new window).

Notice that the file name and the target name each have their own set of quotes; all the other properties are contained in a single set of quotes.

The first two properties, *height* and *width*, are self-explanatory. Just specify the desired height and width of the window (in pixels). The rest of the properties, shown in Table 2-1, can either be set to *yes* or *no*, or *1* or *0* (1 is equivalent to *yes* and 0 is equivalent to *no*.)

If you don't include a particular property in the window-opener code, that property will be set to *no* automatically. For instance, the following code creates a window 200 pixels in height and width, with nothing else in it.

```
aWindow = window.open("page.html","thewindow",
"height=200,width=200");
```

No toolbars, no status bar, just a plain window with *page.html* displayed inside it. If you take this one step further and remove the *height* and *width* properties, however, you will get the default browser window, toolbars and all.

Opening on demand

Now that you understand how to open a window, it's time to get more control. In the c|net article, the email window is launched when you click on either of the two editors' pictures. Achieving this effect takes a little extra work. First put the window-opening

Navigator 4.0 only

In Netscape Navigator 4.0, it is possible to create a window that is "always on top." This is done by adding *alwaysRaised=yes* to the window opening code in the same place you define window height and width.

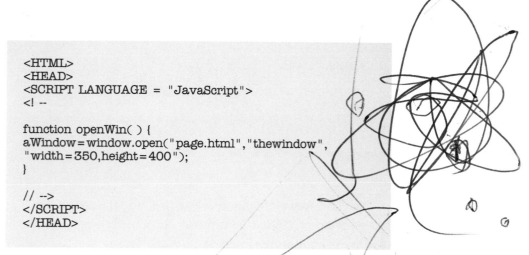

```
<HTML>
<HEAD>
<SCRIPT LANGUAGE = "JavaScript">
<! --

function openWin( ) {
aWindow=window.open("page.html","thewindow",
"width=350,height=400");
}

// -->
</SCRIPT>
</HEAD>
```

Figure 2-7. Defining a function to open a new window.

code inside a function (Figure 2-7) so you can launch your window at will. (See "Writing functions" sidebar.)

Earlier in the chapter, we learned how to change a window's location with a form button. Now that we've defined a function, we can also use a form button to open a new window. Just include the *onClick* event handler inside the button. Inside *onClick,* run the function, as shown in Figure 2-8.

Now for something more interesting: launching the window with a link, as in the c|net example. To do this, you need to create a link that runs the *openWin( )* function when it's clicked. One option is to create a normal link that goes nowhere (using #) and include an *onClick* event handler inside it, as shown in Figure 2-9. Event handlers like *onClick* can be put inside of links, not just form buttons.

```
<BODY>
<FORM>
<INPUT TYPE = "BUTTON" VALUE = "Open Window"
onClick = "openWin( );">
</FORM>
</BODY>
</HTML>
```

Figure 2-8. This form button opens a new window when clicked.

```
<BODY>
<A HREF = "#" onClick = "openWin();">
<IMG HEIGHT = 100 WIDTH = 100 SRC = "image.gif"></A>
</BODY>
</HTML>
```

Figure 2-9. Adding the *onClick* handler to an HREF link.

The best way to do this, however, is to use the JavaScript pseudo-protocol. (*Pseudo* because it's not actually a protocol like *http:* or *ftp:* but it works in the same way.) This is totally different from an event handler; don't get the two confused. Figure 2-10 shows how to use the pseudo-protocol to run our *openWin( )* function.

Common sense dictates that when this link is clicked, the browser will try to find the URL *javascript:openWin( );* and then give you an error because that URL does not exist. But common sense does not prevail. What this *will* do is run any JavaScript code that follows *javascript:* in the link. In this example, the code that follows simply runs the *openWin( )* function, which then proceeds to launch the window. When this link encompasses a graphic, you have created a window-launching graphical button. As you learn more, you will find that this technique applies in many circumstances.

The final touch

There's only one problem with the code we've written so far. c|net has *two* JavaScript links on each page — one for each editor. So they can't "hard-code" the page URL right into the function, as we did above. What's the solution?

```
<BODY>
<A HREF = "javascript:openWin( );">
<IMG HEIGHT = 100 WIDTH = 100 SRC = "image.gif"></A>
</BODY>
</HTML>
```

Figure 2-10. Running the function with the JavaScript pseudo-protocol.

The answer is simple: modify the function so that it takes the name of a page as an *argument*. In this case, the *argument* is named *URL*.

```
function openWin(URL) {
aWindow = window.open(URL,"thewindow","width=350,
height = 400");
}
```

Earlier, we included in the function the URL of the page to be displayed. But, instead of including that URL, why not put a variable there so you can dictate a different page every time? That's what c|net did. In the code above, the variable *URL* has been placed where the static URL goes. This means when you "pass" the name of the page to the function (as *URL*), it will load that page, not the same page every time. Now, when you want to open a specific page using the window opening code, simply pass *openWin( )* the URL of the page:

```
<A HREF - "javascript:openWin('netscape1.html');">
<IMG SRC = "rafe.gif">
</A>
```

This is a good example of how functions, which are a fundamental part of any programming language, can be used to make your scripts more efficient.

Figure 2-11 shows the relevant code from c|net's page. It should all make perfect sense now. First, a function Ⓐ is defined that takes a parameter of *url*. When the function is run a new window called *email* Ⓑ will be opened. To actually open the new windows, an *HREF* tag Ⓒ Ⓓ calls the function and passes the name of the file to be displayed.

Remote control

Remotes are everywhere nowadays: TVs, stereos, garages, and even computers have them. With the advent of JavaScript the remote is now an easy and familiar solution to navigational problems. A remote created in JavaScript works like a TV remote control: It's a handy device for controlling what's on the screen. A JavaScript remote controls your site, or more precisely, the browser in which your site is displayed. Your audience can use it to jump around your site, run a search, and perform a plethora of other tasks. The advantage is that your visitors see a familiar

```
<HTML>
<HEAD>
<TITLE> CNET reviews - individual email client reviews</TITLE>
<SCRIPT>
<! -- hide it
```
Ⓐ `function open_window(url) {`

Ⓑ `email = window.open(url,"eMail","toolbar=0,location=0,directories=0,status=0,`
`menubar=0,scrollbars=0,resizable=0,width=520,height=350");`

`}`

```
// -->
</SCRIPT>
</HEAD>

<BODY>
<IMG SRC = "Images/second.gif" WIDTH = 180 HEIGHT = 35 ALT = "second opinion">
```
Ⓒ `<A HREF = "javascript:open_window('netscape1.html')">`
`<IMG ALIGN = top BORDER = 0 SRC = "Images/rafe.gif" WIDTH = 130 HEIGHT = 110`
`ALT = "Rafe Needleman says...">`
`</A>`
Ⓓ `<A HREF = "javascript:open_window('netscape2.html')">`
`<IMG ALIGN = top BORDER = 0 SRC = "Images/rex.gif" WIDTH = 130 HEIGHT = 110`
`ALT = "Rex Baldazo says...">`
`</A>`
`</BODY>`
`</HTML>`

Figure 2-11. Abbreviated version of HTML for c|net's email review page.

metaphor (the remote) while you save space on all of your pages (no need for navigation bars). Even if you keep your old navigation devices, the remote will complement them nicely.

Web Review has a great looking remote. It uses the metaphor to its fullest: it has the "big buttons" that you find on a TV remote and it allows for a search of the site with the click of a button.

Creating the remote window

To begin, you have to create code to open the remote window. This code is shown in Figure 2-12.

First the function *makeRemote()* Ⓐ is declared. In the next line Ⓑ we create a new window named *remote*, 400 pixels in height

```
A    function makeRemote( ) {
B    remote = window.open(" ","remotewin","width=350,height=400");
C    remote.location.href = "http://webreview.com/remote.html";
D       if (remote.opener == null) remote.opener = window;
E    }
```

Figure 2-12. Function for creating a remote window.

and 350 in width. Because of a bug in Netscape 2 (for the Mac and UNIX), you need to set the location of the window after the window is initially opened. The location must be a full URL, not a relative one. Even though this will only affect a small percentage of your visitors, it's nice to be compatible with the widest range of browsers. So in line **C** the location of the remote is set to a URL.

Finally comes an *if* statement. **D** This line is very important. In JavaScript, if a browser window creates (or opens) a new window, the original browser window is referred to as the new window's *opener*. However, some versions of Navigator don't do this automatically, so this line names the original window *opener* just in case. In Figure 2-13 the large browser window is *opener* and the small window is the *remote* window.

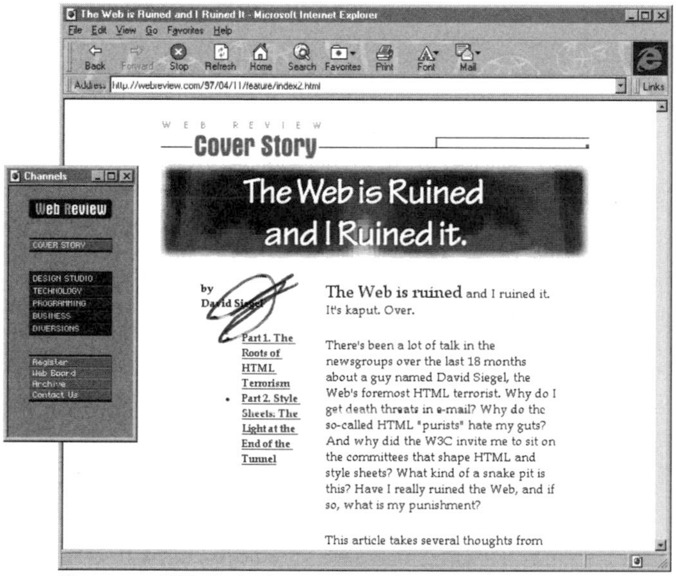

From now on, when the remote window communicates with the original browser window, it will always refer to it as *opener*.

To launch the remote, you can use a link anywhere in the page:

Figure 2-13. *Web Review* **home page and remote.**

```
<A HREF = "javascript:makeRemote( )">Start Remote</A>
```

or put the *onLoad* event handler in the *BODY* tag to display it automatically.

```
<BODY onLoad = "makeRemote( )">
```

```
function go(url) {
opener.location.href = url;
}
```

Figure 2-14. This function redirects links to the *opener* window.

Inside the remote

In the above example we loaded a page called *remote.html* in the new window. This page contains the actual remote code. For the most part, this document contains regular HTML links, with a few exceptions. The most important difference is that you'll be redirecting links to display in the main browser window (*opener*), not the remote window. The function for doing this is very basic, as shown in Figure 2-14.

All *go( )* does is take the URL you pass it and tell the main browser window, *opener*, to go to that URL.

Writing functions

Functions are a core aspect of JavaScript. We just used one in the c|net script, and we'll use them throughout the rest of the book. Every function has this basic look and feel:

```
function function's name (arguments) {
code to be run
}
```

There are four steps to writing a function:

1. Declare a function by simply using the word *function*.
2. Name the function. Whenever you want to use the function later on, you will have to refer to it by name.
3. Give the argument in parentheses. An argument (or parameter) is information that is given directly to the function. Inside the function, arguments can be used just like variables.
4. Finally, within braces, write the code that the function will run.

Your first function

Here's a working example of a (very) simple function:

```
function sayHello( ) {
alert("Hello");
}
```

This function, named *sayHello( )*, will pop up a JavaScript alert box that simply says "Hello," as shown in Figure 2-a.

```
The Amazing Remote <BR>
<A HREF = "javascript:go('index.html')">Front Page</A>
<A HREF = "javascript:go('map.html')">Site Map</A>
```

These links use the JavaScript pseudo-protocol to run *go( )* and redirect the link whenever it is clicked. Include a URL of your choice and the remote will work accordingly.

What this means is that you can treat the *opener* as you would any other window. Changing its location is just one of the many options that you have. Once you understand this basic concept, then you can make your remote do a lot more than redirect links.

To run the function, simply call it by name:

```
sayHello( );
```

Notice the use of parentheses after the function's name; parentheses are always added to the function's name when you run it. When you pass a function arguments, which you will learn to do below, they are placed inside these parentheses.

Figure 2-a.

Using arguments

Let's make this a little more complex and add your name after the word "Hello." To do this, you need to add an argument to the function.

```
function sayHello(your_name) {
alert("Hello" + your_name);
}

sayHello("Susan");
```

Figure 2-b.

This creates a function named *sayHello* with one argument, *your_name*. When this function is run, you have to give it (or "pass" it) your name. When you run the function, add your name in the parentheses. The function will then take the data you pass it — in this example "Susan" — and store it in the variable *your_name* because you specified *your_name* as an argument. Next, the value of *your_name* is appended to "Hello," and an alert box pops up with the text "Hello Susan," as shown in Figure 2-b.

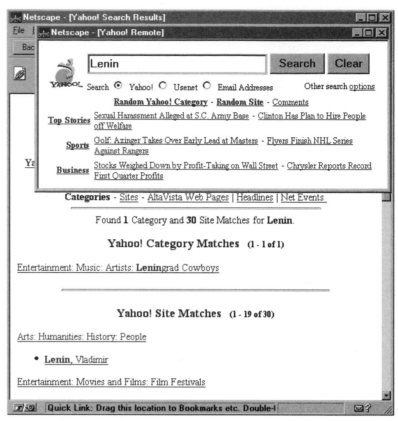

Figure 2-15. Searching in the remote window produces a hit list in the main window.

More power: Adding a search

Many remotes, notably Yahoo's, feature a search function. Adding a search mechanism, or almost any type of form, can be done with a simple trick. Instead of displaying the search results in the current window, you can target the search to the opener window. Figure 2-15 shows how searching for the word "Lenin" in Yahoo's remote window displays the results in the main browser window.

Aside from the modified target, the remote version of the search form is identical to the original version. The first step is to add an extra line to the remote launching code, as shown in Figure 2-16.

```
function makeRemote( ) {
remote=window.open("","remotewin","width=350,
height=400");
remote.location.href="http://webreview.com/remote.html.";
    if (remote.opener == null) remote.opener = window;
remote.opener.name = "opener";
}
```

Figure 2-16. Script for searching from a remote window.

This new line uses the opener's *name* property to name the opener window *opener*. This is like the *NAME* property that you use with frames, but we are assigning the name through JavaScript, not HTML. Just as *TARGET* is used to redirect links and forms to a frame, this line of code lets you use *TARGET* to redirect links and forms from the remote to the opener. For example, a link in the remote can now be redirected to the opener by simply putting *TARGET* = *"opener"* inside a link.

This is just an HTML/JavaScript trick; don't get it confused with the JavaScript *opener* property. The *opener* property is a totally different animal, as we discussed earlier, and is only accessible through JavaScript.

Now place your form in the remote as you would in any other scenario. There is only one thing that needs to be changed:

Wait a second... isn't this redundant?

You may ask, "Why wasn't this target thing done before with links?" The reason is simple: using this method alone excludes almost all of the control that JavaScript has over the opener. Since JavaScript can do more than redirect links, you should first learn how to control the opener through JavaScript rather than through simple, limited HTML. The remote can morph into many different things: a dialog box, a control panel, etc., all of which need JavaScript to work. By combining these two techniques, you get the best of both worlds.

```
<FORM TARGET = "opener"
ACTION = "http://webreview.com/cgi-bin/AT-
webreview_cleansearch.cgi" METHOD="post">
<INPUT TYPE = "text" NAME = "search" SIZE = "13"
MAXLENGTH = "256">
<INPUT TYPE = "hidden" NAME = "sp" VALUE = "sp">
<INPUT TYPE = "image" SRC = "/universal/images/button-
search.gif" BORDER = "0" NAME = "send" VALUE = "search">
</FORM>
```

Figure 2-17. Add the *target* attribute in order to display results in the opener window.

```
<HTML>
<HEAD>
<TITLE>Remote Launching Page</TITLE>
<SCRIPT LANGUAGE = "JavaScript">
<!--
function makeRemote( ) {
remote = window.open("","remotewin","width = 350,
height = 400");
remote.location.href = "http://webreview.com/remote.html";
if (remote.opener == null) remote.opener = window;
remote.opener.name = "opener";
}
//-->
</SCRIPT>
</HEAD>
<BODY>
Remote Launching Page
<BR>
<A HREF = "javascript:makeRemote( )">Open Remote</A>
</BODY>
</HTML>
```

Figure 2-18. Template for the page that launches the remote.

```
<HTML>
<HEAD>
<TITLE>Remote</TITLE>
<SCRIPT LANGUAGE = "JavaScript">
<!--
function go(url) {
opener.location.href = url;
}
//-->
</SCRIPT>
</HEAD>
<BODY>
The Remote
<P>
Links directed to the opener:
<BR>
<A HREF = "javascript:go('index.html')">Front Page</A>
<A HREF = "javascript:go('map.html')">Site Map</A>

Put any form here, but first change its target to "opener."
</BODY>
</HTML>
```

Figure 2-19. Template for the remote page.

the form's target. Since the opener is now named *opener*, make the form's target *opener*, as shown in Figure 2-17. For this example, *Web Review's* search form is used.

The form will now function in the remote as it does in any other page. The difference is that the results of the form (in this example, the search results) will be displayed in the opener, not the remote. The great thing about this method is that it can be used easily with a wide range of forms, not just for searches.

Figure 2-18 shows the page that launches the remote. Figure 2-19 shows the relevant code for the remote document.

3 Controlling Frames

In this chapter

- Targeting frames with JavaScript
- Changing the opener window
- How not to get framed
- Changing several frames with one link
- Rotating pages

Frames powerfully extend the HTML interface by allowing Web authors to carve the browser window into several sections. The best aspect of frames (in my opinion) is that JavaScript has a great deal of control over them. This chapter shows you how to build a more sophisticated interface to your site by using JavaScript to control frames.

The toolbar design

Frames are often used as navigational devices in which a side frame provides a consistent navigational toolbar while content is displayed in the main frame. This classic use of frames is well illustrated in Figure 3-1, the home page of *The Gabby Cabby*. The narrow frame on the left contains several links to content on the site. Clicking on one of these links loads the appropriate document in the large frame on the right. If you clicked on the "City" link, for example, *city.htm* is loaded in the main frame, as shown in Figure 3-2.

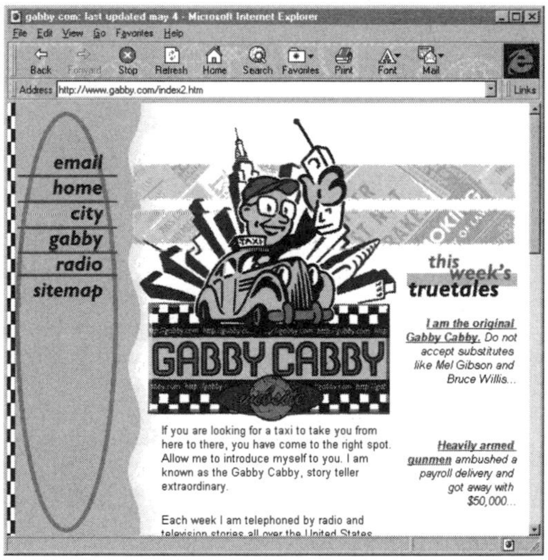

Figure 3-1. The *Gabby Cabby* site *(http://www.gabby.com/)* uses a small navigational frame and a big content frame.

Controlling links in HTML

It's relatively simple to create this effect in HTML. Figure 3-3 shows the frameset document that describes the layout of the document and specifies which documents each frame will display. The *FRAMESET* tag divides this page into two columns: the first (left-hand) column is 133 pixels wide, while the second column takes up the remainder of the browser

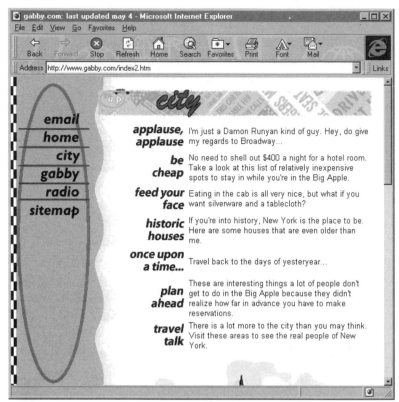

Figure 3-2. Clicking on the "city" link in the navigational frame loads the appropriate document in the content frame.

window. The *FRAME* tags specify the document source and name for each frame. Here the first frame is named *toolbar* and the second frame is named *main*.

Inside the toolbar document, you use the *TARGET* attribute to tell the links where to load their documents. For instance, to load *city.htm* in the big frame when the user clicks on the city link, the HTML is:

```
<A HREF = "city.htm" TARGET= "main">
<IMG SRC="bar3.gif"></A>
```

Controlling links in JavaScript

To target frames in JavaScript, you need to do things a bit differently, though the idea is the same:

```
parent.main.location = "city.htm";
```

```
<HTML>
<HEAD>
<TITLE>
Gabby Cabby
</TITLE>
</HEAD>

<FRAMESET COLS = "133,*">
<FRAME SRC = "frame/toolbar.htm" NAME = "toolbar">
<FRAME SRC = "frame/main.htm" NAME = "main">
</FRAMESET>

</HTML>
```

Figure 3-3. Code for the *Gabby Cabby* home page.

The key here is *main.location*: it tells JavaScript to access the *location* of the frame named *main*, and not that of the current window (which would be *window.location*). You may be puzzled by the use of *parent* here. Whenever you create frames, like *main* and *toolbar*, they become properties of the frameset (the document that defines the frames). Therefore, when you want to access *main* from *toolbar*, you have to climb up to the frameset that defined *toolbar* (which is by default named *parent*) and then access *main* from there. In other words, *parent.main.location.*

Frames and remotes

Now that we have the syntax down, we can use JavaScript to control frames in ways that HTML can't handle. Think back to the remote we created in Chapter 2. If you were to launch a remote from *toolbar*, all of the links in the remote would be targeted back to *toolbar*, not to the frameset. This is because the remote document contains this function:

```
function go(url) {
opener.location.href = url;
}
```

This function is used (refer back to Figure 2-14) to target every link in the remote to the opener. Since *toolbar* is the window (frames are considered windows in their own right) that opened the remote, all of the links will be targeted there. But, of course, you want the links to be targeted to *main*. A simple modification to the code will do the trick:

```
function go(url) {
opener.parent.main.location.href = url;
}
```

The concept here is simple: since *toolbar* is the opener, you can access *main* by climbing up from *toolbar* (*opener*) to the frameset (*parent*) and then down to *main*. To change the whole frameset, thereby replacing all of the frames with the linked document, the same idea holds true.

```
function go(url) {
opener.parent.location.href = url;
}
```

Now you're targeting *toolbar*'s frameset (*parent*) directly.

Expanding and collapsing

Another good reason to use JavaScript is that it lets you expand and collapse your frames. You might want to let users get rid of the *toolbar* frame, in order to save space. All you have to do is create a link in *toolbar* that will change the location of the frameset, *parent*, to the location of *main*. The result is that the document in *main* suddenly takes up the full window.

```
<A HREF = "javascript:parent.location.href =
parent.main.location.href">Expand Article</A>
```

This takes care of the expanding effect. The collapsing part is much easier: just instruct your visitors to click the Back button on the browser (or provide them with one, see "Backing Up and Moving Forward") to return to the framed setup.

Backing up and moving forward

You can create back and forward buttons for frames (and windows in general) with minimal code by accessing the window's history. The history is the list of sites that you've visited during your current browser session. When you press the *back* button on the toolbar, you are traveling one level back in the browser's history. When you press *forward*, the exact opposite occurs. Both of these effects, and more, can be achieved in JavaScript.

```
window.history.go(-1);
```

```
<FORM>
<INPUT
 TYPE = "BUTTON"
 VALUE = "Back"
 onClick = "window.history.go(-1);">
<INPUT
 TYPE = "BUTTON"
 VALUE = "Forward"
 onClick = "window.history.go(1);">
</FORM>
```

Figure 3-4. A form with buttons to go back and forward in the user's history.

This line of code navigates the window one level back in its history. The number that you pass to *go( )* determines how far and in which direction the window will go in the browser's history. If you include a positive 1 instead of a negative 1, you travel forward in the browser's history.

Suppose you want to create two buttons that will achieve the effect of the browser's *forward/back* buttons? How would you do that? Here's a hint: *onClick*. Figure 3-4 shows the code for these two buttons.

Just create two form buttons and include the *onClick* event handler in each of them. Inside *onClick*, just pop in the history navigating code.

Better yet, skip forms and use the JavaScript pseudo-protocol to access the history from ordinary *HREF* links. For example, to create a back button for *main*, all you need is this simple link:

```
<A HREF = "javascript:window.history.go(-1);">Back</A>
```

This instructs JavaScript to travel one level back in the browser's history and display that page. To travel forward, just reverse the number in parentheses:

```
<A HREF = "javascript:window.history.go(1);">
Forward</A>
```

You can control the history of an individual frame, such as *main*, in the same fashion. For example, you can create back and forward buttons in *toolbar* that are targeted to *main*:

TARGET="_parent"
You can also avoid framing by including *TARGET="_parent"* in your anchor tags. But you have to remember to do this for every link in a framed page. With JavaScript, one line in the frameset document takes care of the problem.

```
<A HREF = "javascript:parent.main.history.go(1);">
Forward</A>

<A HREF = "javascript:parent.main.history.go(-1);">
Back</A>
```

Don't get framed

This section ends with an important warning: Don't get framed.
Getting framed will confuse and annoy even the most weathered
Web surfer. It works like this: You link from your *main* frame to a

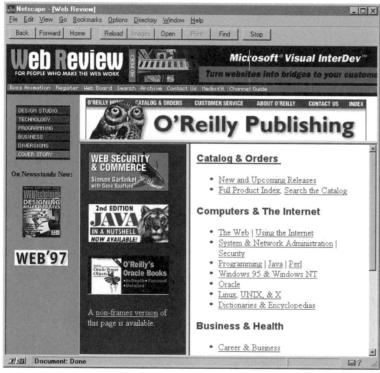

site that's also framed. Now the
user is looking at a framed site
inside one of your frames.
That's it: You've been framed.
Figure 3-5 shows a mock-up
example of *Web Review* framing
the O'Reilly Web site. Of course,
Web Review would never *really*
make such a mistake!

Though this problem may
not surface often, it's just one
of the many scenarios that can
come up when your site relies
heavily on frames. JavaScript
offers a solution, however.
Inside every frameset on your
site, include this line of code:

```
if (parent.location.href !=
window.location.href)
parent.location.href =
window.location.href;
```

Figure 3-5. Framed! In this scenario
***Web Review* frames the O'Reilly site.**

This line makes sure that the current frameset is the one and
only frameset in the browser window, and if it isn't, it makes it
so. Figure 3-6 shows how to use it.

One click, many links

One of the most commonly asked questions is how to change two
frames with one click. If you're using the toolbar/main scenario
we've discussed, it would be useful if clicking on one of the links
in the navigation frame not only displayed the appropriate file in

Designing with JavaScript

```
<SCRIPT LANGUAGE = "JavaScript">
<!--

if (parent.location.href != window.location.href) parent.location.href = window.location.href;

// -->
</SCRIPT>
<FRAMESET COLS = "30%, 70%" FRAMEBORDER = NO BORDER = 0 FRAMESPACING =0>
<FRAME NAME = "toolbar" SRC = "toolbar_document.html">
<FRAME NAME = "main" SRC = "main_document.html">
</FRAMESET>
```

Figure 3-6. Code for a frameset that can't be framed.

the main frame but also changed the display in the *toolbar* frame. A good example is Microsoft's search page. Figure 3-7 shows what users see when they first come to the page.

If you click on "People," two things happen. As you would expect, the main window changes to display the linked page, in this case a search interface to Internet white pages. But the toolbar also changes to reveal a list of links under the "People" heading, as shown in Figure 3-8.

Microsoft's
search page
*http://home.microsoft.com/
exploring/finditfast/*

Figure 3-7. Initial view of Microsoft's search page.

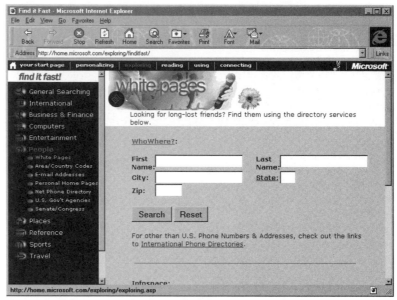

Figure 3-8. Clicking on "People" changes both the main and toolbar frames.

Not surprisingly, there is a little JavaScript code involved in changing the locations of multiple frames. Figure 3-9 shows a function (called *changePages( )*) for changing two frames with one click.

This changes the locations of both the *main* frame and the *toolbar* frame when you pass it the appropriate URLs. For

```
function changePages(toolbarURL, mainURL) {
parent.toolbar.location.href = toolbarURL;
parent.main.location.href = mainURL;
}
```

Figure 3-9. Function to change the contents of two frames with one click.

```
function changePages(toolbarURL,mainURL, anotherURL) {
parent.toolbar.location.href = toolbarURL;
parent.main.location.href = mainURL;
parent.another.location.href = anotherURL;
}
```

Figure 3-10. Function for changing three frames with one click.

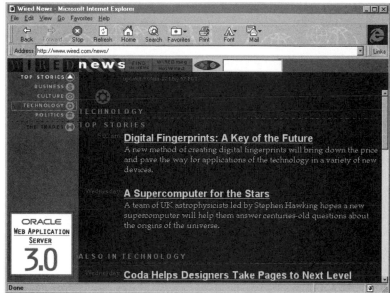

Wired News
http://www.wired.com/news/

Figure 3-11. *Wired News* uses a JavaScript-based ad rotation system in the left frame.

example, to change the location of the *toolbar* frame to *toolbar_document2.html* and the location of the *main* frame to *main_document2.html* create a link with the JavaScript pseudo-protocol that runs the *changePages()* function.

```
<A HREF = "javascript:changePages('toolbar_document2.html',
'main_document2.html');
```

To change additional frames when the user clicks, just add references to those frames in the function, as shown in Figure 3-10.

Rotating pages

Frames are one of the best ways to rotate content. For example, *Wired News'* frames-based advertisement system (shown in Figure 3-11) rotates and displays all of its ads through a small frame on the lower left-hand corner of the screen (it even checks if the user has been active in the last five ads, but we're not going to get into that).

The *Wired News* page is a prime example not only of a good use of JavaScript but also a good use of frames in general. We will use a similar frames-based solution but we will cut down on the number of frames. Figure 3-12 shows the stripped-down frameset.

```
<FRAMESET onLoad = "rotate( )" COLS = "30%, 70%"
FRAMEBORDER = NO BORDER = 0 FRAMESPACING =0>
<FRAMESET ROWS = "*, 200" FRAMEBORDER = NO
BORDER = 0 FRAMESPACING = 0>
<FRAME NAME = "little" SRC = "little.html">
<FRAME NAME = "rotateFrame" SRC = "rotate1.html">
</FRAMESET>
<FRAME NAME = "big" SRC = "big.html">
</FRAMESET>
```

Figure 3-12. Frameset for a simplified version of *Wired News'* page.

This setup consists of three frames: *big, little,* and *rotateFrame.* The *rotateFrame* frame is where the rotated HTML documents are displayed. When the frameset is loaded, a function called *rotate( )* is run. We'll need to define a few variables that control various aspects of the rotation. These are shown in Figure 3-13.

There is a special naming scheme for all of the pages that we'll be rotating. All of these HTML documents need to have the same prefix in their file names, defined by the variable *prefix.* After the prefix, the name of the document should be followed by a number (1 through infinity). In this example we've made the prefix *rotate;* thus to rotate three documents, they need to be named *rotate1.html, rotate2.html,* and *rotate3.html.*

```
var prefix = 'rotate';
var currentPage = 0;
var totalPages = 3;
var lullTime = 5000;
```

Figure 3-13. Variables for the rotation systems.

```
    function rotate( ) {
(A)  if (currentPage < totalPages) currentPage++;
(B)  else currentPage = 1;
(C)  parent.rotateFrame.location.href = prefix + currentPage + '.html';
(D)  setTimeout('rotate( )', lullTime);
    }
```

Figure 3-14. Function *rotate( ).*

Designing with JavaScript

Variable *currentPage* keeps track of which page is being displayed. Variable *totalPages* specifies how many pages will be rotated. It's set to 3 here. Finally *lullTime* specifies the delay between pages (in milliseconds). We've set a 5-second delay (5,000 milliseconds).

After you've defined all of these variables, you need to create a function to rotate all of your pages sequentially. Figure 3-14 shows this function, called *rotate( )*.

This function, which is run as soon as the frames are initially displayed (note the *onLoad* handler in Figure 3-12), begins by determining Ⓐ if the current page, *currentPage*, is less then the total number of pages, *totalPages*. If it is, then it increases *currentPage* by 1; if not, Ⓑ it sets *currentPage* back to 1. The next part Ⓒ sets the location of the *rotate* frame to the document that corresponds with the value of *currentPage*. That is, if *currentPage* is 2,

```
<HTML>
<HEAD><TITLE>A Little Rotation</TITLE>
<SCRIPT LANGUAGE = "JavaScript">
<!--

function rotate( ) {
    if (currentPage < totalPages) currentPage++;
    else currentPage = 1;
parent.rotateFrame.location.href = prefix + currentPage + '.html';
setTimeout('rotate( )', lullTime);
}

var prefix = 'rotate';           // prefix for all rotated pages
var currentPage = 0;
var totalPages = 3;              // total number of rotated pages
var lullTime = 5000;            // lull time for display of each page

// -->
</SCRIPT>
</HEAD>
<FRAMESET onLoad = "rotate( )" COLS = "30%, 70%" FRAMEBORDER = NO BORDER = 0
FRAMESPACING =0>
    <FRAMESET ROWS = "*, 200" FRAMEBORDER = NO BORDER = 0 FRAMESPACING = 0>
    <FRAME NAME = "little" SRC = "little.html">
    <FRAME NAME = "rotateFrame" SRC = "rotate1.html">
    </FRAMESET>
<FRAME NAME = "big" SRC = "big.html">
</FRAMESET>
</HTML>
```

Figure 3-15. Source for content rotation system.

the location of the *rotate* frame is *rotate2.html* ("rotate" + 2 + ".html"). Then, the *setTimeout( )* method ⓓ reruns the *rotate( )* function after waiting the amount of time specified in *lullTime.*

Timing the rotation

The *setTimeout( )* method is JavaScript's way of timing the execution of different events. In this example, it is used to control the timing for the rotation of pages in a frame. It is a staple for any JavaScript programmer who wishes to add timed events (such as a countdown clock in a game) to any of his or her creations. Here's a quick overview of how to use it:

```
setTimeout('code to run', time to wait in milliseconds);
```

The first argument is the code you want to run after the timeout is over; this must be inside quotes. The second argument specifies how long *setTimeout( )* should wait before running the code that you gave it; this is always in milliseconds.

Figure 3-15 shows the full source for the rotation system.

4

Forms and Functions

Before you do much with JavaScript, you have to understand its interface. In many cases, the interface you will be dealing with is a form and its elements: select menus, radio buttons, text inputs, to name a few. In this chapter, we'll create a fun JavaScript twist on the classic Madlibs game. Then, in a more practical mode, we'll learn how to use JavaScript to validate forms

Getting to know that form

Before we get into our examples, let's take a moment to understand how JavaScript accesses forms. If you know how to create a form in HTML, then you're halfway there. Let's begin by creating a basic form, shown in Figure 4-1, and show you how to use JavaScript to access the information inside that form.

Whenever you refer to anything in JavaScript, you refer to it by name. In most cases, the name of an HTML object (like a form) is determined by the *NAME* attribute of its tag. For example, this

```
<HTML>
<HEAD><TITLE>A Form</TITLE></HEAD>
<BODY>
<FORM NAME = "simple">
<INPUT TYPE = TEXT NAME = "stuff" >
<INPUT TYPE = BUTTON VALUE = "Okay">
</FORM>
</BODY>
</HTML>
```

Figure 4-1. A simple form containing a text input and submit button.

47

form's name is *simple*. Inside this form, there is a text input field and a button. The text input is named *stuff* but the button doesn't have a name.

So how do we access the text that the user types into *stuff*? Well, we have to climb the JavaScript tree that we learned about in Chapter 1. As you know, everything on the page is part of an object called *document*. When you refer to something in the *document* object, such as a form, it's always a property of the *document* object. Since we know the form's name, *simple*, accessing it through JavaScript is easy: *document.simple*. To get to the text input, you have to climb a little higher. Just as the form is a property of the document, the form's elements (e.g. the text

Try *this*

When you refer to a specific form object, such as *document.simple.stuff.value*, it takes a lot of typing to access that last little element. There is a commonly used shortcut that uses a simple word to save you all of this typing: *this*. Understand that *this* can be used in place of an object's own name. In real life, for example, you refer to yourself as "I," not by your full name. Similarly, a form (or any object) can refer to itself using *this*. When you refer to the form in Figure 4-1 using its full name, it looks like this:

```
document.simple
```

But if you are working inside the form, e.g. if you are in an event handler in the *FORM* tag, you can refer to it as:

```
this
```

This concept is one of the more difficult ones to understand, especially for a beginning JavaScripter, but try to follow the logic to see how it works. Here goes: A button inside the form can also refer to the form using the *this* statement, but in a slightly different way:

```
this.form
```

This example inverts the usual construction. Here, *this* refers to the button itself and *form* refers to the form in which the button is contained. Using this method of naming things, you can pass *this.form* (which is equivalent to *document.simple*, the form's name) to a function that will work with the form.

     Designing with JavaScript

input and button) are properties of the form. Therefore, to refer to the value of text input named *stuff*, you have to say, "Give me the *value* of the text input named *stuff* inside the form named *simple* inside the *document*." In JavaScript, that looks like this:

```
document.simple.stuff.value
```

To display this information, treat it as you would a variable. For instance, you can put it inside a dialog box, like so:

```
alert(document.simple.stuff.value);
```

Once you understand this syntax you can write many interesting scripts, such as the Madlibs script in the next section.

```
<SCRIPT LANGUAGE = "JavaScript">

function showStuff(form) {
alert(form.stuff.value);
}

</SCRIPT>

<FORM NAME = "simple">
<INPUT TYPE = TEXT NAME = "stuff" >
<INPUT TYPE = BUTTON VALUE = "Okay" onClick = "showStuff(this.form);">
</FORM>
```

Here's a working example. When the form's button is clicked, the *onClick* event handler passes the form, which can be referred to as *this.form* from inside the button, to function *showStuff( )*. As we all know, *this.form* is another way of saying *document.simple*, the form's full name. When *this.form* arrives at *showStuff( )*, it becomes variable *form*. From now on, at least inside this function, the form can be referred to as *form*, and not by its full name, *document.simple*. Remember how we had to type out *document.simple.stuff.value* to access the text input? Now we can refer to is as *form.stuff.value* and pass that to *alert( )*.

The truth is, this (often confusing) method doesn't really save a great amount of typing. The reason that you need to know this, however, is that almost all the scripts on the Web use this method with their forms. If you plan on learning to script by studying examples, as most scripters do, then you first need to know how the example works.

Madlibs: America's favorite party game

Madlibs: America's favorite party game... 20 years ago. A bit passé today, it's still a great way to understand how to combine forms with JavaScript. If you're not familiar with the game, here's how it works: You enter verbs, nouns, adjectives, and various parts of speech into a form. The words that you enter into the form are inserted into a prefabricated story: a poem, an advertisement, the Gettysberg address, pretty much anything that fits into a few pages. The resulting story is an often humorous and always unpredictable mélange of words.

Filling out the form

We begin by creating a form to gather all of our parts of speech from the user. The words entered into this form will eventually be plugged into a story and displayed in a separate window through JavaScript.

This form, shown in Figures 4-2 and 4-3 is named *madlibs* and consists of 6 text inputs, each of them placed next to a corresponding part of speech. The first text input, *input1*, for example,

Figure 4-2. The Madlibs form asks users to provide various words.

```
<FORM NAME = "madlibs">
<TABLE BORDER = 0>

<TR><TD>Plural Noun:</TD>
<TD><INPUT TYPE = "TEXT" NAME = "input1"></TD></TR>

<TR><TD>Part of Body:</TD>
<TD><INPUT TYPE = "TEXT" NAME = "input2"></TD></TR>

<TR><TD>Verb:</TD>
<TD><INPUT TYPE = "TEXT" NAME = "input3"></TD></TR>

<TR><TD>Name:</TD>
<TD><INPUT TYPE = "TEXT" NAME = "input4"></TD></TR>

<TR><TD>Polictician:</TD>
<TD><INPUT TYPE = "TEXT" NAME = "input5"></TD></TR>

<TR><TD>Adjective:</TD>
<TD><INPUT TYPE = "TEXT" NAME = "input6"></TD></TR>
</TABLE>
```

Figure 4-3. HTML for the Madlibs form.

should contain a plural noun. The names of each of these text inputs are very important: they will be needed when we assemble the final story.

After all of these text inputs have been filled out, a function will combine them with the story and then display that story in a separate window. Before you get to this function, you'll want to create a button to run it. This can be done using a form button:

```
<INPUT TYPE = "BUTTON" VALUE = "Create Story"
onClick ="makeLibs( )">
```

or with a standard link:

```
<A HREF = "javascript:makeLibs( )">Create Story</A>
```

Creating the story

Figure 4-4 shows the story that results when the user's responses to the form are combined with the JavaScript shown in Figure 4-5.

Figure 4-5 consists of a function **Ⓐ** called *makeLibs( )*. First a new variable named *story* **Ⓑ** is created. This variable is given a combination of text input values from the form and prefabricated story material. Combining all of this information in the correct

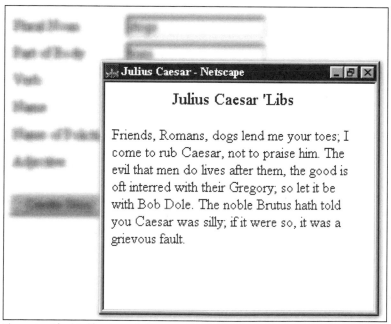

Figure 4-4. The Madibs story window.

```
Ⓐ  function makeLibs( ) {
Ⓑ  var story = "<HEAD><TITLE> Julius Caesar</TITLE></HEAD>" +
    "<BODY BGCOLOR = '#FFFFFF'>
    <FONT SIZE = 4>Julius Caesar</FONT><P>" + "Friends, Romans, " +
    document.madlibs.input1.value + ", lend me your " +
    document.madlibs.input2.value + "; I come to " + document.madlibs.input3.value +
    " Caesar, not to praise him. " + "The evil that men do lives after them, the good is
    oft interred with their " + document.madlibs.input4.value + "; " + "so let it be with
    " + document.madlibs.input5.value + ". " + "The noble Brutus hath told you
    Caesar was " + document.madlibs.input6.value + "; if it were so, it was a grievous
    fault. ";
Ⓒ  libsWin = window.open("," "","width=300,height=250,scrollbars=yes");
Ⓓ  libsWin.document.write(story);
Ⓔ  libsWin.document.close( );
    }
```

Figure 4-5. The MadLibs code

order results in the final product: a Mablibs story. Let's take a look at one of the lines added to *story* to understand how this works:

```
"Friends, Romans, " + document.madlibs.input1.value +
" lend me your " +
```

This line serves one and only one purpose: to combine the static story text with a value entered in the form. This phrase begins, "Friends, Romans," then continues by adding the entered value from the first text input: *document.madlibs.input1.value* (the value of the text input named *input1* inside the form named *madlibs* inside the document), next the words "lend me your" are added.

Let's say, for the sake of example, that you entered the word "dogs" into *input1*. The resulting string of text would say "Friends, Romans, dogs, lend me your..." This same procedure is applied to create the rest of the story.

After the story is compiled and placed in variable *story*, it needs to be displayed. This is accomplished in the last three lines of the function.

First, a new window (300 x 250 pixels) is created Ⓒ and named *libsWin*. Next, *document.write( )* is used Ⓓ to print the information in *story* into the new window. Notice that instead of saying

Designing with JavaScript

```
<HTML>
<HEAD><TITLE>Madlibs</TITLE>
<SCRIPT LANGUAGE = "JavaScript">

function makeLibs( ) {
story = "<HEAD><TITLE>Julius Caesar</TITLE></HEAD>" + "<BODY BGCOLOR =
'#FFFFFF'><<FONT SIZE = 4>Julius Caesar</FONT><P>" + "Friends, Romans, " +
document.madlibs.input1.value + " lend me your " +
document.madlibs.input2.value + "; I come to " +
document.madlibs.input3.value + " Caesar, not to praise him. " + "The evil that men do
lives after them, the good is oft interred with their " + document.madlibs.input4.value +
"; " + "so let it be with " + document.madlibs.input5.value + ". " + "The noble Brutus
hath told you Caesar was " + document.madlibs.input6.value + "; if it were so, it was a
grievous fault. ";
libsWin = window.open("","","",width=300,height=250,scrollbars=yes");
libsWin.document.write(story);
libsWin.document.close( );
}
</SCRIPT>
</HEAD>
<BODY BGCOLOR = "#FFFFFF">
<FORM NAME = "madlibs">
<TABLE BORDER = 0>
<TR><TD>Plural Noun:</TD><TD><INPUT TYPE = "TEXT" NAME = "input1"></TD></TR>
<TR><TD>Part of Body:</TD><TD><INPUT TYPE = "TEXT" NAME = "input2"></TD></TR>
<TR><TD>Verb:</TD><TD><INPUT TYPE = "TEXT" NAME = "input3"></TD></TR>
<TR><TD>Name:</TD><TD><INPUT TYPE = "TEXT" NAME = "input4"></TD></TR>
<TR><TD>Polictician:</TD><TD><INPUT TYPE = "TEXT" NAME = "input5"></TD></TR>
<TR><TD>Adjective:</TD><TD><INPUT TYPE = "TEXT" NAME = "input6"></TD></TR>
</TABLE>
<P>
<!-- This button runs the function that compiles the story -->
<INPUT TYPE = "BUTTON" VALUE = "Create Story" onClick ="makeLibs( )">
</FORM>
</BODY>
</HTML>
```

Figure 4-6. The complete MadLibs script.

document.write(story), the function says *libsWin.document.write (story)*. If you said *document.write(story)*, you would display the story in the current document, not the new window's document. By climbing the tree to the new window, *libsWin*, the information is displayed there.

The last line **E** is a minor but important detail: it tells the window that you've finished writing to it and that it should display what you sent it. This is often referred to as *closing the* *stream.* Although not usually needed when using *document.write( ),* it is required if you're writing to any window but the current one.

This light-hearted Madlibs example shows you how JavaScript can take static information and automate it, often without a great deal of work. I hope you'll be able to use this script as a starting point for more useful ideas. (Or maybe Madlibs are just what you were looking for.) Figure 4-6 shows the entire script.

Stop that form!

Let's face it, if your site is doing well, your traffic is increasing. If your traffic is increasing, then so is the load on your server. There is a way to alleviate this higher volume of traffic when you're dealing with forms and other server-based interaction. The general term for this is *forms validation,* but there's more to it than that. Using JavaScript to validate your forms saves your server from needless work, improves the quality of data that users provide, and results in a better interface for your visitors.

Basic forms validation deals with catching the form before it's sent, processing what has been entered, and deciding whether or not to continue sending the form. This can all be done using a few basic functions.

Catching the form

To catch a form before it is submitted you'll need to incorporate the *onSubmit* event handler. This special event handler is designed specifically to catch a form for validation. Figure 4-7 shows a form that asks users to send in a comment. Figure 4-8 shows the code for this simple form.

Figure 4-7. The "Send us a message" form.

```
<FORM NAME = "theform" onSubmit = "return
isReady(this)" METHOD=POST ACTION = "/cgi-bin/">
<IMG SRC = "send_message.gif"><P>
<TEXTAREA NAME = "message" ROWS = 6 COLS = 20
WRAP></TEXTAREA><P>
<INPUT TYPE = SUBMIT VALUE = " Submit ">
<INPUT TYPE = RESET VALUE = " Reset ">
</FORM>
```

Figure 4-8. The HTML for the form.

Designing with JavaScript

Notice the placement of the *onSubmit* event handler — right in the form tag. This is the only place you can use *onSubmit*. When the user submits this form, either by clicking the submit button or pressing the Enter key, the code inside the *onSubmit* handler is run. This form passes itself to *isReady( )*. Here's the important part: if the code that *onSubmit* runs returns a *true* value, then the form will continue being submitted. If the code returns a *false* value, the form will be stopped. To better understand what this means, take a look at the function that validates the form.

Validation is the name of the game

In our example, the *isReady( )* function (Figure 4-9) is run whenever a user attempts to submit the form. The function Ⓐ requires that a form be specified. In the form in Figure 4-8, *this* was passed to the function, indicating the current form.

The function first checks the value of the text area Ⓑ named *message*. This line says, "If the value of the form element named *message* is not blank, allow the submission to continue." (Blank is denoted by empty quotes.) This is where *true* and *false* come into play. If *message* is not blank, the function returns *true*, which tells the form that it can continue its submission. If *message* is blank (that is, the user submitted the form with no message), than the *else* condition Ⓒ applies and the next three lines of code are run.

First an alert box, shown in Figure 4-10, asks you to include a message. Ⓓ After the user clicks OK, the script *focuses* the text area (*message*). Ⓔ This means that the browser brings up the part of the page with the text area and places the cursor

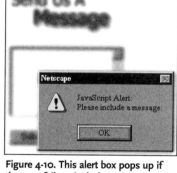

Figure 4-10. This alert box pops up if the user fails to include a message.

```
Ⓐ  function isReady(form) {
Ⓑ  if (form.message.value != "") return true;
Ⓒ  else {
Ⓓ  alert("Please include a message.");
Ⓔ  form.message.focus( );
Ⓕ  return false;
      }
   }
```

Figure 4-9. The is*Ready( )* function.

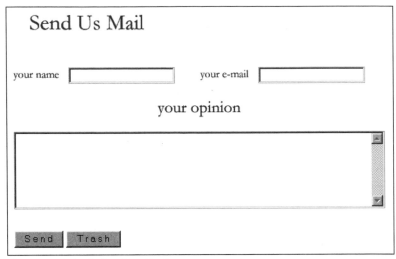

Figure 4-11. A simple form for collecting user comments.

there so the user can type. *Focus* is built into most form elements and makes it much easier for visitors to fix any errors made when filling out the form. Finally, the function returns *false* **F** so the submission is canceled.

This is very rudimentary validation. Determining if a form element is blank is just the beginning, as you'll see throughout the rest of this chapter.

Is that really your email?

One of the most commonly used forms on the Web is the email form. An email form takes a name, an email address, and a message. Often you'll receive a message through one of these forms with no email address or an improper address. When this becomes a recurring theme, it can become an annoyance. That's when it's time to call on JavaScript.

The generic email form

Figure 4-11 shows your run-of-the-mill email form. Users enter their name, email and comments, and click the submit button. As you can see from the code in Figure 4-12, this form uses a CGI script to process the form. It's simplified (no tables or images) for this example so it will be easier to understand.

```
Ⓐ <FORM NAME = "mailform" onSubmit = "return
      isReady(this)" ACTION = "cgi-bin/mailform.cgi">
Ⓑ your name: <INPUT NAME = "fullname" TYPE = TEXT>
Ⓒ your email: <INPUT NAME = "address" TYPE = TEXT>
Ⓓ <P>your opinion:<P><TEXTAREA NAME = "opinion"
      ROWS = 6 COLS = 64 WRAP></TEXTAREA>
Ⓔ <P><INPUT TYPE = SUBMIT VALUE = " S e n d ">
Ⓕ <INPUT TYPE = RESET VALUE = " T r a s h ">
Ⓖ </FORM>
```

Figure 4-12. This form validates that the user has filled out the name, email, and message.

The *onSubmit* event handler runs the *isReady( )* function when the form is submitted, but this time *isReady( )* does a lot more than validate a single element. It actually sends the elements to functions that determine if the elements have been filled out correctly. We'll be focusing on three different form elements: *address*, which contains the user's email address; *fullname*, which contains the visitor's name; and *opinion*, which contains the actual content of the message.

The *isReady( )* function (shown in Figure 4-13) depends on smaller functions to validate specific form elements — anything from detecting a valid email address to making sure a form element is not left blank. After creating the smaller functions, you can write a master function, like *isReady( )*, to run them.

That's not an email address!

As with our earlier validation function (Figure 4-9), the function in Figure 4-13 starts by declaring the function with a parameter called *form*. Ⓐ The rest of the function is divided into three *if* statements, each of which runs another function. The first *if* statement runs a function called *isEmail( )*, which determines if a form element contains a proper email address.

For *isEmail( )* to do anything, it needs to look over a form element. In this script, we've passed the form's *address* element Ⓑ to *isEmail( )*. This is the form element where users enter their email addresses.

```
Ⓐ  function isReady(form) {
Ⓑ    if (isEmail(form.address) == false) {   // a real email
Ⓒ      alert("Please enter your email address.");
Ⓓ      form.address.focus( );
Ⓔ      return false;
      }
Ⓕ    if (isFilled(form.fullname) == false) {  // a full name?
Ⓖ      alert("Please enter your name.");
Ⓗ      form.fullname.focus( );
Ⓘ      return false;
      }
Ⓙ    if (isFilled(form.opinion) == false) {   // a message/opinion?
Ⓚ      alert("Please enter your opinion.");
Ⓛ      form.opinion.focus( );
Ⓜ      return false;
      }
Ⓝ    return true;
    }
```

Figure 4-13. The *isReady()* master function calls the smaller functions *isEmail* and *isFilled*.

If *isEmail( )* determines that *address* is a valid email address —
a valid email address contains both an @ symbol and at least one
period — then *isEmail( )* returns *true* and the validation continues.
If the user has not entered a valid email address in this field,
however, the next three lines of code in the *if* statement are run.
This code simply brings up an alert box Ⓒ telling the user to enter
an email address, brings the user to the *address* element Ⓓ using
focus( ), and stops the submission by returning *false*. Ⓔ

Similarly, the two other *if* statements run a function called
isFilled( ), which checks to see whether the *fullname* Ⓕ and *opinion*
Ⓙ areas have been correctly filled out. If they have, the script
returns *true* Ⓝ and submission continues. If not, an alert is raised, Ⓖ
Ⓚ the form is focused, Ⓗ Ⓛ and form submission is halted. Ⓘ Ⓜ

Inside *isEmail( )*

So far so good, but how do the validation functions verify that the
user entered valid data? To answer that, let's look at *isEmail( )*.
Figure 4-14 shows the function.

```
Ⓐ  function isEmail(elm) {
Ⓑ      if (elm.value.indexOf("@") != "-1" &&
Ⓒ          elm.value.indexOf(".") != "-1" &&
Ⓓ          elm.value != "")
Ⓔ      return true;
Ⓕ      else return false;
Ⓖ  }
```

Figure 4-14. The is*Email( )* function.

When you look closely at this function, you may wonder where variable *elm* comes from. Remember for *isEmail( )* to do anything you need to pass it a form element to examine. In the *isReady( )* function, the *address* element is passed to *isEmail( )* (Figure 4-13 Ⓑ).

When the form element arrives at the *isEmail( )* function, it is given a new, shorter name—*elm*. Instead of saying *address*'s full name—*document.mailform.address*—we can now refer to it simply as *elm*. The same goes for any form element that you pass to *isEmail( )*. There's a good reason for all of this passing of variables and form elements: you can use *isEmail( )* over and over to check different form elements in different forms.

Where's the @?

As mentioned before, *isEmail( )* takes any form element that you pass it and searches for an @ sign and a period, and makes sure the form element is not blank. If there is an @ sign and a period, then the element contains some sort of email address and the function returns *true*. If the element has no @ sign, no period, or is blank, *isEmail( )* returns *false* to the *if* statement that ran it, thereby stopping the submission.

A valid email address can be anything from *billg@microsoft.com* to *nobody@nowhere.com*. The point is, *isEmail( )* makes sure that some sort of email address is in the form element that you pass it. You'd be surprised how many people who would otherwise ignore the email field include their legitimate addresses when this type of validation is used.

Let's talk Booleans

In programming, the words *true* and *false* are called *Booleans*. One useful aspect of Booleans is that they can be shortened when used to determine if something is true or false in an *if* statement. For instance, *isEmail( )* returns a Boolean after determining whether or not *address* is a valid email address. The *if* statement that is used to handle it,

```
if (isEmail(form.address) == false)
```

is actually the same as a

```
if (!isEmail(form.address))
```

The exclamation point in front of the function is just a short way of saying "If this is false." Similarly,

```
if (isEmail(form.address) == true)
```

is the same as

```
if (isEmail(form.address))
```

Including nothing, other than a value, tells the *if* statement to test if the value is true. It's not that you can't live without knowing this shorthand, but you'll see it used a lot on the Web and it's good to know what this shorthand means.

This *isEmail( )* function uses a common JavaScript function (or method) called *indexOf( )* to search through the form element. Here's an example of how it works. Take a variable called *question* that contains the sentence "Will you find me?"

```
question = "Will you find me?";
```

You can now use *indexOf( )* to search through the sentence. To look for the word "me," run the *indexOf( )* method, with a search for "me" on the variable *question*.

```
question.indexOf("me");
```

What does this give you? The number 14. That's right, *indexOf( )* returns the placement of the word (by character) in the string of text. Consider that the first character, "W," is character 0. If you count all the way up to the "m" in "me," you'll see that "m" is the 14th character in the sentence. Using this method, you can find the placement of any character inside a string of text. What

```
if (isFilled(form.fullname) == false) {
    alert("Please enter your name.");
    form.fullname.focus();
    return false;
}
```

Figure 4-15. Calling *isFilled( )* from *isReady( )*.

happens if *indexOf( )* doesn't find "me" in *question*? It returns a
value of -1. If you apply this logic to an email address, you will
understand how *isEmail( )* uses *indexOf( )*.

The *if* statement in *isEmail( )* Ⓑ uses similar logic to do its
work. If there is an @ sign in the email address element, then a
search for @ will not return a -1. Therefore, as long as the returned
value is not -1, there must be an @ sign somewhere in the email
address element. Similarly, the next line of the *if* statement Ⓒ
uses *indexOf( )* to search for a period. Then it checks to make sure
the field is not blank. Ⓓ If everything is cool, *isEmail( )* returns
true; Ⓔ if not, it returns *false*. Ⓕ

Fill in the blanks

After making sure the form contains a valid email address,
isReady( ) checks the email form's remaining elements: *fullname*
and *opinion*. It does this using the function *isFilled( )*, which
determines if a form element is empty or not. Figure 4-15 shows
how the function is used in *isReady( )* to check the name field.
The *fullname* element, which contains the visitor's name, is
passed to *isFilled( )*.

```
Ⓐ  function isFilled(elm) {
Ⓑ      if (elm.value == "" ||
Ⓒ          elm.value == null)
Ⓓ      return false;
Ⓔ      else return true;
    }
```

Figure 4-16. The *isFilled( )* function.

Because *isFilled( )* is just checking for *any* content, it's a simple function, as shown in Figure 4-16. When a form element, such as *fullname*, is passed to *isFilled( )*, the element is given a shorter name: *elm*. **Ⓐ** This is exactly what happens in *isEmail( )*. Next, the function looks at the element **Ⓑ** **Ⓒ** and determines if it is blank or not. If the element has nothing in it, **Ⓓ** *isFilled( )* returns *false*. Otherwise **Ⓔ** it returns *true*. If *isFilled( )* returns *false*, *isReady( )* pops up an alert box and focuses the form element.

The big picture

Now that you understand how individual elements are validated, you're ready to look at the big picture: *isReady( )*. When it comes time to validate your forms, *isReady( )* is the only thing you will need to modify; the validation functions are designed to play along. You may wonder where the separate validation functions, like *isFilled( )* and *isEmail( )*, are kept. As a habit, you should place them right above *isReady( )*.

So let's look again at *isReady()*, which we've repeated as Figure 4-17.

```
Ⓐ  function isReady(form) {
Ⓑ  if (isEmail(form.address) == false) { // a real email?
Ⓒ  alert("Please enter your email address.");
Ⓓ  form.address.focus( );
Ⓔ  return false;
       }
Ⓕ  if (isFilled(form.fullname) == false) { // a full name?
Ⓖ  alert("Please enter your name.");
Ⓗ  form.fullname.focus( );
Ⓘ  return false;
       }
Ⓙ  if (isFilled(form.opinion) == false) { //a message/opinion?
Ⓚ  alert("Please enter your opinion.");
Ⓛ  form.opinion.focus( );
Ⓜ  return false;
       }
Ⓝ  return true;
       }
```

Figure 4-17. The *isReady( )* function.

Designing with JavaScript

```
<HTML>
<HEAD><TITLE>Send Us Mail</TITLE>
<SCRIPT LANGUAGE = "JavaScript">
<! --
// Check for email address: look for [@] and [.]
function isEmail(elm) {
   if (elm.value.indexOf("@")  != "-1" &&
      elm.value.indexOf(".")  != "-1" &&
      elm.value != "")
   return true;
   else return false;
}
// Check for null and for empty
function isFilled(elm) {
   if (elm.value == "" ||
      elm.value == null)
   return false;
   else return true;
}
function isReady(form) {
   if (isEmail(form.address) == false) {        // is address element a real email address?
   alert("Please enter your email address.");
   form.address.focus( );
   return false;
   }
   if (isFilled(form.fullname) == false) {      // is fullname element filled?
   alert("Please enter your name.");
   form.fullname.focus( );
   return false;
   }
   if (isFilled(form.opinion) == false) {       // is opinion element filled?
   alert("Please enter your opinion.");
   form.opinion.focus( );
   return false;
   }
return true;
}
// -->
</SCRIPT>
</HEAD>
<BODY BGCOLOR = "#FFFFFF">
<FORM NAME = "mailform" onSubmit = "return isReady(this)" ACTION = "cgi-bin/mailform.cgi">
your name: <INPUT NAME = "fullname" TYPE = TEXT>
your email: <INPUT NAME = "address" TYPE = TEXT>
<P>your opinion:<P><TEXTAREA NAME="opinion" ROWS = 6 COLS = 64 WRAP></TEXTAREA>
<P><INPUT TYPE = SUBMIT VALUE = " S e n d ">
<INPUT TYPE = RESET VALUE = " T r a s h ">
</FORM>
</BODY>
</HTML>
```

Figure 4-18. Complete source code for the form validation script.

Before your form is submitted, it is passed to *isReady( )* Ⓐ for validation. Next, a series of *if* statements validate the individual elements of the form. Finally, if all of the form elements are filled out correctly, *isReady( )* returns *true* Ⓝ and the form is submitted.

There is a distinct pattern to each element's validation: it's all in the *if* statement. Basically, each element has its own *if* statement. Let's go through the process of constructing one of these *if* statements.

To begin with, we place the name of the element to be validated inside an *if* statement. Then the element is passed to a validation function. The form is:

```
if (validation function's name(form element's name) ==
false) {
```

For example, if you want to make sure that the *fullname* element is filled, you'll pass that element to *isFilled( )*:

```
if (isFilled(form.fullname) == false)
```

If the element passes validation, meaning it is filled, then *isFilled( )* will return *true*. If the element is blank, then *isFilled( )* will return *false*. Since the *if* statement tests for a *false* value, the code that follows (in braces) will be run only if the validation function returns *false*.

The code that follows the *if* statement alerts visitors of their mistake and then brings them to the element in question. You tell JavaScript what message to put in the alert box by passing the message to the *alert* function. Ⓒ Ⓖ Ⓚ

Finally, bring the visitor to the form element using *focus( )* Ⓓ Ⓗ Ⓛ and return *false* to stop the submission. Ⓔ Ⓘ Ⓜ

Figure 4-18 shows the entire HTML page for validating a form in this way.

Validate this!

For your experimental pleasure, here are a few other functions that you may find useful in validating your forms. All of these can be plugged right in, just like *isEmail( )* and *isFilled( )*.

Is it an integer? The function shown in Figure 4-19 can be used to check over a form element and determine if it is a positive integer. If it's not an integer, the function will return *false*.

```
function isInt(elm) {
var elmstr = elm.value + " ";
   if (elmstr == " ") return false;
   for (var i = 0; i < elmstr.length; i++) {
      if (elmstr.charAt(i) < "0" ||
         elmstr.charAt(i) > "9") {
      return false;
      }
   }
return true;
}
```

Figure 4-19. *isInt( )* checks to see if an element contains a positive integer.

```
function isPhone(elm) {
var elmstr = elm.value + " ";
   if (elmstr.length != 12) return false;
   for (var i = 0; i < elmstr.length; i++) {
      if ((i < 3 && i > -1) ||
         (1 > 3 && i < 7) ||
         (i > 7 && i < 12)) {
         if (elmstr.charAt(i) < "0" ||
            elmstr.charAt(i) > "9") return false;
      }
      else if (elmstr.charAt(i) != "-") return false;
   }
return true;
}
```

Figure 4.20. *isPhone( )* checks to see if an element contains a phone number.

Is it a phone number? The function shown in Figure 4-20 will return *true* for any complete phone number with a three digit area code. It should be in the form: xxx-xxx-xxxx. Sorry Bjorn, this only takes into account U.S. phone numbers.

5

Getting in Line with Arrays

Arrays are the great organizers of information. This chapter will give you a gentle introduction to arrays: what they are, how they work, and how to use them. Then we'll see examples of arrays in action. First you'll learn to randomize your site: sounds, images, and text will never be the same. Next, we'll use arrays to convert numbers from the *Date* object to the names of days and months. Finally, we'll combine arrays with forms to create a simple navigational device that will save space and help organize your site.

The array concept

Think of an array as a straight line of people, each holding something in his or her hands. Since the line is completely straight, each person can be addressed by a number. When you ask, "Would the first person in line please show me what's in your hands?" the person at the front of the line will show you what he or she is holding. When you ask, "Would the 99th person in the line please show me what's in your hands?" the 99th person in line will show you what he or she is holding. This is very useful since you don't have to know anyone's name, just their place in line. This is a concept practiced all over the world: Ever been to a deli?

To relate this to JavaScript you have to change the terms around a little. The line of people is an *array*. Each person in the line is an *element* of the array. Finally, the object in each person's hands is the data stored in each element.

To create an array in JavaScript, just create a new *Array* object:

```
var people = new Array( );
```

This creates a new array called *people*. Each element of the array is accessed by placing the number of the element in brackets. So the first element of the *people* array looks like this:

```
people[0];
```

The first element of the array is indicated by 0, not 1. (Except in Netscape 2, of course; see the sidebar "Arrays are everywhere except in Netscape 2.") To give some data to the first element of the *people* array, simply use the same format that you use with regular variables:

```
people[0] = "my data";
```

Here the value of the first element in the array is "my data." Simple, right? Now let's apply these array concepts to some real scripts.

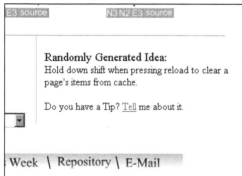

Figure 5-1. JavaScript Tip of the Week's randomly generated idea.

Being unpredictable

Did you ever want to enliven your site by adding a random quote, image, or sound? You could have randomly selected quotes, or background music…you could even build a random sentence out of random nouns, adjectives, and verbs. Besides being a good way to spiff up your site, creating a randomizing script is a good way to learn about arrays and to learn more about functions and variables.

The first step in the process of creating randomly generated "stuff" is to create an array (or list) of words, quotes, images, or other HTML-related objects. First, you need to have some information that you want to randomize; this can be anything from simple words to embedded sounds, graphics, or Java applets.

Figure 5-1 shows a picture of my JavaScript Tip of the Week Web site *(http://webcoder.com/tip/)*. Notice that a randomly generated idea is displayed at the bottom of the page. A different idea is displayed every time you visit, no server-side includes or CGI required.

```
Ⓐ var ideas = new Array( );
Ⓑ ideas[0] = "Type \"about:cache\" into your browser to
     find everything that is stored in your cache.";
Ⓒ ideas[1] = "Type \"about:mozilla\" to get an odd
     message from the Netscape team.";
Ⓓ ideas[2] = "Hold down Shift when pressing Reload to
     clear a page\'s items from cache.";
Ⓔ ideas[3] = "Type \"view-source:\" preceding a
     document\'s URL to automatically view its source.";
```

Figure 5-2. Array for the JavaScript Tip of the Week's randomly generated idea.

Here are the four ideas included in my array:

- Type "about:cache" into your browser to find everything that is stored in your cache.
- Type "about:mozilla" to get an odd message from the Netscape team.
- Hold down Shift when pressing Reload to clear a page's items from cache.
- Type "view-source:" preceding a document's URL to automatically view its source.

Everything you just learned about arrays is going to be used to rearrange these tips. The first step is to put all of the tips in an array, as shown in Figure 5-2. First a new array Ⓐ called *ideas* is created. The next four lines give the values of each of the four elements in the array.

Once you've put the tips in an array, accessing them is easy. Below, *document.write( )* has been used to print out the "about:cache" tip:

```
document.write(ideas[0]);
```

Since the "about:cache" tip is in the first element of the array Ⓑ passing that element to *document.write( )* prints out that tip. Passing *ideas[1]* Ⓒ to *document.write( )* would print out the "about:mozilla" tip, *ideas[2]* Ⓓ would print out the "Shift-Reload" tip, and *ideas[3]* Ⓔ would print out the "view source" tip.

Arrays are everywhere, except in Netscape 2

Arrays are not supported in the oldest version of JavaScript, which is part of Netscape 2. They are supported, however, in Netscape 3 and later and in Internet Explorer 3 and later. But, unless you want to alienate those of us laggards still using the older versions of Netscape, you'll have to find a way around this.

The workaround involves user-defined objects, something we'll explore in some depth in Chapter 12, *Advanced Applications*. For now, just accept the fact that the code below, which is in the form of a function, will create and manage arrays like a true array does.

Array constructor function

```
function makeArray(len) {
    for (var i = 0; i < len; i++) this[i] = null;
this.length = len;
}
```

Making an array of four tips using this function is almost identical to the method used with the true array object shown in Figure 5-2.

```
var ideas = new makeArray(4);
ideas[0] = "Type \"about:cache\" into your browser to find everything
          that is stored in your cache.";
ideas[1] = "Type \"about:mozilla\" to get an odd message from the
          Netscape team.";
ideas[2] = "Hold down Shift when pressing reload to clear a page\'s items
          from cache.";
ideas[3] = "Type \"view-source:\" preceding a document\'s URL to
          automatically view its source.";
```

The most visible difference is that you are making a new *makeArray( )* object as opposed to an *Array( )* object. There is one other difference: you are required to tell *makeArray( )* the number of elements in the array. In this scenario, the array has 4 elements, so the first line is:

```
var ideas = new makeArray(4);
```

The rest of this example will assume that you are using this backwards-compatible method.

```
function rand(n) {
seed = (0x015a4e35 * seed) % 0x7fffffff;
return (seed >> 16) % n;
}
var now = new Date( )
var seed = now.getTime( ) % 0xffffffff
```

Figure 5-3. A random number generator.

Making random numbers

Now that you have your tips (or words, images, or whatever else) in an array, you need to randomize them. For this, we will use a random number generator (naturally). The one we'll use relies on the system clock to produce a random value. Figure 5-3 shows the function that creates random numbers.

At this point, I'm going to assume you're not too interested in the mathematical details of this. To put it simply, this function takes the current time in milliseconds, multiplies that by a large (hexadecimal) number, and takes the remainder of the resulting value divided by your number. This leaves you with an integer (whole number) from 0 to your number. The last line of this function is simple but important. It returns the random number, which means that the random number will be placed where you originally run the function. So running the random number generator like this

```
document.write (rand (5));
```

prints a random number 0 through 4 on the page. It's as if the function is just an automated random number variable. You will find that *return* can be used in many other functions to simulate a variable.

Now you need to apply the random number generator to the array of tips, but how? Take the total number of tips in the array, determined by using the *length* property, and send that to the random number generator. The *length* property of the array gives you the total number of elements in the array. Think back to the people analogy; it's like the number of people in the line.

```
rand (ideas.length);
```

```
<HTML>
<HEAD>
<TITLE>Randomly Generated Idea</TITLE>

<SCRIPT LANGUAGE = "JavaScript">

// The Array Function

function makeArray(len) {
    for (var i = 0; i < len; i++) this[i] = null;
this.length = len;
}

// This is where the array of text/images/sounds is created.

var ideas = new makeArray(4);
ideas[0] = "Type \"about:cache\" into your browser to find everything that is stored in
your cache.";
ideas[1] = "Type \"about:mozilla\" to get an odd message from the Netscape team.";
ideas[2] = "Hold down Shift when pressing Reload to clear a page\'s items from cache.";
ideas[3] = "Type \"view-source:\" preceding a document\'s URL to automatically view
its source.";

// The random number generator.

function rand(n) {
seed = (0x015a4e35 * seed) % 0x7fffffff;
return (seed >> 16) % n;
}
var now = new Date( )
var seed = now.getTime( ) % 0xffffffff

</SCRIPT>

</HEAD>

<BODY>
Today's Randomly Generated Idea is:
<P>

<SCRIPT LANGUAGE = "JavaScript">

// Where you place this is where the random object will be displayed.

document.write(ideas[rand(ideas.length)])
</SCRIPT>

</BODY>
</HTML>
```

Figure 5-4. Code for a page that writes a random element to a page.

You have a random number, but you need to grab the element that corresponds to that random number out of the array. Since the random number returned is 0 through 3, you can use that to access the elements of the array. Put the random number code where the number of the array element goes and presto — random tips:

```
document.write (ideas [rand (ideas.length)])
```

Figure 5-4 gives the entire source for the randomly generated idea page.

Random sounds and images, too

You are not limited to using words: you can use images, embeds, other HTML-related objects, or any combination of these. Simply plug your object directly into the array. If you want a random sound track, for instance, try this format:

```
var music = new makeArray(4);
music[0] = "<EMBED AUTOSTART = TRUE HIDDEN = TRUE
SRC = 'rave.mid'>";
music[1] = "<EMBED AUTOSTART = TRUE HIDDEN = TRUE
SRC = 'pop.mid'>";
music[2] = "<EMBED AUTOSTART = TRUE HIDDEN = TRUE
SRC = 'prelude.mid'>";
music[3] = "<EMBED AUTOSTART = TRUE HIDDEN = TRUE
SRC = 'take5.mid'>";
```

This creates an array of four embeds. To print them out in a random fashion just follow the same steps as you did with the words. Keep in mind that this array is named *music*, not *ideas*, and the code must reflect that.

Doing the date right

Back in Chapter 1, you learned about the *Date* object. You learned how to access different units of time, how to display the current day, and how to find the difference (in days) between two dates. What you did not learn, however, was how to display a fully formatted date on the page (e.g. Friday, January 1, 1999). Figure 5-5 uses the "associative" powers of arrays to solve this little problem.

Essentially, the script associates JavaScript's numerically formatted dates with ones that you and I understand. The day of the week, for instance, is a number 0 through 6 when taken

```
<HTML>
<HEAD><TITLE>Doing the Date Right</TITLE>
</HEAD>
<BODY BGCOLOR = "#FFFFFF">
<SCRIPT LANGUAGE="Javascript">
<! --

A  // Array function
   function makeArray(len) {
   for (var i = 0; i < len; i++) this[i] = null;
   this.length = len;
   }

B  // Array of day names
   var dayNames = new makeArray(7);
   dayNames[0] = "Sunday";
   dayNames[1] = "Monday";
   dayNames[2] = "Tuesday";
   dayNames[3] = "Wednesday";
   dayNames[4] = "Thursday";
   dayNames[5] = "Friday";
   dayNames[6] = "Saturday';

C  // Array of month Names
   var monthNames = new makeArray(12);
   monthNames[0] = "January";
   monthNames[1] = "February";
   monthNames[2] = "March";
   monthNames[3] = "April";
   monthNames[4] = "May";
   monthNames[5] = "June";
   monthNames[6] = "July";
   monthNames[7] = "August";
   monthNames[8] = "September";
   monthNames[9] = "October";
   monthNames[10] = "November";
   monthNames[11] = "December";

   //Elements of Date object assigned to variables
D     var now = new Date( );
E     var day = now.getDay( );
F     var month = now.getMonth( );
G     var year = now.getYear( );
H     var date = now.getDate( );

I  //Code to print Date as Monday, July 4, 1997
   document.write(dayNames[day] + ", " + monthNames[month] + " " + date + ",
   19" + year);

   // -->
   </SCRIPT>
   </BODY>
   </HTML>
```

Figure 5-5. Script to print date as Monday, July 4, 1997.

directly from the *Date* object. This script has an array named *dayNames* **B** that contains the full names of each day of the week. (The first element, *dayNames[0]*, contains the word "Sunday"; the second element, *dayNames[1]*, contains the word "Monday"; and so on.)

When the script asks for the day of the week from JavaScript, *now.getDay( )*, what's returned is a number 0 through 6. In this script, the numeric day is stored in variable *day*. **E** So if it's Thursday, *day* will be 4. If you plug 4 into *dayNames* you'll access *dayNames[4]*, which contains "Thursday," which is what we want to display.

This process is also used for the month names, which have their own array, *monthNames*. **C** If it's July, *now.getMonth( )* returns 6, which is stored in variable *month*. **F** Plugging that number into the *monthNames* array gives you "July."

The last line **I** is the most important; it displays the formatted date on the page by inserting the numeric date values into their corresponding arrays, as previously explained.

Thus if the value of *day* is 1, the value of *month* is 6, the value of *date* is 4, and the value of *year* is 97, the script displays "Monday, July 4, 1997."

Note that the year and the day of the month do not need special formatting (although "19" preceeds the two-digit year value).

Jumpin' jive

In the real world, there is never enough space; but that doesn't have to be true of the Web world. In my opinion, the select menu (the pop-up menu in a form) is the object of choice when you want to save space on a Web site. As shown in Figure 5-6, select menus can contain lots of options but take up very little space when they're not being used. You often see select menus in forms for "multiple choice" questions on forms. Teletext's home page features a JavaScript jump list that lets users see all available options and quickly pick one. With JavaScript, it's all done locally and there's no waiting for the server to process the information.

In this section, we'll learn how to use JavaScript to add this "jumpin' jive" functionality to your page. There are three steps to this script:

Teletext

http://www.teletext.com

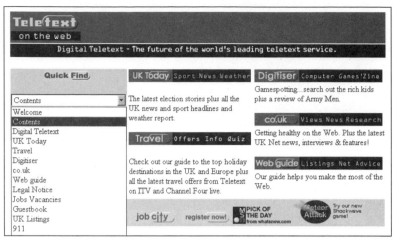

Figure 5-6. Teletext features a jump list to the major areas of the site.

- Create arrays for the names and URLs of your pages;
- Display the form on your page;
- Create the "jump" code.

Creating the arrays

To begin the select menu, you need to create two arrays. The first array contains the names of the pages that you want to appear in the select menu. The second array, used in tandem with the first, contains the URLs of those pages. To make this compatible with Netscape 2, as opposed to Internet Explorer or any later version of Netscape, you will need to use an array constructor function, shown in Figure 5-7. This function is different than the one we used before (with the random script) because we will be giving the data to the arrays in a different way, and the function must accommodate that.

```
function makeArray( ) {
var args = makeArray.arguments;
   for (var i = 0; i < args.length; i++) {
   this[i] = args[i];
   }
this.length = args.length;
}
```

Figure 5-7. Array constructor function for "jumpin' jive."

Designing with JavaScript

```
// The pages array
var pages = new makeArray("Select a Page",
    "This Week",
    "Tip Repository",
    "The Book",
    "The Hut ",
    "E-Mail");

// The urls array
var urls = new makeArray(" ",
    "this_week/",
    "tip_week_past.html",
    "the_book/",
    "the_hut/",
    "e-mail.html");
```

Figure 5-8. The two arrays used in the "jumpin jive" script.

Unlike the arrays in the random script, the arrays in the jump menu script are created all at once, not element by element. In Figure 5-8, examine the *pages* array closely. The data for this array is passed directly to the array constructor function. "Select a Page" is the data in the first element of the array, *pages[0]*; "This Week" is the data in the second element of the array, *pages[1]*, etc.

The first arrays, *pages,* contains the page names, or descriptions, to be displayed in the select menu. The second array, *urls,* contains the URLs that correspond to those descriptions. For example, "This Week" is the second element in the *pages* array; selecting "This Week" in the select menu will load the page at *this_week/* because they are both the second elements in the arrays. Note that the first element in the pages

```
Ⓐ document.write('<FORM><SELECT NAME = "menu"
Ⓑ     onChange="goPage(this.form)">');
Ⓒ for (var i = 0; i < pages.length; i++) {
Ⓓ     document.write('<OPTION>' + pages[i]);
    }
Ⓔ document.write('</SELECT></FORM>');
```

Figure 5-9. Code for creating the select script.

array, "Select a Page," does nothing since the corresponding element in the *urls* array is empty. "Select a Page" serves to notify visitors that "yes, you *can* click here."

Displaying it on the page

Now the select menu needs to be displayed on the page. What better way to do this than with JavaScript? You can even automate the process so that you don't need to rewrite the names of all those pages. Figure 5-9 shows the code.

This looks confusing at first glance, so let's go through it step by step. The first line **Ⓐ** begins to display the select menu on the

How the array constructor works

Admittedly, the syntax of the array constructor function in Figure 5-7 doesn't appear to make much sense, at least not without any explanation. Though we're not going to delve deeply into the object-oriented aspect of the function, we are going to skim the surface. Let's start by understanding that this array constructor function takes its data in the following format:

```
var myArray = new makeArray(1st argument, 2nd argument, 3rd argument);
```

Each argument that you pass the function becomes an element of the array. The first argument becomes the first element, *myArray[0]*, the second argument becomes the second element, *myArray[1]*, etc. This is different from the previous array constructor function, which allowed us to add elements individually.

```
var args = makeArray.arguments;
```

The array constructor function begins by taking the total number of arguments passed to it, *makeArray.arguments*, and giving that to a variable named *args*. In JavaScript, when you pass arguments to a function, they become properties of that function. So, when you pass *makeArray( )* arguments, those arguments become properties of *makeArray( )*. The property containing the function's arguments, named *arguments*, is an array itself. If you create a new array named *stuff* using *makeArray( )* and pass it the following arguments

```
var stuff = new makeArray("Stuff", "More Stuff", "Even More Stuff");
```

you can access those arguments (after the fact) like so:

```
makeArray.arguments[0] // contains "Stuff"
makeArray.arguments[1] // contains "More Stuff"
makeArray.arguments[2] // contains "Even More Stuff"
```

page, giving it the name *menu*. Then comes the *onChange* Ⓑ event handler. Whenever a user selects an item in the menu, the script will run a function called *goPage( )*, which loads the selected page in the browser window.

Next Ⓒ comes a *for* loop to display all of the options and page names. The *for* loop repeats a specified block of code over and over until a condition is met.

The *for* loop begins by creating a variable, *i*, and setting it equal to 0. Then the code inside brackets is run once. After the code inside brackets is run (we'll get to that shortly), the loop asks, "Is *i* less than the length of the pages array?" If it is, the

It may seem odd to treat the function like an object, but in JavaScript functions are considered objects. (Normally, when you pass arguments to a function, they are put inside variables contained in the parentheses where the function is defined; this is simply another way of doing things.)

This is only the beginning: arguments that are properties of the *makeArray( )* function now need to become part of the *stuff* array. This task is accomplished with a *for* loop:

```
for (var i = 0; i < args.length; i++) {
this[i] = args[i];
}
```

This loop creates one element in the *stuff* array for every argument that was passed to the function. Keep in mind that the arguments in the function, *makeArray.arguments*, were given to variable *args* in the first line of the function (to save typing). To access the first argument which will be the first element of the *stuff* array, you would say *args[0]* (this returns the word "Stuff"). By setting *this[0]* — which is really *stuff[0]* — equal to *args[0]*, you are filling the first element of the newly created *stuff* array with the value contained in the first argument passed to the function (*makeArray( )*). This process is continued for each of the arguments that were passed to the function, thereby filling up the *stuff* array.

```
this.length = args.length;
```

After the array has been filled, it is given a *length* property, something that is essential to all arrays. Once this step is completed, the array is complete.

```
stuff[0] // contains "Stuff"
stuff[1] // contains "More Stuff"
stuff[2] // contains "Even More Stuff"
```

```
Ⓐ  function goPage(form) {
Ⓑ    var i = form.menu.selectedIndex;
Ⓒ      if (i != 0) {
Ⓓ        window.location.href = urls[i];
        }
      }
```

Figure 5-10. The *goPage( )* function.

value of *i* is increased by one (*i*++), and the loop repeats until *i* is equal to the length of the *pages* array.

So how are the page descriptions and their options displayed? Each time the loop repeats, *document.write( )* Ⓓ displays an option and one of the page descriptions from the *page* array. For example, the first time the *for* loop runs, *i* is equal to 0. When you plug *i* (or 0) into the pages array, it looks like this: *pages[0]*, and you get the first element of the array, i.e., "Select a Page." The second time through the loop, you get the second element in the array, "This Week." Since each time the loop repeats, variable *i* is increased by 1, all the rest of the descriptions (and their options) are displayed until the end of the *pages* array is reached. After all of the options for the select menu are displayed on the page, the select menu and the form are closed off. Ⓔ

Jumping to the page

The last step in creating the select menu is to create the function that jumps to the selected page. As you learned earlier, a form can pass itself to a function. In the *goPage( )* function shown in Figure 5-10, the select menu's form is passed to the function Ⓐ as variable form.

The function uses the *selectedIndex* property Ⓑ of the select menu (named *menu*) to determine which option is selected. For example, if the first option is selected, the value of *selectedIndex* is 0. If the second option is selected, the value is 1. The function will use this information to determine which URL to deliver.

Since the first option in the select menu, "Select a Page," does nothing, the function does not change the page if the *selectedIndex* is 0. Placing this line within an *if* statement Ⓒ lets

How do I get this to work with frames?

Make the line that says

> window.location.href = urls[i];

reference a frame instead of the current window. Like this:

> parent.frame.location.
> href = urls[i];

Where *frame* is the name of the frame that you want changed.

```
<HTML>
<HEAD>
<TITLE></TITLE>
<SCRIPT LANGUAGE = "JavaScript">
<! --
// Array Function
function makeArray( ) {
var args = makeArray.arguments;
   for (var i = 0; i < args.length; i++) {
   this[i] = args[i];
   }
this.length = args.length;
}
// This array holds the descriptions and names of the pages.
var pages = new makeArray("Select a Page",
   "This Week",
   "Tip Repository",
   "The Book",
   "The Hut ",
   "E-Mail");
// This array hold the URLs of the pages.
var urls = new makeArray("",
   "this_week/",
   "tip_week_past.html",
   "the_book/",
   "the_hut/",
   "e-mail.html");
// This function determines which page is selected and goes to it.
function goPage(form) {
i = form.menu.selectedIndex;
   if (i != 0) {
   window.location.href = urls[i];
   }
}
// -->
</SCRIPT>
</HEAD>
<BODY>
Choose A Page and Jump:<BR>
<SCRIPT LANGUAGE = "JavaScript">
<! --
// The select menu will be displayed wherever you place this code.
document.write('<FORM><SELECT NAME = "menu" onChange = "goPage(this.form)">');
   for (var i = 0; i < pages.length; i++) {
   document.write('<OPTION>' + pages[i]);
   }
document.write('</SELECT></FORM>');
// -->
</SCRIPT>
</BODY>
</HTML>
```

Figure 5-11. Source code for the select menu script.

us tell the function to change the window location only if *i* does not equal 0.

The last line **D** is the most important, since it brings you to the URL you selected using *window.location*. Here's where the *urls* array comes into play. By matching the selected option with an entry from the *urls* array, the script determines which document to load. For instance, if you select the second option ("This Week") the select menu will return a *selectedIndex* of 1. Since the *urls* array and the *pages* array mirror each other, "This Week" corresponds to *this_week/*.

Figure 5-11 shows the complete code for the "jumpin' jive" script.

6

Too Many Browsers?
Not Really

A long time ago, life was simple. There was standard HTML and there was NCSA Mosaic. Then came Netscape with their HTML "extensions" and suddenly sites started labeling themselves "Enhanced for Netscape," meaning "this site looks lousy in Mosaic." By the time Microsoft came along with Internet Explorer, Mosaic was effectively dead, and Netscape and Microsoft were locked in a war to extend HTML in a way that would make one of their products the dominant browser.

Fortunately, they both handle JavaScript, albeit to different extents, so it becomes the job of JavaScript to differentiate between the two. This chapter is all about making your site as friendly as possible to each browser, even different versions of those browsers.

What browser is that knocking at my door?

Before you learn how JavaScript differentiates one browser from another, you need to understand the different ways that JavaScript can get information from the browser. This applies to both Netscape Navigator and Internet Explorer.

The *navigator* object

JavaScript identifies browsers through the *navigator* object. Though "navigator" is the name of Netscape's browser, it serves the same function in IE's implementation of JavaScript. There's a lot of information that you can get from the *navigator* object, all of which will be taught in this chapter. Table 6-1 shows three of the most useful properties for getting information about browsers, versions, and operating systems.

Properties of the browser object

The property	What it refers to
navigator.appName	The browser's name.
navigator.appVersion	The brower's version.
navigator.userAgent	The browser's "userAgent."

Table 6-1.

Without any context, the significance of these may not hit home. So Table 6-2 shows some examples of what you actually get when you use these properties on different browsers.

Now you should begin to see the power behind these properties: they can determine the application name, version, and platform for any browser.

The first of these, *navigator.appName*, is the most straight-forward: It tells you the name of the browser and nothing more. If you are using Netscape Navigator, the value of *appName* will be "Netscape." If you are using Internet Explorer, the value will be "Microsoft Internet Explorer."

Results of *navigator* properties on different browsers

Browser	appName	appVersion	userAgent
Netscape 3.01 on a PPC Mac	Netscape	3.01 (Macintosh; I; PPC)	Mozilla/3.01 (Macintosh; PPC)
Netscape 4.0 on Windows 95	Netscape	4.0 (Win95; I)	Mozilla/4.0 (Win95; I)
Internet Explorer 3.0 on Windows 95	Microsoft Internet Explorer	2.0 (compatible; MSIE 3.01; Windows 95)	Mozilla/2.0 (compatible; MSIE 3.01; Windows 95)
Internet Explorer 4.0 on Windows 95	Microsoft Internet Explorer	4.0 (compatible; MSIE 4.0; Windows 95)	Mozilla/4.0 (compatible; MSIE 4.0; Windows 95)

Table 6-2.

The second property, *navigator.appVersion*, returns the version number as well as the browser's platform. When you ask Netscape 4.0 for its *appVersion*, it will return "4.0 (Win95; I)."

The third property, *navigator.userAgent*, essentially combines the first two properties. The user agent is not new to the browser world; it was around long before JavaScript. Many servers use the information gathered from the user agent to determine which browsers are being used on their sites. For the most part, however, we will be dealing with *appName* and *appVersion*.

You can access all of these properties without any extra work. For example, to print out the name of a browser, stored in *navigator.appName*, all you need to do is pass it to *document.write( )*.

```
document.write("Welcome all " + navigator.appName +
"users.");
```

This, however, is relatively pointless. The point of checking browser identities is to tailor your pages (or your entire site) for different browsers. The rest of this chapter is all about doing just that.

Browser name and number

The browser's name and major version number (2, 3, 4, etc.) almost always determine which features a browser supports. For example, IE 3 does not support Microsoft's Dynamic HTML but IE 4 does. Netscape 2 and IE 3 do not support JavaScript image replacement but Netscape 3 and 4 and IE 4 do. If you know what browser and version you're dealing with, you know a lot about what kind of documents you can serve.

The method of browser "detection" that you will learn here is only one of many. In almost all cases, however, this is the most robust and versatile method.

To determine the browser's name and version, we'll use two of the properties you learned about earlier: *appName* and *appVersion*. To make the script shorter, the values of these properties are given to two variables, as shown in Figure 6-1.

```
A  bName = navigator.appName;
B  bVer = parseInt(navigator.appVersion);
```

Figure 6-1. Values of *appName* and *appVersion* are given to variables.

A note about Internet Explorer 3

If you look at Internet Explorer 3.01's *appVersion*, you will notice that something is askew. Instead of giving you what you would expect, "3.01 (Win95)", which stands for version 3.01 running on Windows 95, it gives you "2.0 (compatible; MSIE 3.01; Windows 95)." The reason for this is that when Internet Explorer originally came out, it tried to be compatible with Netscape 2.0 and its implementation of JavaScript. Being compatible with Netscape 2.0 meant having an *appVersion* that returned the same as Netscape 2.0 would.

```
Ⓐ  if (bName == "Netscape" && bVer == 4) {        // Is it Netscape version 4?
Ⓑ    document.write("This is Netscape 4.0");        // If it is, then say so.
   }
Ⓒ  else ("This is not Netscape 4.0");              // If it's not, say that.
```

Figure 6-2. Checking for Netscape 4.0 and printing the results.

First Ⓐ the browser's name is given to variable *bName*. The second line Ⓑ gives the browser's version to variable *bVer*. This line also does something else — it uses a built-in JavaScript function, *parseInt( )*, to extract the integer value (whole number) from *navigator.appVersion*. It works like this: The *appVersion* of Netscape 3.01 on a Power Mac is "3.01 (Macintosh; I; PPC)". When this is passed to *parseInt( )*, the returned value is simply 3, an integer. The *appVersion* of Internet Explorer 4.0 for Windows 95 is "4.0 (compatible; MSIE 4.0b1; Windows 95)." When this is passed to *parseInt()*, the returned value is 4.

Matching up names and numbers

Now that you have the browser name and its major version number, you need to match up those names and numbers. This is done with *if* statements. Figure 6-2 shows an *if* statement that detects the presence of Netscape 4.0 using the *bName* and *bVer* variables defined above.

This *if* statement compares both the browser's name and version: If the browser name is "Netscape" and the version is 4, Ⓐ then this must be Netscape 4. If that's the case, the code within braces is run Ⓑ (print "This is Netscape 4.0" to the page). If the browser is not Netscape 4, then it defaults to the code following *else.* Ⓒ

```
Ⓐ  if (bName == "Netscape" && bVer >= 4) br = "n4";                          // Netscape 4?
Ⓑ  else if (bName == "Netscape" && bVer == 3) br = "n3";                     // Netscape 3?
Ⓒ  else if (bName == "Netscape" && bVer == 2) br = "n2";                     // Netscape 2?
Ⓓ  else if (bName == "Microsoft Internet Explorer" && bVer >= 4) br = "e4";  // IE 4?
Ⓔ  else if (bName == "Microsoft Internet Explorer") br = "e3";              // IE 3?
Ⓕ  else br = "n2";          // if none of these are found, default to Netscape 2
```

Figure 6-3. Detecting the five major browsers.

```
<HTML>
<HEAD>
<TITLE>A Page</TITLE>
<SCRIPT LANGUAGE = "JavaScript">
<! --
bName = navigator.appName;
bVer = parseInt(navigator.appVersion);
if (bName == "Netscape" && bVer >= 4) br = "n4";
else if (bName == "Netscape" && bVer == 3) br = "n3";
else if (bName == "Netscape" && bVer == 2) br = "n2";
else if (bName == "Microsoft Internet Explorer" &&
    bVer >= 4) br = "e4";
else if (bName == "Microsoft Internet Explorer") br = "e3";
else br = "n2";
```

Figure 6-4. HTML document with version detection.

By combining a series of *if* statements similar to the one in Figure 6-2, you can detect any browser (that supports JavaScript). Figure 6-3 shows how to use *if* statements to piece together the identity of the browser. Anything from Netscape 4 (or greater) all the way down to IE 3 is detected.

When the browser's name and version are matched up, variable *br* is set to one of five strings: *n4, n3, n2, e4, e3*. If the browser is Netscape 4, Ⓐ then *br* is "n4." If it's Netscape 3, Ⓑ *br* is set to "n3." If it's Netscape 2, Ⓒ *br* equals "n2." If the browser is IE 4, Ⓓ *br* is "e4." Any earlier versions of Internet Explorer Ⓔ set *br* to "e3." If none of these browsers are found, Ⓕ the default value for *br* is *n2*: Netscape 2.

With this information, you can begin tailoring your pages to fit any or each of these browser's needs. Figure 6-4 shows the start of an HTML document with the basic version detection script.

The page now has a working knowledge of what browser is being used, and it's time to make use of that. The variable *br* has identified the browser as one of five possible browsers: *n4, n3, n2, e4, or e3*. You already know what these stand for, so let's put them to work. Keep this template page in mind for the rest of the chapter.

Different browsers, different needs

Telling your visitors to "choose the Netscape-enhanced site" or to "click here if you have Internet Explorer" doesn't cut it anymore.

How do I detect Netscape or IE 5.0 (and beyond)?

By now, you should understand the concept behind the *if* statements and how they use *bName* and *bVer*. To determine if a browser is version number 5, for instance, check its *bVer*.

```
If (bName == "Netscape"
&& bVer == 5) br = "n5";
```

Using greater than/equal to, you can determine if a browser is at least, if not more than, a particular version. This *if* statement looks for anything that's Netscape version 3 or above and puts it in the *n3* category:

```
if (bName == "Netscape"
&& bVer >= 3) br = "n3";
```

Why not do the choosing for your visitors automatically and save them the trouble?

Bits and pieces: Tailoring parts of your page

Say your site uses a Netscape 3 feature, such as dynamic images (this is also supported in IE 4). The effect of dynamic images will be appreciated by those with Netscape, but visitors with other browsers, such as IE 3, will be barraged with error messages. Instead of making different pages for browser-specific features like this, why not deploy the browser-detection script?

Figure 6-5 shows how to customize one graphic link on a page. Figure 6-6 shows what this page looks like in IE 3 and Netscape 3.

First, put a trimmed-down browser-detection script in the head of your page. Since you're looking for Netscape 3-compatible browsers (that includes IE 4), you don't need to include *if* statements for IE 3, Netscape 4, or any other browser.

```
<HTML>
<HEAD>
<TITLE>A Page</TITLE>
<SCRIPT LANGUAGE = "JavaScript">
<! --

bName = navigator.appName;
bVer = parseInt(navigator.appVersion);
if ((bName == "Netscape" && bVer >= 3) ||
(bName == "Microsoft Internet Explorer" && bVer >= 4)) br = "n3";
else br = "n2";
// -->
</SCRIPT>
</HEAD>
<BODY BGCOLOR = "#FFFFFF">
<A HREF = "home.html"
onMouseOver = "if (br == 'n3') document.home.src = 'home_on.gif';">
<IMG BORDER = 0 HEIGHT = 35 WIDTH = 111 NAME = "home"
   SRC = "home_off.gif"></A>
</BODY>
</HTML>
```

Figure 6-5. Customizing a graphic link within an HTML document.

Designing with JavaScript

If the browser is Netscape 3 Ⓐ or IE 4 Ⓑ (| | means *or*), variable *br* is set to "n3." In all other cases, Ⓒ *br* is *n2*.

For the sake of simplicity, the body of the page is very brief. When the mouse moves over the image link Ⓔ, the code inside the *onMouseOver* event handler Ⓓ is run. This code uses the dynamic image feature of JavaScript to change the image (named *home*) to a highlighted state. The important part of this is the *if* statement inside the event handler. It only allows the image to be put in a highlighted state if variable *br* is equal to *n3*, meaning that the browser is capable of handling dynamic images.

For many of your pages, a simple *if* statement like this can save you a lot of trouble. As you start experimenting with JavaScript features that only work in certain browsers, you should find this lesson's basic principles useful.

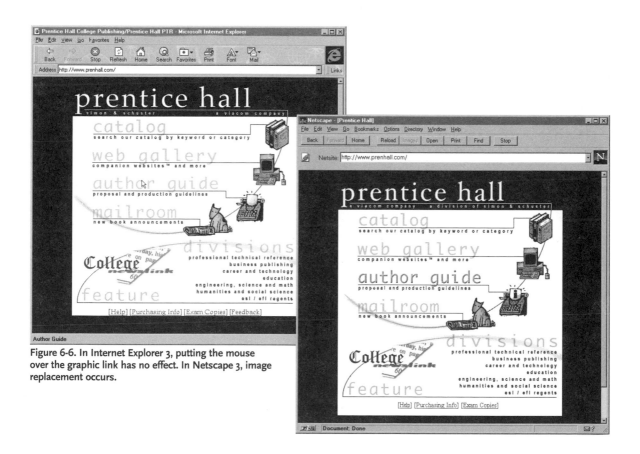

Figure 6-6. In Internet Explorer 3, putting the mouse over the graphic link has no effect. In Netscape 3, image replacement occurs.

The single-frame method

If you use a lot of browser-specific features on your site, then you may want to tailor more than just parts of a page. You may want a totally different page; especially if you're employing features that significantly effect the layout and function of your pages. If this is the case, then the single-frame method is for you.

The back-up black hole

You may wonder, "Why not just direct browsers to different pages using *window.location?*" The reason is what I call the back-up black hole. If you create a special page to direct browsers to their browser-specific pages, when a user presses the back button from any of those pages (which returns you to the redirection page) they will be directed right back to the referring page. This is quite unprofessional and can confuse your visitors.

The single-frame method is the easiest and most reliable way to direct different browsers on your site to different pages; it's also transparent. If you enter a site that uses the single-frame method, a script detects your browser type, creates a single frame for you, and displays a browser-specific page inside that frame. Because it is a single frame, you don't see any frame borders, just the page. A page full of ActiveX controls and other IE-related technologies could be kept "safe" from Netscape using this method.

For this example, we are going to direct IE 4 users to a page that makes extensive use of IE's implementation of "Dynamic HTML," and direct the rest of the pack to a Dynamic HTML-free page. The full HTML is shown in Figure 6-7.

This script takes place in the head of the document that defines the single frame. First, the browser's name and version are determined. Since we only need to know if someone is using IE 4 or not, one *if* statement **B** will do the job. If IE 4 is detected, then variable *br* is set to "e4"; for any other browser, *br* is set to "n2."

Next, a single frame is created for each browser type. If it's IE 4, then the script creates a single frame that displays *index_dynamichtml.html* **C** (the page that uses IE's implementation of Dynamic HTML.) If it's not IE 4, the script creates a different frame **D** that displays *index_nodynamichtml.html*. Since you're not redirecting the browser to a different page, but instead creating a single frame for each page, all of this is transparent to the visitor.

What about the frame borders? Not a problem. When the frameset is created, the first row is set to 100% and the second to nothing. Therefore, when the single frame is defined it will take up the full browser window. Suprisingly, leaving out the second frame does not result in any adverse effects. There's another added value to the single-frame method: since you're using frames, though only one, you now have the ability to set the margin heights and widths of your pages.

```
<HTML>
<HEAD>
A <BASE TARGET="_top">
<SCRIPT LANGUAGE = "JavaScript">
<!--
bName = navigator.appName;
bVer = parseInt(navigator.appVersion);
B if (bName == "Microsoft Internet Explorer" && bVer >= 4) br = "e4";
else br = "n2";

C // Frame for IE 4 with Dynamic HTML.
if (br == "e4") {
document.write('<FRAMESET ROWS = "100%, *" FRAMEBORDER = NO BORDER = 0');
document.write('MARGINHEIGHT=5 MARGINWIDTH=5>');
document.write('<FRAME SRC = "index_dynamichtml.html" SCROLLING = AUTO>');
document.write('</FRAMESET>');
}

D // Frame for every other browser.
else {
document.write('<FRAMESET ROWS = "100%, *" FRAMEBORDER = NO BORDER = 0>');
document.write('MARGINHEIGHT=5 MARGINWIDTH=5>');
document.write('<FRAME SRC = "index_nodynamichtml.html" SCROLLING = AUTO>');
document.write('</FRAMESET>');
}

// -->
</SCRIPT>
</HEAD>
E <BODY BGCOLOR = "#FFFFFF">
This page is what non-JavaScript enabled browsers see.
</BODY>
</HTML>
```

Figure 6-7. HTML for the single-frame method.

When using this method, it is advisable to include $<BASE$ $TARGET = "\_top">$ Ⓐ in the head of your HTML documents, so that the single frame will be cleared whenever a link is followed.

What about browsers *sans* JavaScript? This is always an issue: What if someone doesn't have a JavaScript-capable browser or has JavaScript turned off? The single-frame method takes into account these two scenarios. After closing the script (and the head), create the HTML you want to serve to these users. Ⓔ

This works because if the browser does not support JavaScript, or has it turned off, everything between the *SCRIPT* tags (and comments) will be ignored.

Checking for plug-ins

In Netscape 3 and greater, JavaScript has the ability to detect which plug-ins are installed in a browser and which file types (Director, MIDI, .au, etc.) a browser will support. The two objects that allow for this are *nagivator.plugins* and *navigator.mimeTypes*. The first object contains the names and descriptions of all the plug-ins installed in the browser. The second, *navigator.mimeTypes*, determines which file types the browser can handle. For the most part, this second object is what you will be working with.

Names with a purpose

The names that the browser receives for different file types, also called MIME types, have odd-looking names. For example, a *.dcr* document, the type Shockwave understands, is MIME type *application/x-director*. A VRML document's MIME type is *x-world/x-vrml*. The MIME types that a browser supports almost always determine which plug-ins are installed. If the MIME type *application/x-director* is supported by your browser, then the Shockwave plug-in is most likely installed.

```
Ⓐ  if (navigator.mimeTypes["application/x-director"]) {      // If MIME exists...
Ⓑ  document.write("You have Shockwave!");
    }
Ⓒ  else document.write("You do not have Shockwave.");        // If it doesn't...
```

Figure 6-8. Checking for MIME types.

Figure 6-9. Netscape 3 users with Shockwave see the movie.

How do I find the MIME type for...

If you go into Netscape's *General Preferences/Helpers* menu, or into IE's *View/Options/Programs/File Types* menu, you will be able to find the MIME types for different documents, such as audio, MIDI, etc. Typing "about:plugins" into the location input of Netscape 3, or selecting Netscape's *Help/About Plugins* menu will also spit out a list of all installed plug-ins and their respective MIME types.

To make use of JavaScript's ability to detect MIME types, simply give *nagivator.mimeTypes* the file type that you are looking for, as shown in Figure 6-8. If the file type is found, the object returns *true*; otherwise, it returns *false*.

Notice that the MIME type in question, *application/x-director*, is (sort of) passed to the object. **Ⓐ** The *if* statement determines if the Shockwave MIME type is present in the browser. If it is, then the message "You have Shockwave!" is written to the screen; **Ⓑ** if not, the screen says, "You do not have Shockwave." **Ⓒ**

To make this more useful, you may want to display a Shockwave movie if the file type is found and display a link to download Shockwave if it is not found. Another thing to keep in mind is that this only works in Netscape 3 and greater, so a little version detection can be used to make this more compatible with other browsers.

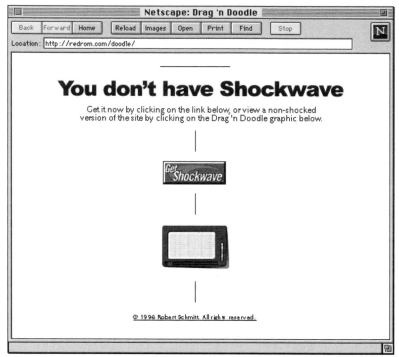

Figure 6-10. Netscape 3 users without Shockwave see a page that links to a non-shocked version of the site and to Macromedia's Shockwave download page. Since we know these users don't have Shockwave, they aren't given a link to the shocked site.

Would you like Shockwave with that?

Let's create a script that creates dramatically different pages depending on the user's configuration. Here are the possibilities:

- If the browser is Netscape 3 or higher and Shockwave is found, display the Shockwave movie (Figure 6-9).
- If the browser is Netscape 3 or higher and Shockwave is not found, display a page that links to the Shockwave download page and to a non-shocked version of the site (Figure 6-10).
- If the browser is IE, show the movie if Shockwave is found, or download the Shockwave ActiveX control if Shockwave is not found (Figure 6-11).
- If the browser is not Netscape 3 or higher or Internet Explorer, display a page that gives users options to enter the shocked or non-shocked versions of the site.

This way, all Netscape 3 and greater users will be taken care of, all IE users will have Shockwave automatically downloaded as a control, and anybody else will be able to decide what they want to do. The script is shown in Figure 6-12.

First, put the browser into one of three categories using the browser detection script: Netscape 3 and greater, IE 3 and greater, and anything else. Ⓐ

Then, if the browser is Netscape 3 or greater and the MIME type is detected, display a Shockwave movie. Ⓑ

If the browser is Netscape 3 or greater but the MIME type is not detected, display a link to download the Shockwave plug-in or an alternative (e.g., an image). Ⓒ

If the browser is IE, then display the Shockwave ActiveX control, which will be automatically downloaded to the browser (and the movie will be played). Ⓓ Most of the popular plug-ins have an ActiveX control as well as a plug-in. For less popular plug-ins, this option may not be one available, in which case you may want to remove that *if* statement.

Finally, if there's no way for JavaScript to detect the presence of Shockwave, display a page with all possible options, so users can decide on their own what to do. Ⓔ

Figure 6-11. IE users will download the Shockwave ActiveX control if Shockwave is not already installed.

Using this example, a simple method of detecting plug-ins/MIME types and displaying them can be deduced. Follow this and your use of plug-ins is sure to be well received by users of all browsers.

Beyond the browser

JavaScript is not limited to detecting browsers and plug-ins, it can also determine on what operating system a browser is running. When you look at the *navigator.appVersion* property, you see more than just the browser's version: you see the the operating

```
<HTML>
<HEAD>
<TITLE>A Page with a Plug-In</TITLE>
</HEAD>
<BODY>
<SCRIPT LANGUAGE = "JavaScript">
<! --

bName = navigator.appName;
bVer = parseInt(navigator.appVersion);
```
A // Determine which browser is being used.
```
if (bName == "Netscape" && bVer >= 3) br = "n3";
else if (bName == "Microsoft Internet Explorer" && bVer >= 3) br = "e3";
else br = "n2";
```
B // Display plug-in on page if detected in Netscape 3+.
```
if (br == "n3" && navigator.mimeTypes["application/x-director"]) {
document.write('<EMBED SRC = "movie.dcr" HEIGHT = 320 WIDTH = 240>');
}
```
C // Display link to download plug-in in Netscape 3+.
```
else if (br == "n3") {
document.write('<A HREF = "http://www.macromedia.com/shockwave/">
   Download</A> Shockwave!');
}
```
D // For IE, you may want to display an ActiveX control, otherwise remove this.
```
else if (br == "e3") {
document.write('<OBJECT CLASSID = "clsid:166B1BCA-3F9C-11CF-8075-
   444553540000"');
document.write('CODEBASE = "http://active.macromedia.com/director6/cabs/
   sw.cab#version=6,0,0,159"');
document.write('WIDTH = "240" HEIGHT = "320" NAME = "Shockwave" ID = "movie">');
document.write('<PARAM NAME = "SRC" VALUE = "movie.dcr">');
document.write('<PARAM NAME = "BGCOLOR" VALUE = "#000000">');
document.write('</OBJECT>');
}
```
E // Otherwise, display plug-in by default.
```
else {
document.write('<A HREF = "shockwave.html">Enter Shocked site</A>');
document.write('<P><A HREF = "noshockwave.html">Enter Plain Site</A>');
document.write('<P><A HREF = "http://www.macromedia.com/shockwave/">
   Download Shockwave</A>');
}

// -->
</SCRIPT>
</BODY>
</HTML>
```

Figure 6-12. Code for Shockwave detection script.

appVersion values for common operating systems

Operating system	*appVersion*
Windows 95	Win95; I
Windows 3.1	Win16; I
Macintosh PPC	Macintosh; I; PPC
Sun (Unix)	X11; I; SunOS
Linux (Unix)	X11; I; Linux

Table 6-3.

system as well. Table 6-3 shows *appVersion* values for five common operating systems. (The browser versions have been taken out, since they are irrelevant.)

With this knowledge, you can create simple functions to determine which OS your visitor is using. For example, Figure 6-13 shows a function that uses *indexOf( )* to determine if a browser is running on Windows 95.

You can use this function, which returns *true* if the browser is running on Windows 95, to tailor parts of your page, just as you did with the browser detection script. Here, if the platform is Windows 95, the script prints: "You're running Windows 95."

```
if (isWin95( )) document.write("You\'re running Windows 95");
```

Think of it this way: if it's in the *appVersion*, you can detect it. If you're looking to detect all Power Macs, notice that the *appVersion* for Power Macs contains the letters "PPC." Knowing this, you can use *indexOf( )* to create a function, shown in Figure

Pesky details
As shown in Table 6-2, Netscape and IE report Windows 95 as "Win95" and "Windows 95," respectively. Searching for "95" bridges the gap.

```
function isWin95( ) {
    if (navigator.appVersion.indexOf("95") != -1)
    return true;
    else return false;
}
```

Figure 6-13. Is the platform Windows 95?

```
function isPPC( ) {
   if (navigator.appVersion.indexOf("PPC") != -1)
   return true;
   else return false;
}
```

Figure 6-14. Is the computer a PowerPC-based Mac?

```
function isWin31( ) {
   if (navigator.appVersion.indexOf("16") != -1)
   return true;
   else return false;
}
```

Figure 6-15. Is the computer a Windows 3.x machine?

6-14, which will detect all Power PC-based Macs. Or use it to create a function to identify Windows 3.x PCs (Figure 6-15).

This ability opens up many doors. Say your company develops software for Windows 95, Windows 3.1, and Power Mac. When visitors come to download your software, save them the trouble of picking the OS; do it for them with JavaScript. Figure 6-16 shows you how.

You can easily combine OS detection and browser detection, or OS detection and plug-in detection. They're all interchangeable. Never again will your visitors have to make decisions based on their software (and hardware); you can do it for them.

```
if (isWin95( )) {
document.write('<A HREF ="dl32.exe">Get</A>
   our software for Windows 95.');
}
else if (isWin31( )) {
document.write('<A HREF = "dl16.exe">Get</A>
   our software for Windows 3.1.');
}
else if(isPPC( )) {
document.write('<A HREF = "dl.hqx">Get</A>
   our software for Macintosh.');
}
```

Figure 6-16. Identify the user's platform and write the appropriate HTML on the fly.

7

Dynamic Images

In this chapter
- The *image* object
- Image rollovers
- Multiple rollovers
- Image billboard

*S*tatic images aren't a great deal of fun: they're pretty, but they don't *do* anything. What if you could take all the static images on your Web site and bring them to life without Java, Shockwave, or any other high-bandwidth technology? This dream can finally be realized thanks to a feature in JavaScript called "dynamic images." Rollovers, clickable images, and interactive animations are just a few lines of code away with this JavaScript technology. Though it was not introduced until Netscape 3 (and IE 4), creative (and often cool) uses of this JavaScript feature can be found on sites all over the Web.

The dynamic image

As the name suggests, the "dynamic image" feature gives JavaScript the ability to change an image right on the page. One moment you could be seeing an image of a sprawling metropolis and the next moment it could be replaced with a serene forest. The point is, any image on your site can be made dynamic with a little bit of JavaScript code and some imagination.

Care to dance? Working with the image object

In an HTML document, images, like forms, are considered by JavaScript to be objects. Let's illustrate this by creating an image in HTML and then controlling it through JavaScript:

```
<IMG NAME = "cupholder" HEIGHT = 85 WIDTH = 86
BORDER = 0 SRC = "cupajoe.gif">
```

This is your basic *IMG* tag, it has *NAME*, *HEIGHT*, *WIDTH*, *BORDER*, and *SRC* properties. For now, we'll be focusing in on two of these: *SRC* and *NAME*. The first property, *SRC*, contains the name of the image file that you want displayed (we all know that). The second property may seem a little odd. Normally, you don't put a *NAME* property in the *IMG* tag. So why is it there? Because to access this image through JavaScript, it's helpful to know its name. Since this image's name is *cupholder,* you can refer to it like this in JavaScript:

```
document.cupholder
```

As you can see, the image object, *cupholder*, is a property of the document object. Now for the fun part. Since you have access to the image object through JavaScript, you also have access to its properties. For example, to change the actual image file that's being displayed in the image, just change its *SRC* property.

```
document.cupholder.src = "cupajoesteam.gif"
```

If you did this, the old image file *cupajoe.gif* would disappear and in its place you'd see *cupajoesteam.gif*. The image changes directly on the the page, no redrawing required. There's only one problem: before the new image is displayed it has to load, and as anybody without a T1 will tell you, that takes time. Fortunately, there's a way to preload images so they'll be displayed as soon as you ask for them. To do this, you have to create a new image object. But instead of creating your image in HTML with the *IMG* tag, you create an image in "memory" with the JavaScript *Image* object.

```
var cup = new Image( );
cup.src = "cupajoesteam.gif";
```

This creates a new image object named *cup* with a *SRC* property of *cupajoesteam.gif*. Instead of loading *cupajoesteam.gif* and displaying it on the page, however, the image is loaded and then stored in cache. Now that the image has been preloaded, we can replace the image in *cupholder* (the image object that's physically on the page) with the image in *cup* (the image in cache) without any delay.

```
document.cupholder.src = cup.src;
```

This sets the *SRC* property of *cupholder* equal to the *SRC* property of *cup*, thereby replacing the image on the page with the one that's

Changing the source of the image object replaces one image with another.

```
<HTML>
<HEAD>
<SCRIPT LANGUAGE= "JavaScript">
<! --
Ⓐ var cup = new Image( );
Ⓑ cup.src = "cupajoe.gif";
Ⓒ var cupsteam = new Image( );
Ⓓ cupsteam.src = "cupajoesteam.gif";
// -->
</SCRIPT>
</HEAD>
<BODY BGCOLOR = "#FFFFFF">
Ⓔ <A HREF = "#"
Ⓕ onMouseOver = "document.cupholder.src = cupsteam.src"
Ⓖ onMouseOut = "document.cupholder.src = cup.src">
Ⓗ <IMG NAME = "cupholder" HEIGHT = 85 WIDTH = 86
    BORDER = 0 SRC = "cupajoe.gif"></A>
<BR>
<FONT SIZE = 2>A Cup of Joe</FONT>
</BODY>
</HTML>
```

Figure 7-1. Source for changing an image on *mouseOver* and *mouseOut*.

preloaded. Combine this with some event handlers and these image changes can become interactive. Let's create a small HTML document to show how this can be done. Take a look at Figure 7-1. First we'll create two new image objects — one called *cup* Ⓐ and one called *cupsteam* Ⓒ and preload their image files — *cupajoe.gif* Ⓑ and *cupajoesteam.gif* Ⓓ respectively.

Now we need to create a physical image object on the page using the *IMG* tag Ⓗ. The preloaded images will be displayed where we place this image tag. Let's name it *cupholder*, and use the coffee cup image, *cupajoe.gif*, as its (initial) image file. To make the image change when the mouse moves over it, surround it with a link Ⓔ and add some event handlers.

The first of these event handlers, *onMouseOver* Ⓕ (which is triggered when the mouse moves over the image), changes *cupholder*'s source to *cupsteam*'s source (*cupajoesteam.gif*). Now if

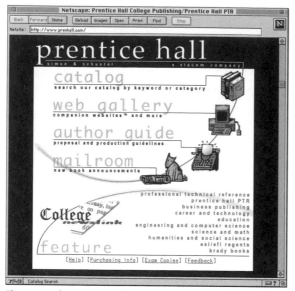

Figure 7-2. The Prentice Hall site in its quiet state.

you move the mouse over the coffee cup image, steam will start to rise from it. The second event handler, *onMouseOut* (which is triggered when the mouse moves off the image), changes *cupholder*'s image to *cup*'s *cupajoe.gif* . So when the mouse is moved off the image, the steam rising from the coffee cup suddenly disappears.

This is a basic example of dynamic images in action. The following scripts will expand upon this and show you some of the best real-world examples.

Image rollovers

For some reason, people love images that change when the mouse is moved over them. Perhaps it's because the "rollover" effect is used in so many desktop programs and multimedia titles, or perhaps it signifies to them that, "Yes, something will happen if you click here." Maybe people just like eye candy. Whatever the reason, image rollovers are an interesting effect to add to your site.

One of the most compelling examples of the rollover is the combination of the static image and the animated image (an animated GIF). To illustrate this, let's take a look at Prentice

Figure 7-3. Active "web gallery" image.

Figure 7-4. Active "author guide" image.

Hall's Web site, which does a great job of combining the two.

When you first enter the site, everything is static, as shown in Figure 7-2. When you roll over the image links, however, that quickly changes. If you move your mouse over the "Web Gallery" link (Figure 7-3), the text of the image suddenly lights up and the cartoon computer starts its screen saver. Move over to the "Author Guide" (Figure 7-4) and the typewriter next to it starts typing away numbers and letters. Mousing over "Catalog" (Figure 7-5) puts an image on the book, and when you go down to "Mailroom" (Figure 7-6) the dog even wags its tail and blinks (now you're excited).

So how does this work? Let's analyze the setup. Each rollover in the menu is actually a separate image, consisting of the words and image; it's not one giant image map. There are a total of four rollovers, each consisting of two image files. For example, the "Author Guide" element has both an active and inactive image. Figure 7-7 shows the inactive image and Figure 7-8 shows the active (animated) GIF.

Let's begin the rollover script by employing some browser detection. Since dynamic images only work in Netscape 3+ and IE 4+, we need to look out for older browsers. Figure 7-9 shows this code.

Next we need to preload all of the images, active and inactive alike. This is accomplished by creating image objects

Figure 7-5. Active "catalog" image.

Figure 7-6. Active "mailroom" image.

Figure 7-7. The plain "Author Guide" graphic.

Figure 7-8. The animated GIF file used for the active "Author Guide" image.

for all of our images, just like we did in the last script. This is shown in Figure 7-10.

The first set of image objects, beginning with *img1on*, preloads the image files that will be displayed when the mouse moves over a given rollover. Notice that all of these image objects have the same suffix: *on*. The actual image files that correspond to these image objects also have similar names, but they don't need to (e.g. *catalogon.gif* with *img1on*).

The second set of image objects, beginning with *img1off*, preload the image files that are displayed when the mouse is moved off a given rollover. Notice they share a similar suffix as well: *off*.

As you can see, the source for *img1on* is *catalogon.gif*; the source for *img1off* is *catalogoff.gif*.

The names of all the image objects (not the image files) should be left unchanged, unless of course you want to add more rollovers. For example, if you want five rollovers instead of four, add them using the same naming system with the on/off suffix, like so:

```
bName = navigator.appName;
bVer = parseInt(navigator.appVersion);
   if ((bName == "Netscape" && bVer >= 3) ||
       (bName == "Microsoft Internet Explorer" &&
       bVer >= 4)) br = "n3";
   else br = "n2";
```

Figure 7-9. Browser detection code.

```
if (br== "n3") {
imglon = new Image( );           // Create four image objects for the
imglon.src = "catalogon.gif";    // active images; the images displayed
img2on = new Image( )            // when the mouse moves over the rollovers.
img2on.src = "galleryon.gif";
img3on = new Image( );
img3on.src = "authoron.gif";
img4on = new Image( );
img4on.src = "mailon.gif";

imgloff = new Image( );          // Create four image objects for the
imgloff.src = "catalogoff.gif";  // inactive images; the images displayed
img2off = new Image( );          // when the mouse moves off the rollovers.
img2off.src = "galleryoff.gif";
img3off = new Image( );
img3off.src = "authoroff.gif";
img4off = new Image( );
img4off.src = "mailoff.gif";
}
```

Figure 7-10. Creating the image objects.

```
img5on = new Image( );
img5on.src = "anotherimageon.gif";
img5off = new Image( );
img5off.src = "anotherimageoff.gif";
```

After you've preloaded all these images, you have to create the images and their links on the page (the actual rollover), shown in Figure 7-11.

This is the first rollover in the menu, "Catalog," because its name is *img1*. **C** Notice that the *onMouseOver* and *onMouseOut* event handlers **A B** pass the name of the image to two functions (we'll get to those in a minute). We need three more images (and links) to complete the menu, each named *img2*, *img3*, etc.

```
      <A HREF = "catalog.html"
A  onMouseOver = "imgAct('img1')"
B  onMouseOut = "imgInact('img1')">
C  <IMG NAME = "img1" BORDER = 0 HEIGHT = 71
       WIDTH = 500 SRC="catalogoff.gif"></A>
```

Figure 7-11. Creating an image and its link with event handlers.

```
Ⓐ  function imgAct(imgName) {
Ⓑ      if (br== "n3") {
Ⓒ          document[imgName].src = eval(imgName + "on.src");
        }
    }
```

Figure 7-12. The *imgAct( )* function.

When the mouse is moved over an image, *onMouseOver* runs
the *imgAct( )* function, shown in Figure 7-12.

This function takes the name of the image that you pass it
and gives it to variable *imgName*. Ⓐ If the browser is Netscape 3
or later, Ⓑ the function changes the source of the image in
imgName by adding the *on* suffix to it. For example, when the
mouse is moved over the first rollover, "Catalog," *imgAct( )* is

```
<HTML>
<HEAD><TITLE>Teach An Old Dog New Tricks: Image Rollovers</TITLE>
<SCRIPT LANGUAGE = "JavaScript">
<! --
Ⓐ  bName = navigator.appName;        // Detect if browser is Netscape 3 + or IE 4 +.
    bVer = parseInt(navigator.appVersion);
    if ((bName == "Netscape" && bVer >= 3) ||
        (bName == "Microsoft Internet Explorer" && bVer >= 4)) br = "n3";
    else br = "n2";
Ⓑ  // Create image objects, preload all active and inactive images.
    if (br== "n3") {
        img1on = new Image( );           // Create four image objects for the
        img1on.src = "catalogon.gif";    // active images; the images displayed
        img2on = new Image( );           // when the mouse moves over the rollovers.
        img2on.src = "galleryon.gif";
        img3on = new Image( );
        img3on.src = "authoron.gif";
        img4on = new Image( );
        img4on.src = "mailon.gif";
Ⓒ      img1off = new Image( );          // Create four image objects for the
        img1off.src = "catalogoff.gif";  // inactive images; the images displayed
        img2off = new Image( );          // when the mouse moves off the rollovers.
        img2off.src = "galleryoff.gif";
        img3off = new Image( );
        img3off.src = "authoroff.gif";
        img4off = new Image( );
        img4off.src = "mailoff.gif";
    }
```

Figure 7-14. Complete source for Prentice Hall's rollover page.

Designing with JavaScript

```
function imgInact(imgName) {
    if (br== "n3") {
    document[imgName].src = eval(imgName + "off.src");
    }
}
```

Figure 7-13. The *imgInact( )* function.

passed the name *img1*. When the *on* suffix is added to that name, the result is *img1on*, which is the name of the active image object for the "Catalog" rollover (see Figure 7-10).

Once the name of the image object is determined, the physical image (rollover) on the page, *document.img1*, is changed to that image file. Ⓒ So in the case of the "Catalog" link, *imgAct( )* changes the image source to *catalogon.gif*.

```
Ⓓ function imgAct(imgName) {          // Function to "activate" images.
      if (br == "n3") {
          document[imgName].src = eval(imgName + "on.src");
      }
  }
Ⓔ function imgInact(imgName) {        // Function to "deactivate" images.
      if (br == "n3") {
          document[imgName].src = eval(imgName + "off.src");
      }
  }
  // -->
  </SCRIPT>
  </HEAD>
  <BODY BGCOLOR = "#FFFFFF">
Ⓕ <A HREF = "catalog.html" onMouseOver = "imgAct('img1')"
      onMouseOut = "imgInact('img1')">
  <IMG NAME = "img1" BORDER = 0 HEIGHT = 71 WIDTH = 500 SRC = "catalogoff.gif"></A>
  <A HREF = "gallery.html" onMouseOver = "imgAct('img2')"
      onMouseOut = "imgInact('img2')">
  <IMG NAME = "img2" BORDER = 0 HEIGHT = 71 WIDTH = 500 SRC = "galleryoff.gif"></A>
  <A HREF = "author.html" onMouseOver = "imgAct('img3')"
      onMouseOut = "imgInact('img3')">
  <IMG NAME = "img3" BORDER = 0 HEIGHT = 71 WIDTH = 500 SRC = "authoroff.gif"></A>
  <A HREF = "mail.html" onMouseOver = "imgAct('img4')"
      onMouseOut = "imgInact('img4')">
  <IMG NAME = "img4" BORDER = 0 HEIGHT = 71 WIDTH = 500 SRC = "mailoff.gif"></A>
  </BODY>
  </HTML>
```

Conversely, when the mouse is moved off the image, the function *imgInact( )* is run. This function is shown in Figure 7-13.

The function *imgInact( )* does the same thing as *imgAct( )*, except it adds the *off* suffix to the name that its passed, thus displaying the inactive image file — *catalogoff.gif*, in this case.

To put it all together, let's look at the complete source file in Figure 7-14. First we detect if the browser in Netscape 3 or Internet Explorer 4 or later. **A** Next we create image objects for the four "active" images **B** and the four "inactive" images. **C** Then we have the *imgAct( )* **D** and *imgInact( )* **E** functions. Finally we create the links. **F** In each link, *imgAct( )* is run when the user places the mouse over the image and *imgInact( )* is run when the mouse leaves the image. The first link passes *img1* to these functions; the second link passes *img2* to the functions, and so on.

The function *imgAct( )*, which is invoked by the *mouseOver* handler, changes the image to the source for the "on" image object. The function *imgInact( )*, which is triggered by the *mouseOut* event handler, changes the image to the source for the "off" image object. Thus putting the mouse over the link displays the active image and moving the mouse off the image displays the inactive image.

Two birds, one stone: Multiple rollovers

Playing around with one image at a time is OK, but how about two images, or three, or more? One of the best examples of multiple images reacting to one action can be found at IBM's Web site.

The menu at the top of the page makes use of rollovers to mimic Windows' behavior. In Windows, when you leave your mouse over a tool, a description of the tool pops up; when you move the mouse, the description disappears. On IBM's site, as shown in Figure 7-15, when you move your mouse over a menu option, the option lights up *and* a Windows-like description of the link pops up as well. Move to a different menu option and the description changes.

So how does it work? As you can probably guess, it's similar to the rollover script, but with a few differences. In addition to preloading the active and inactive images, the tool-tip images have to be preloaded. Also note that directly below the menu bar

Figure 7-15. Placing the mouse over menu options highlights the option (circled) and displays a descriptive graphic.

is a clear image 600 pixels in length and about 20 pixels in height: this image is replaced by the descriptive graphic.

If you've already set up some rollovers, all you need to do is add a few lines to the script. Once you've created image objects for each of your primary active/inactive images, you need to create some for your secondary images (the tool-tip graphics). Figure 7-16 shows a simplified version of the script that IBM uses.

First you create image objects for the active, **A** inactive, **B** and secondary **C** image files. For the sake of space, this script only shows the first two rollovers in IBM's menu: "IBM News" and "Products." Notice that, like the active and inactive images, the secondary images have the same suffix: *ad*.

After you've created all your image objects, you need to create the physical images on the page. In addition to the inactive "News" **F** and "Products" **G** images, you will also have to create a placeholder image for the secondary images. **H** The placeholder does not have to be blank; it just works well in IBM's situation.

In the real layout, all of these images are carefully organized with a table, but for our purposes it's not important. Notice that the placeholder image is named *holder*; this will be important

```
<HTML>
<HEAD><TITLE>Two Birds, One Stone: Multiple Rollovers</TITLE>
<SCRIPT LANGUAGE = "JavaScript">
<! --

bName = navigator.appName;
bVer = parseInt(navigator.appVersion);
if ((bName == "Netscape" && bVer >= 3) ||
    (bName == "Microsoft Internet Explorer" && bVer >= 4)) br = "n3";
else br = "n2";

if (br == "n3") {
    img1on = new Image( );
    img1on.src = "newson.gif";          // Active News Image
    img2on = new Image( );
    img2on.src = "productson.gif";      // Active Products Image

    img1off = new Image( );
    img1off.src = "newsoff.gif";        // Inactive News Image
    img2off = new Image( );
    img2off.src = "productsoff.gif";    // Inactive Products Image

    img1ad = new Image( );
    img1ad.src = "newstip.gif";         // Secondary News Image
    img2ad = new Image( );
    img2ad.src = "productstip.gif";     // Secondary Products Image
}
```

Figure 7-16. HTML for changing two images with one event.

when we rewrite *imgAct( )* and *imgInact( )* to accommodate the secondary image.

The only difference between the new and the old versions of *imgAct( )* Ⓓ is the addition of one line:

```
document["holder"].src = eval(imgName + "ad.src");
```

This line changes the placeholder image, *document.holder*, to one of the secondary images. For instance when the "IBM News" rollover runs this function, it passes its name, *img1*, as variable *imgName*. The *on* suffix is added to the name, and the active image is displayed. To change the placeholder image, the following line appends the *ad* suffix to the rollover's name (now it's *img1ad*) and the secondary image is displayed in the physical placeholder image.

Designing with JavaScript

```
function imgAct(imgName) {
    if (br == "n3") {
        document[imgName].src = eval(imgName + "on.src");
        document["holder"].src = eval(imgName + "ad.src");
    }
}
function imgInact(imgName) {
    if (br == "n3") {
        document[imgName].src = eval(imgName + "off.src");
        document["holder"].src = "clear.gif";
    }
}
// -->
</SCRIPT> </HEAD>
<BODY BGCOLOR = "#FFFFFF">
<! -- News Rollover -->
<A HREF = "catalog.html" onMouseOver = "imgAct('img1')"
    onMouseOut = "imgInact('img1')">
<IMG NAME= "img1" BORDER = 0 HEIGHT = 19 WIDTH = 93 SRC = "newsoff.gif"></A>
<! -- Products Rollover -->
<A HREF = "catalog.html" onMouseOver = "imgAct('img2')"
    onMouseOut = "imgInact('img2')">
<IMG NAME= "img2" BORDER = 0 HEIGHT = 19 WIDTH = 84 SRC = "productsoff.gif"></A>
<! -- Placeholder Image -->
<IMG NAME = "holder" HEIGHT = 17 WIDTH  = 600 SRC = "clear.gif">
</BODY>
</HTML>
```

The modified *imgInact( )* function Ⓔ also has an added line, but it simply changes the placeholder image back to the default image, *clear.gif*:

```
document["holder"].src = "clear.gif";
```

An image billboard

Take image replacement, a link, and three arrays: what do you get? A JavaScript billboard. The billboard saves space while being useful and fun to look at.

The JavaScript billboard is reminiscent of the billboards you pass as you drive home from work, the difference being that it rotates and it's on your Web site.

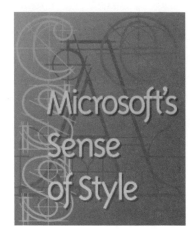

Figure 7-17. Three images of a rotating billboard.

Figure 7-17 shows the images for a billboard that displays three different images, with a two-second delay between each. Depending on which image you click on, you'll be brought to a different link.

There are three main parts to the billboard script: the images, the URLs, and the rotator function. Let's begin, as usual, by defining some variables for the billboard, as shown in Figure 7-18. As a precautionary measure, all of the variables are inside an *if* statement that verifies that the browser is Netscape 3+ or IE 4+ before the script is started (because older browsers don't support dynamic images).

The first variable, *boardSpeed*, determines how long (in milliseconds) the billboard should display an individual image before the next one is displayed. You can change this to your heart's content. The script creates one other variable, *boardNum*, to keep track of which image/link combination the billboard is currently displaying.

Next, all the billboard's images should be preloaded in the form of arrays. Figure 7-19 shows an array called *billboards*. These images are the essence of the billboard.

You can use any number of images you want; this example only uses three. (If you want to add transitions to the display of each image, animated GIFs are your best bet.) Once you've preloaded your images, specify where you want them to link

```
bName = navigator.appName;
bVer = parseInt(navigator.appVersion);
if ((bName == "Netscape" && bVer >= 3) ||
   (bName == "Microsoft Internet Explorer" &&
   bVer >= 4)) br = "n3";
else br = "n2";

if (br == "n3") {
   boardSpeed = 2000;
   boardNum = 0;
```

Figure 7-18. Creating variables for the billboard.

when they are displayed in the billboard. As shown in Figure
7-20, that's another array.

Each of these URLs correspond to the images in the billboard
array; for instance, *news.gif* links to *news/index.html*. Now that
you have all of your data in arrays, you need the rotator function,
shown in Figure 7-21, which automates the billboard.

This function begins by displaying the current billboard
image on the page. The current billboard image is defined by
boardNum. For example, if *boardNum* is 0, we are on the first
billboard image; if it's 1, we're on the second, etc. When you plug
this number into the *billboards* array, you get the current image.
After the image is displayed, *boardNum* is increased by 1 so that
when the function is run again, the next billboard image will be
displayed. If the value of *boardNum* is greater than the total
number of billboard images, it's set back to 0. Finally, this
function uses *setTimeout( )* to pause for a specified number of
milliseconds (the value is in *boardSpeed*) and the function is run
again, repeating the process of changing the billboard image.

```
billboards = new Array( );
billboards[0] = new Image( );
billboards[0].src = "news.gif";       // news image
billboards[1] = new Image( );
billboards[1].src = "archives.gif";   // archives image
billboards[2] = new Image( );
billboards[2].src = "contents.gif";   // contents image
```

Figure 7-19. The image array.

```
url = new Array( );
url[0] = "news/index.html";      // URL for news image
url[1] = "archives/index.html";  // URL for archives image
url[2] = "contents/index.html";  // URL for contents image
}
```

Figure 7-20. The URL array.

The last function, shown in Figure 7-22, is very simple; it just brings you to the proper URL when the billboard is clicked on.

Now you need to create an image for the billboard on the page; this needs to be named *billboard*. This image will also have an HREF tag that runs *jumpBillboard( )* so when it's clicked the visitor will be brought to a page (the one that corresponds with the currently displayed image).

```
<A HREF = "javascript:jumpBillboard( )">
<IMG onLoad = "if (br == 'n3')
    setTimeout('rotateBoard( )', boardSpeed)"
    NAME = "billboard" BORDER = 0 HEIGHT = 100
    WIDTH = 150 SRC = "news.gif"></A>
```

Once you have the billboard on the page, you need a way to start it rotating. The best way to do this is to place an *onLoad* event handler inside the *BODY* tag, so that as soon as the document loads, the *rotateBoard( )* function will be run (and the billboard will start rotating). The code is shown in Figure 7-23

```
function rotateBoard( ) {
if (boardNum < billboards.length - 1) boardNum++;
   else boardNum = 0;
   document.billboard.src = billboards[boardNum].src;
   setTimeout('rotateBoard( )', boardSpeed);
}
```

Figure 7-21. The rotator function.

```
function jumpBillboard( ) {
window.location.href = url[boardNum];
}
```

Figure 7-22. Function to load the correct URL when an image is clicked on.

Designing with JavaScript

```html
<HTML>
<HEAD>
<TITLE>The Billboard</TITLE>
<SCRIPT LANGUAGE = "JavaScript">

bName = navigator.appName;
bVer = parseInt(navigator.appVersion);
    if ((bName == "Netscape" && bVer >= 3) ||
      (bName == "Microsoft Internet Explorer" && bVer >= 4)) br = "n3";
    else br = "n2";

    if (br == "n3") {
    boardNum = 0;
    boardSpeed = 2000;

    billboards = new Array( );
    billboards[0] = new Image( );
    billboards[0].src = "news.gif";
    billboards[1] = new Image( );
    billboards[1].src = "archives.gif";
    billboards[2] = new Image( );
    billboards[2].src = "contents.gif";

    url = new Array( );
    url[0] = "news/index.html";
    url[1] = "archives/index.html";
    url[2] = "contents/index.html";
    }
function rotateBoard( ) {

if (boardNum < billboards.length - 1) boardNum++;
    else boardNum = 0;
    document.billboard.src = billboards[boardNum].src;
    setTimeout('rotateBoard( )', boardSpeed);
}

function jumpBillboard( ) {
window.location.href = url[boardNum];
}

</SCRIPT>
</HEAD>
<BODY BGCOLOR = "#FFFFFF" onLoad = "if (br == 'n3') setTimeout('rotateBoard( )',
    boardSpeed)">
<! -- The billboard image and link. -->
<A HREF = "javascript:jumpBillboard( )">
<IMG
NAME = "billboard"
BORDER = 0
HEIGHT = 100
WIDTH = 150
SRC = "news.gif"></A>
</BODY>
</HTML>
```

Figure 7-23. Complete code for the billboard rotator.

8

Customizing a Site with Cookies

The infamous cookie. It began as an innocent device that webmasters could use to remember things about individual visitors. With cookies, site visitors were not just an anonymous crowd; they became individuals. Now a site could remember your name, your last visit, or even your favorite color (now we're talking). But soon the denizens of the Web realized they preferred to remain "anonymous surfing entities." In some circles, the cookie became as taboo as spam. It's up to you to decide whether you wish to use cookies on your site. Either way, this chapter will teach you the basics and get you started with a tasty group of examples.

What's a cookie?

A cookie is a small, customized piece of information that a Web site stores on a visitor's hard drive. Through a browser, a cookie can be stored, retrieved, and deleted. A cookie has only one purpose: to remember information about an individual visitor.

Before you start working with cookies, there are a few "rules" you should be aware of. First, each cookie file can store a maximum of 300 cookies, with a maximum of 4 kilobytes per cookie. Each domain (*yahoo.com*, for instance), is allowed only 20 cookies. Figure 8-1 shows what a cookie file looks like.

The core functions

At this point, you may wonder how JavaScript accesses cookies. Like almost everything else in JavaScript, cookies are accessible through an object. The *document.cookie.* object does not directly

```
# Netscape HTTP Cookie File
# http://www.netscape.com/newsref/std/cookie_spec.html
# This is a generated file!  Do not edit.

www.tunes.com    FALSE    /tunes-cgi/tunes          FALSE    905994061         TUNES_ID          716_10
.techweb.com     TRUE     /wire/news/mar   FALSE    942189160         TechWeb  204.148.41.69.85862276
www.twoclicks.com         FALSE    /cgi-bin/         FALSE    883612799         no_visits_tabdemo
www.redwagon.com          FALSE    /        FALSE    2137622400        CATEGORY          1
.disney.com      TRUE     /        FALSE    946684799         DISNEY   204.148.41.693787842399972347
.msnbc.com       TRUE     /        FALSE    937396800         MC1      GUID=a079@c14@c@811d@bcfd@@@@f
.msn.com         TRUE     /        FALSE    937396800         MC1      GUID=a079@c14@c@811d@bcfd@@@@f
.netscape.com    TRUE     /        FALSE    946684799         NETSCAPE_ID       1000e010,1015db9e
.realaudio.com   TRUE     /        FALSE    946684740         uid      2041425684248469558
.pacbell.com     TRUE     /        FALSE    946684799         INTERSE  204.148.41.6915544842575097
www.realaudio.com         FALSE    /        FALSE    946511999         RoxenUserID       0xd6f
.timecast.com    TRUE     /        FALSE    946684740         uid      20418307842994210597
.microsoft.com   TRUE     /        FALSE    937422000         MC1      GUID=a079@c14@c@811d@bcfd@@@@f
.adobe.com       TRUE     /        FALSE    946684799         INTERSE  204.148.41.692103685655480271
get.real.com     FALSE    /        FALSE    946511999         RoxenUserID       0x136d3e
204.236.5.1      FALSE    /        FALSE    946511999         RoxenUserID       0x3b72f
.nrsite.com      TRUE     /        FALSE    946598400         NRid     DNquTTJk1CGSvkiqjsU7cG
www.coffeehaus.net        FALSE    /        FALSE    946511999         RoxenUserID       0x1651
.doubleclick.net          TRUE     /        FALSE    1920499140        IAF      34beddb
www.jbutler.com  TRUE     /        FALSE    888608232         VISITOR_ID        2826
```

Figure 8-1. Contents of a cookie file.

Where do you keep your cookies?

It depends on your platform and browser. If you are running Netscape on a Windows machine, look for a file called *cookies.txt* in Netscape's Program directory. If you're running Netscape on a Mac, you'll find a file called *Magic Cookie* in Netscape's Program folder. If you are running Internet Explorer on a Wintel machine, you will find all of your cookies stored in separate files in the *Windows\ Cookies* directory.

connect to the hard drive; it merely reflects all the cookies stored there. While you can work directly with the *document.cookie* object, I've written three commonly used functions to save you the trouble: *setCookie( )*, *getCookie( )*, and *delCookie( )*.

Saving a cookie

The *setCookie( )* function, shown in Figure 8-2, is used to create a cookie and then save a value to that cookie.

To use this function properly, you need to pass it three things: a name, a value, and an expiration date. The name and the value are easy; the expiration date takes a little more work. Figure 8-3 shows the code for setting an expiration date 31 days in the future. First, a new *Date* object, *exp*, is created. Then we take the current time in milliseconds, found with *exp.getTime( )*, and add the equivalent of 31 more days.

After you have the expiration date, you can create the cookie by running *setCookie( )* and passing it three things: a name ("myname"), a value ("myvalue"), and the expiration date *(exp)*.

```
function setCookie(name, value, expires) {
document.cookie = name + "=" + escape(value) + "; path=/" +
((expires == null) ? "" : "; expires=" +
   expires.toGMTString( ));
}
```

Figure 8-2. The *setCookie()* function.

```
var exp = new Date( );
exp.setTime(exp.getTime( ) + (1000 * 60 * 60 * 24 * 31));
setCookie("myname", "myvalue", exp);
```

Figure 8-3. Code for setting the expiration date 31 days in the future.

Retrieving a cookie

Once you have a cookie saved, you need a way to retrieve it.
The *getCookie( )* function (as shown in Figure 8-4) scans through
document.cookie until it finds the cookie in question and then
returns that cookie's value.

Though the *getCookie( )* function is clearly more complex
than *setCookie( )*, it's easier to use. To retrieve the value of the
cookie named "myname," just pass *getCookie( )* the cookie's name:

```
getCookie("myname");
```

If the cookie exists, the value will be returned. If it does not exist,
null will be returned. You can treat *getCookie( )* like a variable:
passing it, displaying it, etc. To display the value of the cookie on
the page, for example, combine it with *document.write( )*:

```
document.write(getCookie("myname"));
```

This displays the value of the "myname" cookie: "myvalue." As
you will see later in this chapter, you can do a lot more than
simply display a cookie's value on the page.

Days of milliseconds

The 31 days, in milliseconds, is
found by multiplying 1000
milliseconds by 60 seconds by 60
minutes by 24 hours by 31 days. To
save your cookie for a year, for
example, change the "31" to "365."

```
function getCookie(name){
var cname = name + "=";
var dc = document.cookie;
if (dc.length > 0) {
   begin = dc.indexOf(cname);
      if (begin != -1) {
         begin += cname.length;
         end = dc.indexOf(";", begin);
            if (end == -1) end = dc.length;
               return unescape(dc.substring(begin, end));
      }
   }
return null;
}
```

Figure 8-4. The *getCookie( )* function.

Getting that cookie

How is an individual cookie retrieved? It all happens within the *getCookie( )* function. Although it looks complex, the logic of this function is quite simple. For easy reference, here it is again:

```
A  function getCookie(name){
B    var cname = name + "=";
C    var dc = document.cookie;
D    if (dc.length > 0) {
E      begin = dc.indexOf(cname);
F      if (begin != -1) {
G        begin += cname.length;
H        end = dc.indexOf(";", begin);
I        if (end == -1) end = dc.length;
J        return unescape(dc.substring(begin, end));
       }
     }
K    return null;
   }
```

Let's begin by understanding that the *document.cookie* object is simply a string of text reflecting the names and values of the cookies stored on the hard drive. Below is a sample *document.cookie* object; this is what we're really dealing with:

```
dummycookie=dummyvalue; myname=myvalue; anotherdummy=anothervalue
```

We'll use this dummy *document.cookie* information for the rest of this example. As you can see, the *document.cookie* object contains a long string of names and values. The name and value of each cookie are separated by an equal sign, and the individual cookies are separated from each other by semicolons. This is a reflection of the cookies on the hard drive, but filtered through the *document.cookie* object.

Only cookies created by your domain will appear in *document.cookie* — all the rest are hidden to prevent you from stealing other domains' cookies. The *getCookie( )* function searches through this string of text, finds the correct cookie name ("myname"), and retrieves the cookie's value ("myvalue").

To begin with, **B** the function adds an equal sign to the name of the cookie you are trying to retrieve. If you are looking for "myname," the name becomes "myname=". Then the new name is given to variable *cname*.

Next, *document.cookie* (the long string of cookie names and values) is given to variable *dc* ⓒ (from now on *document.cookie* will be referred to as *dc*). This is a workaround for a bug that results in a performance hit if *document.cookie* is accessed repeatedly.

An *if* statement ⓓ then determines if anything exists in *dc* by verifying that the length (in characters of text) is greater than 0. If the length of *dc* is 0, there are no cookies and the function skips everything else and returns null. If the length is greater than 0, the function continues.

Next, the *indexOf( )* method ⓔ is used on *dc* to find the location of the cookie's name. (Note: *indexOf( )* is discussed in the "Searching for an email address" section of Chapter 4.) If the cookie name is found using *indexOf( )*, the location of the name in characters is given to variable *begin*. This is very important: *begin* is being used to "mark" the location of the cookie's name, and ultimately the cookie's value, inside the string of cookie names and values.

Now think back to your *dc* object. If it looks like this

```
dummycookie=dummyvalue; myname=myvalue; anotherdummy=anothervalue
```

and if *cname* (the cookie's name) is "myname –" *begin* will equal 24 (counting starts with 0). If you count the number of characters from the beginning of *dc* to the first character in "myname =" you will come up with 24: the exact location of the cookie's name in *dc*. If *indexOf( )* does not find the cookie name in *dc*, it gives *begin* a value of -1.

If *begin* is -1, ⓕ the function returns *null*. ⓚ If the name is found, however, *begin* is increased ⓖ by the length of the cookie name, *cname*. For your cookie, whose name is "myname =" and is seven characters long, *begin* is now 31. If you count 31 characters from the beginning of *dc*, you will find that you end up smack dab on the value of your cookie.

Now that the function knows where the value of the cookie begins, it needs to figure out where it ends. Since all cookies in *dc* are separated by semicolons, the cookie — and therefore its value — must end at a semicolon. For this reason, *indexOf( )* performs a search on *dc* again, ⓗ but this time it's searching for a semicolon. Another difference is that the search is instructed to start at *begin*, the beginning of the cookie's value. The placement of the semicolon (the end of the cookie's value) is then given to variable *end*. In our example, *end* is 38, the location of the semicolon following "myvalue."

Both the beginning and the end of the cookie's value have been determined, so it's a simple task to grab the value in between. Using the *substring( )* method ⓘ on dc, the value of the cookie is finally extracted and returned.

Deleting a cookie

The *delCookie( )* function, shown in Figure 8-5, is used to delete a cookie from the cookie file.

Just pass *delCookie( )* the name of the cookie you want deleted and the function takes care of it for you. The function simply sets your doomed cookie's value to nothing and expiration to a past date, thus deleting the cookie. Try it with:

```
delCookie("myname");
```

Now that you know how to set, get, and delete cookies, what do you do with these new abilities? The following scripts will start you off with some useful examples of cookies in action. Before you jump into these scripts, though, experiment with the cookies template document, shown in Figure 8-6.

Remember, to access cookies through JavaScript, you will need a combination of these three functions in your documents.

A welcome mat for new visitors

Most sites make no distinction between new visitors and long-time regulars. But wouldn't it be nice to take new visitors by the hand, show them around the site, and get them oriented? That's a perfect job for cookies. In this script, we're going to automatically determine if someone has visited the site before and create a special welcome message for new visitors. A good example of this is the Microsoft Network, which identifies new users and gives them the proper technologies to view the site. Figure 8-7 shows this welcome mat.

Persona grata, persona non grata

This script makes use of only one cookie, which we'll call the *welcome* cookie. There are three possible values for this cookie:

- "Null" means the cookie does not exist and the visitor has never been to the site (at least the browser has not).

```
function delCookie(name) {
document.cookie = name + "=; expires=Thu, 01-Jan-70
   00:00:01 GMT" +  "; path=/";
}
```

Figure 8-5. The *delCookie( )* function.

```
HTML>
<HEAD>
<TITLE>The Cookie Jar</TITLE>
<SCRIPT LANGUAGE = "JavaScript">
<! --

// Use this function to retrieve a cookie.
function getCookie(name){
var cname = name + "=";
var dc = document.cookie;
if (dc.length > 0) {
   begin = dc.indexOf(cname);
   if (begin != -1) {
      begin += cname.length;
      end = dc.indexOf(";", begin);
      if (end == -1) end = dc.length;
      return unescape(dc.substring(begin, end));
   }
}
return null;
}

// Use this function to save a cookie.
function setCookie(name, value, expires) {
document.cookie = name + "=" + escape(value) + "; path=/" +
((expires == null) ? "" : "; expires=" + expires.toGMTString( ));
}

// Use this function to delete a cookie.
function delCookie(name) {
document.cookie = name + "=; expires=Thu, 01-Jan-70 00:00:01 GMT" +  "; path=/";
}

// -->
</SCRIPT>
</HEAD>
<BODY BGCOLOR = "#FFFFFF">
<SCRIPT LANGUAGE = "JavaScript">
<! --

var exp = new Date( );                              // make new date object
exp.setTime(exp.getTime( ) + (1000 * 60 * 60 * 24 * 31));    // set it 31 days ahead
setCookie("myname", "myvalue", exp);                // save the cookie
document.write(getCookie("myname"));                // retrieve and display cookie on page
delCookie("myname");                                // delete cookie

// -->
</SCRIPT>
</BODY>
</HTML>
```

Figure 8-6. Template for saving, retrieving, and deleting cookies.

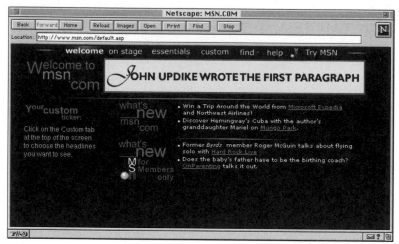

Figure 8-7. MSN presents this welcome screen to new users.

- "Welcome" means the visitor has been to the site before but still wants to be welcomed.
- "Nowelcome" means the visitor has been to the site before and does not want to be welcomed.

Let's begin by defining some variables: the expiration date of the welcome cookie, the name of the welcome cookie, and the welcome message.

As shown in Figure 8-8, you first need to set the expiration date of the welcome cookie Ⓐ and give it to *exp*. In this example, the welcome cookie's expiration date Ⓑ is one year. The cookie's name Ⓒ is in variable *cookieName* and doesn't need to be changed. The most important of these variables is *theMessage*, Ⓓ which contains the HTML that first-time visitors will see.

```
Ⓐ var exp = new Date( );
Ⓑ exp.setTime(exp.getTime( ) + (24 * 60 * 60 *
     1000 * 365));
Ⓒ var cookieName = '_welcome';
Ⓓ var theMessage = 'Since this this is your first
     time here...';
```

Figure 8-8. Defining name, value, and expiration date for a cookie.

Displaying the welcome mat

Now we need to create a function that determines whether or not the visitor is new and, if so, displays the welcome message. This function, called *showWelc( )*, is shown in Figure 8-9.

If a visitor has never been to your site before, then the *welcome* cookie will be *null* because it doesn't exist. If the cookie value is *null* or "welcome," the welcome message is displayed using *document.write( )* and the *welcome* cookie is reset to "welcome" so it doesn't expire (at least not for 365 more days). If the *welcome* cookie is set to "nowelcome," then the cookie is reset to that same value to keep it fresh.

Toggling the welcome mat

So how do you turn the *welcome* cookie off (that is, set its value to "nowelcome")? We need to create a function that toggles the value of the *welcome* cookie between "welcome" and "nowelcome." This function, *toggleWelc( )*, is shown in Figure 8-10. Whenever this function runs, it toggles the value of the *welcome* cookie between "welcome" and "nowelcome" using an *if* statement. In other words, it toggles the display of the welcome message.

Working in conjunction with *toggleWelc( )*, is *showForm( )*, shown in Figure 8-11. The purpose of this function is to display a small form that allows the visitors to disable the welcome message. A sample form is shown in Figure 8-13. If the *welcome* cookie is *null* or "welcome," then the form and its accompanying text (which you can modify) are displayed.

Welcome hints

Make sure your welcome message has a purpose — don't simply say "Welcome." Supply your visitors with some links telling them about the site, perhaps a message about how to get around, or even a special table of contents designed to be less confusing for first-timers.

```
function showWelc( ) {
   if (getCookie(cookieName) == null ||       // Is the cookie value null
      getCookie(cookieName) == "welcome") {   // or "welcome"?
   setCookie(cookieName, "welcome", exp);     // If so, set the welcome cookie
   document.write(theMessage);                // and display the greeting
   }
   else {
   setCookie(cookieName, "nowelcome", exp);   // Otherwise, set to "nowelcome"
   }
}
```

Figure 8-9. The *showWelc( )* function.

```
function toggleWelc( ) {
    if (getCookie(cookieName) == "welcome") {       // Is the cookie set to welcome?
    setCookie(cookieName, "nowelcome", exp);        // If so, set it to nowelcome
    }
    else {
    setCookie(cookieName, "welcome', exp);          // Otherwise, set it to welcome
    }
}
```

Figure 8-10. The *toggleWelc( )* function.

The form is simply a single checkbox that runs *toggleWelc( )* — via the *onClick* event handler — each time the box is clicked. The whole script is put together in Figure 8-12. Notice that the welcome message and toggle form are displayed where you run *showWelc( )* and *showForm( )*. This puts most of your code in the head of your document, out of the way of your HTML.

Forms that remember

Picture the following scenarios:

- You're in the process of filling out a lengthy form, and you only have two more elements to fill in, when suddenly your laptop runs out of batteries.
- You've signed up for a new service where you must enter your user ID and password every time you want to enter member-only chat areas.

These scenarios and many others could be vastly improved for want of one thing: forms that remember what the user typed.

Making form elements remember input is not a complicated process. First, place the following event handlers inside all of

```
function showForm( ) {
    if (getCookie(cookieName) == null ||
        getCookie(cookieName) == "welcome") {
    document.write('<FORM><INPUT TYPE = "CHECKBOX" onClick = "toggleWelc( )">');
    document.write('Don\'t show this welcome message again.</FORM>');
    }
}
```

Figure 8-11. The *showForm( )* function.

```
<HTML>
<HEAD>
<SCRIPT LANGUAGE = "JavaScript">
<! --

// IMPORTANT: Always include the three core cookie functions: getCookie( ),
// setCookie( ), and delCookie( ).


// Use this function to retrieve a cookie.
function getCookie(name){
var cname = name + "=";
var dc = document.cookie;
   if (dc.length > 0) {
   begin = dc.indexOf(cname);
      if (begin != -1) {
      begin += cname.length;
      end = dc.indexOf(";", begin);
         if (end == -1) end = dc.length;
         return unescape(dc.substring(begin, end));
      }
   }
return null;
}


// Use this function to save a cookie.
function setCookie(name, value, expires) {
document.cookie = name + "=" + escape(value) + "; path=/" +
((expires == null) ? "" : "; expires=" + expires.toGMTString( ));
}


// Use this function to delete a cookie.
function delCookie(name) {
document.cookie = name + "=; expires=Thu, 01-Jan-70 00:00:01 GMT" + "; path=/";
}


// Function to display welcome message if new visitor.
function showWelc( ) {
   if (getCookie(cookieName) == null ||
      getCookie(cookieName) == "welcome") {
   setCookie(cookieName, "welcome", exp);
   document.write(theMessage);
   }
   else {
   setCookie(cookieName, "nowelcome", exp);
   }
}
```

Figure 8-12. Source code for the welcome mat application.

```
// Function to toggle welcome message.
function toggleWelc( ) {
   if (getCookie(cookieName) == "welcome") setCookie(cookieName, "nowelcome", exp);
   else setCookie(cookieName, "welcome", exp);
}

// Function to display a form that allows welcome message to be toggled.
function showForm( ) {
   if (getCookie(cookieName) == null ||
      getCookie(cookieName) == "welcome") {
   document.write('<FORM><INPUT TYPE = "CHECKBOX" onClick = "toggleWelc( )">');
   document.write('Don\'t show this welcome message again.</FORM>');
   }
}

var exp = new Date( );
exp.setTime(exp.getTime( ) +  (24 * 60 * 60 * 1000 * 365));
var cookieName = '_welcome';

// Your welcome message:
var theMessage = 'Since this this is your first time here...';

// -->

</SCRIPT>

</HEAD>

<BODY BGCOLOR = "#FFFFFF">
<SCRIPT LANGUAGE = "JavaScript">
<! --

// Place this where you want the welcome message to be displayed.
showWelc( );

// -->
</SCRIPT>

<SCRIPT LANGUAGE = "JavaScript">
<! --

// Place this where you want the welcome message "toggle form" to be displayed.
showForm( );

// -->

</SCRIPT>

</BODY>
</HTML>
```

Figure 8-12. Source code for the welcome mat application (continued from previous page).

Figure 8-13. The *showForm( )* function adds a checkbox that lets users disable the welcome message on future visits.

the form elements (text inputs only) to which you wish to add this feature.

```
onFocus = "getValue(this)"
onBlur = "setValue(this)"
```

The *onFocus* and *onBlur* event handlers are complementary to each other. The *onBlur* handler is triggered whenever the user leaves a form element; this is usually after the information has been entered. *onBlur* runs a function — *getValue( )* — that stores the user's information in a cookie. When the user returns to that element (either by clicking or tabbing to it), the *onFocus* event handler is triggered and the previous value of that form element is taken from the cookie and inserted into that element.

Place *getValue( )* and *setValue( )* — the two functions that save and retrieve this information — in the head of the document along with the three core cookie functions. Figure 8-14 shows *getValue( )* and *setValue( )*.

The *setValue( )* function takes the form element as argument *element*. It then creates a cookie with *element.name* and *element.value* as the name and value of the cookie, respectively.

The complementary *getValue( )* function also takes the form element as argument *element*. It then uses *element.name* to retrieve the previously stored value of that form element with the *getCookie( )* function. That value is given to variable *value*. If *value* is not *null* — that is, if there is a cookie with a value for the

```
function setValue(element) {
setCookie(element.name, element.value, exp);
}

function getValue(element) {
var value = getCookie(element.name);
   if (value != null) element.value = value;
}
```

Figure 8-14. The *getValue( )* and *setValue( )* cookies.

Custom
Web Review
The customizable version
of *Web Review* is located at:
*http://webcoder.com/
customwr.html*

form element — *element.value* is set equal to *value*, thereby displaying the saved value in the form element.

Figure 8-15 shows the form with text displayed in the focused field.

Figure 8-16 shows the code for a three-element form that shows how these functions can be used together.

Customize your entire site

So far we've learned how to customize a message based on users' activity (the welcome mat) and how to remember the text the user has entered. But much more is possible. Using cookies, forms, and JavaScript, I created a prototype version of *Web Review* that remembers each user's name, interests, and what content they've already read.

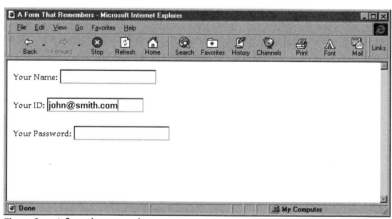

Figure 8-15. A form that remembers.

```
<HTML>
<HEAD>

<TITLE>A Form That Remembers</TITLE>

<SCRIPT LANGUAGE = "JavaScript">
<! --

// IMPORTANT: Include here the three core cookie functions: getCookie( ),
// setCookie(), and delCookie( ).

// Function to retrieve form element's value.
function getValue(element) {
var value = getCookie(element.name);
   if (value != null) element.value = value;
}

// Function to save form element's value.
function setValue(element) {
setCookie(element.name, element.value, exp);
}

var exp = new Date( );
exp.setTime(exp.getTime( ) + (1000 * 60 * 60 * 24 * 31));

// -->
</SCRIPT>

</HEAD>

<BODY BGCOLOR = "#FFFFFF">

<FORM ACTION = "/cgi-bin/enter.cgi">
<P>
Your Name:
<INPUT TYPE = "TEXT" NAME = "yourname" onFocus = "getValue(this)"
   onBlur = "setValue(this)">
<P>
Your ID:
<INPUT TYPE = "TEXT" NAME = "yourid" onFocus = "getValue(this)"
   onBlur = "setValue(this)">
<P>
Your Password:
<INPUT TYPE = "TEXT" NAME = "yourpassword" onFocus = "getValue(this)"
   onBlur = "setValue(this)">
</FORM>

</BODY>
</HTML>
```

Figure 8-16. Code for a form that remembers.

Where everybody knows your name

In order to customize *Web Review,* users need to fill out a form that collects their information. This information will be used to generate the custom view of the site. Figure 8-17 shows this form.

Web Review is divided into five channels: business, design, diversions, programming, and technology. So after asking for your name and email address, the site asks you what your level of interest is in each of these areas. In this example, I've rated

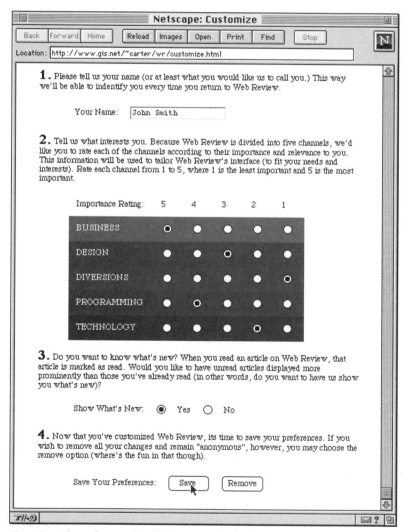

Figure 8-17. The preferences form for the customized *Web Review.*

Designing with JavaScript

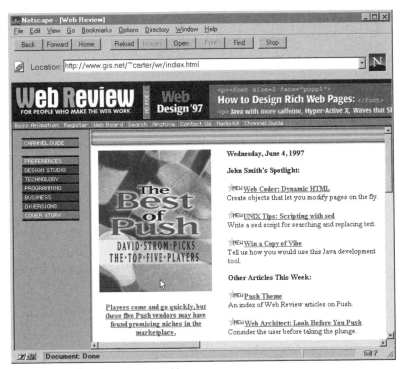

Figure 8-18. *Web Review's* customized home page.

business 5 (the highest), programming 4, and so on. You'll see in a moment what *Web Review* does with this information.

After telling *Web Review* your interests, you are asked if you'd like to be shown what's new on the site. This is not just any "What's New" feature; this one knows which articles you've read (and those you have not) and logs them to a cookie. So this page shows what's new to *you*, not just what's new on the site.

Once you've completed this three-step process, you are given the option to discard your changes or save them. If you save them, you return to *Web Review's* front page where you'll find a site that knows who you are, what you like, and what you've read, as shown in Figure 8-18.

The first thing you'll notice is that three articles are placed at the top of the page under the spotlight heading. These are new articles in your highest-rated channels. In this example, all of the programming-related articles have been placed under the spotlight because when I rated my favorite channels, programming came in at 4. There are no business stories in the spotlight even though business was rated highest, because there were no new business articles in this issue.

The rest of the articles are listed below the spotlight and are categorized by "freshness," with the unread articles displayed more prominently than read articles. In fact, all of the articles you have read are recorded in a log, which you can access at any time (you can actually see a listing of all the articles you've read).

I'm not going to attempt to explain how all of this was done, but I can give you two rules to live by when designing an application similar to this.

Rule #1: Conserve your cookies

The first rule that you must follow is this: conserve your cookies. This is because you can have only 20 cookies per domain. This is not a problem when you are dealing with a few pieces of information, but when you're keeping track of multiple channel ratings and logging all read articles, you have to manage your space carefully. To preserve space, I use a technique called the *chip*. With this technique, you are able to store chips of information within an individual cookie (get it? cookie, chip).

First I set an expiration date for the whole menagerie:

```
var exp = new Date( );
exp.setTime (exp.getTime( ) + (24 * 60 * 60 * 1000 * 31));
```

Then I use the *setChip( )* function, to save a chip, passing it a cookie name, a chip name, and a value.

Then, I use the *getChip( )* function, to retrieve a chip, passing it a cookie name and chip name.

Finally, I use the *delChip( )* function, to delete a chip when I'm done with it. These functions are shown in Figure 8-19.

Always remember that when you use any of these functions, you will need to have the core cookie functions, *getCookie( )* and *setCookie( )*, in the script as well.

Rule #2: Organize and code your data logically

The second rule I follow (with any application) is to organize my data logically. You may wonder, for example, how all of the data

```
function setChip(cookie, name, value) {
var dc = getCookie(cookie);
var cv = getChip(name);
var cn = name + '=';
   if (cv != null) {
   var start = dc.indexOf(cn);
      if (start != -1) {
      var end = dc.indexOf('|', start);
      setCookie(cookie, dc.substring(0, start) + cn + value + '|' + dc.substring(end + 1,
         dc.length), exp);
      }
   }
   else {
      if (dc != null) dc += cn + value + '|';
      else dc = cn + value + '|';
   setCookie(cookie, dc, exp);
   }
}
// EXAMPLE USAGE
setChip("CookieName", "ChipName", "ChipValue");

function getChip(cookie, name){
var cn = name + '=';
var dc = getCookie(cookie);
   if (dc != null) {
   var start = dc.indexOf(cn);
      if (start != -1) {
      start += cn.length;
      var end = dc.indexOf('|', start);
         if (end != -1) return unescape(dc.substring(start, end));
      }
   }
return null;
}
// EXAMPLE USAGE
getChip("CookieName", "ChipName");

function delChip(cookie, name) {
var dc = getCookie(cookie);
var cv = getChip(name);
var cn = name + '=';
   if (cv != null) {
   var start = dc.indexOf(cn);
   var end = dc.indexOf('|', start);
   setCookie(cookie, dc.substring(0, start) + dc.substring(end + 1, dc.length), exp);
   }
}
// EXAMPLE USAGE
delChip("CookieName", "ChipName");
```

Figure 8-19. The *setChip( )*, *getChip( )*, and *delChip( )* functions.

```
newArticle ('Web Architect: Look Before You Push',      // title
    '/97/04/18/arch/index.html',                         // url
    'Consider the user before taking the plunge.',       // subtitle
    2,                                                    // channel
    970418);                                              // date
```

Figure 8-20. An entry in the article database.

in the articles is made accesible to JavaScript and the cookie. This is accomplished with a small object-oriented database of articles contained in a script on the front page of the site. This database contains article objects for each article in the current issue. Before I did anything, I identified which aspects of the articles the script would need to work with the articles. These are the attributes that I came up with:

- Title
- URL
- Subtitle
- Channel
- Date

After I determined what the script needed to know about each article, I created an *article object* with all of these properties (you'll learn more about creating objects in Chapter 12). Once I did this, adding an article to the article database was not a difficult task. Figure 8-20 shows the logical format for an article entry.

With all of this information in the database, all relevant information for each article is now available to the script. The page-creation script can now judge how the article should be displayed: if it should be displayed in the spotlight (because the article's channel was rated highest by the user), if it should be marked new (because the title is not in the article log), and so on.

Finally, look at the entire "Custom Web Review" script on the CD. With an understanding of object-oriented scripting (Chapter 12) and an understanding of how to organize your information programmatically, creating an application like this is a feasable, and quite manageable, project.

9

Dynamic
HTML

Take JavaScript's power over the page and square it; that's what you get with the capabilities of Dynamic HTML. As we've learned throughout this book, there is an object model in JavaScript (the JavaScript tree) that reflects the contents of an HTML document and allows those contents to be modified to a certain extent.

With Dynamic HTML, the object model greatly expands, encompassing almost every aspect of the page. Dynamic HTML also adds absolute positioning of HTML, a more powerful event model, and useful add-ons that allow you to play multichannel stereo sound among other things.

At the time of this book's publication, there was not yet a standard for the Dynamic HTML document object model. Because of this, the syntax discussed here is based on Microsoft's proposed object model as it appears in Internet Explorer 4. Netscape Navigator's object model, at least through version 4.0x, supports only two major aspects of Dynamic HTML: absolute positioning and a more powerful event model. Because of these differences, this chapter focuses mainly on IE's object model (which has a good chance of becoming the standard). Netscape's comparable features are described in a final section, "Netscape 4's object model," which shows how to use them.

Dynamic HTML and style sheets

Cascading style sheets and the Dynamic HTML object model are powerful partners. Style sheets give you more more control over the look and feel of your pages. Style sheets let you more accurately specify fonts, point sizes, and margin widths; they even allow you to position text and other objects at exact coordinates on the page.

We can begin to understand how style sheets, and the page in general, are accessible to JavaScript with the Dynamic HTML object model by playing around with this ordinary line of text:

```
I will grow.
```

Before we can control this text through JavaScript, we need to isolate it as an individual HTML *element*. This can be done by surrounding the text with a standard HTML tag, such as *P*, *A*, *DIV*, or *SPAN*, and by giving it a name with the *ID* attribute, which is similar to the *NAME* attribute. Once the text is contained within HTML tags, it becomes a malleable object that JavaScript can manipulate.

```
<DIV ID = "grow">
I will grow.
</DIV>
```

For example, to change the point size of this text, which we've named *grow*, we can access its *style* property (a part of all HTML elements in Dynamic HTML) and from there change its *fontSize* property. This is the same property that style sheets use to control font size (*font-size*); all of the *style* properties of HTML elements have style sheet counterparts. To change the size of this text to 24 points (that's right, you can specify a specific point size, not just HTML's relative sizes), only one line of JavaScript is needed. Here we've changed the *fontSize* property to 24.

```
document.all.grow.style.fontSize = 24;
```

Obviously, *fontSize* is a property of *style* and *style* is a property of *grow*, but *document.all* seems a little askew. We already know that the *document* object is the current page, so why doesn't *grow* branch directly off of that? In the Dynamic HTML object model you can't use the name of the HTML element (directly) to access it through JavaScript. You must first go through the *all* property, which is a collection of all the elements in the body of the document. You always access your HTML elements through *document.all*.

In truth, Internet Explorer's Dynamic HTML object model is not drastically different from what you've already learned (though there are *a lot* of additional objects). It is important, however, to know how to access individual HTML elements through the

**All about
style sheets**
For a general introduction to
style sheets, see the "Style
sheets in depth" section.

HTML element
The term *HTML element*
refers to any specific piece of
content surrounded by a tag.

Designing with JavaScript

Common style properties

Style property	What it controls
fontSize	The point size of the text's font (e.g. 12, 24)
fontWeight	The weight of the text's font (e.g. bold, italic)
fontFamily	The family of the text's font (e.g. Times, Arial)
color	The color of the text's foreground (e.g. red, blue)
background	The color of the text's background

Table 9-1.

object model, as we've done here, because they are a vital part of Dynamic HTML. You also need to understand how to control the styles (through style sheets) of those HTML elements.

Table 9-1 lists five common style-sheet-based properties that you can modify on the fly. Remember to use the correct syntax with these properties when controlling HTML elements: *document.all.elementName.style.propertyName.*

Style sheets in depth

Now that you have a basic understanding of the Dynamic HTML object model in Internet Explorer, it's time to explore style sheets in greater depth. In this section we're going to create a true style sheet with styles for active links (a link is active when the mouse is placed over it) and for inactive links (the normal state of links). The inactive links will be 16-point, black text; the active links will be underlined, 18-point, blue text. After we've created these styles, we'll use JavaScript to apply them interactively through the Dynamic HTML object model. Figure 9-1 shows what this page looks like when a user places the mouse over one of the links.

We'll begin by creating a style sheet with styles named *on* and *off*. These will contain the text styles for the active and inactive links. Figure 9-2 shows the HTML for this page.

Style sheet properties

For a more comprehensive list of style-sheet-based properties, see Microsoft's documentation on the *style* object at *http://www.microsoft.com/workshop/ author/dynhtml/dhtmo285.htm.*

Figure 9-1. The attributes of links change when the mouse is placed over them.

Where are the ID attributes for all of these links?

If you've been paying close attention, you may wonder, "Where are the ID attributes for all of these links?" We used a little trick that should be familiar to you by now: the *this* statement. With *this*, you don't have to give an HTML element an ID attribute if your code is located inside that element's tag. In this case, the code that changes each element's appearance is inside an event handler within the *A* tag. Instead of refering to the tag by its full name, you can simply say *this*. So, *element.Name.className = 'on'* becomes *this.className = 'on.'*

If you're not familiar with style sheets, you'll see that they are very intuitive. The *STYLE* tag Ⓐ defines the style sheet. The two styles (or classes) we're creating are named *on* and *off*: in the style sheet, these are represented as *.on* Ⓑ and *.off*. Ⓕ The information that follows these names in brackets defines the look of that particular style.

For the *on* style, the font size Ⓒ is 18, the text decoration Ⓓ is an underline, and its color Ⓔ is blue. The *off* style has a smaller font size Ⓖ of 16, no text decoration, Ⓗ and its color Ⓘ is black.

Once you've defined these styles, the rest comes together with a minimal amount of code. Take a look at the "Customers" Ⓙ link: in its *A* tag, you'll notice the inclusion of the *CLASS* attribute, Ⓚ which is used to assign a style to the text on the page. In the "Customers" link, as in all of the links, the CLASS attribute is set to the *off* style, so all of the properties of that style will be applied to the text of the link.

All that's left are the *onMouseOver* Ⓛ and *onMouseOut* Ⓜ event handlers, which change the style of the text when the mouse is moved over the link. When the mouse is moved over the "Customers" link, for example, this code is run:

```
this.className ='on';
```

This sets the *CLASS* attribute's name, *className*, of the "Customers" link to *on*. In other words, it applies all of the properties of the *on* style to the text in the link (blue, 18 pt, underlined). Since all of the links have this code, the same effect

```
      <HTML>
      <HEAD>
(A)   <STYLE>

(B)   .on {
(C)      font-size: 18;
(D)      text-decoration: underline;
(E)      color: blue;
      }

(F)   .off {
(G)      font-size: 16;
(H)      text-decoration: none;
(I)      color: black;
      }

      </STYLE>

      <BODY STYLE = "font-family: Arial">
      <H1>Learn more about our company</H1>
      <UL>

      <LI>
(J)   <A HREF = "customers.html"
(K)      CLASS = "off"
(L)      onMouseOver = "this.className ='on';"
(M)      onMouseOut = "this.className = 'off';">Customers
      </A>

      <LI>
      <A HREF = "products.html"
         CLASS = "off"
         onMouseOver = "this.className ='on';"
         onMouseOut = "this.className = 'off';">Products
      </A>

      <LI>
      <A HREF = "techs.html"
         CLASS = "off"
         onMouseOver = "this.className ='on';"
         onMouseOut = "this.className = 'off';">Technologies
      </A>

      </UL>
      </BODY>
      </HTML>
```

Figure 9-2. Code for a page that changes the type style of "active" links.

```
<OBJECT ID = "stocks" CLASSID = "clsid:333C7BC4-460F-11D0-BC04-0080C7055A83">
<PARAM NAME = "DataURL" VALUE = "stocks.txt">
<PARAM NAME = "UseHeader" VALUE ="TRUE">
</OBJECT>
```

Figure 9-3. The object tag for the data binding control.

happens when the mouse is moved over any of the links (and the *off* style is restored when the mouse is moved off the links).

Data binding

No longer do you need complex CGI scripts or massive SQL databases to maintain a simple database on a Web page. Dynamic HTML provides controls that let your Web pages access data on the server with minimal hassle. In short, data binding allows you to hook up data on your server (a simple text file) with HTML content on your pages.

Before you do anything with data binding, place a data binding control on your page. The HTML tag shown in Figure 9-3 is all you need. You can put this anywhere in your page; it's not visible.

The ID attribute of the control is important: this is the name you will be using to access all of the data. In this example, the name of the control is *stocks*. The location of your data is specified by the *DataURL* parameter. In this example, the data is

Symbol,	Company,	Quote:FLOAT,	Change:FLOAT,	Volume:INT
HWP,	Hewlett-Packard,	55.375,	-.25,	2552200
IBM,	IBM,	143.625,	.75,	2005800
AAPL,	Apple Computer,	16.5625,	.01875,	2057300
NSCP,	Netscape,	27.00,	-.375,	1466100
MSFT,	Microsoft,	99.00,	.625,	7665900
AOL,	America Online,	43.75,	-.25,	1397600

Figure 9-4. The *stocks.txt* data file.

Designing with JavaScript

```
Ⓐ  <TABLE BORDER = "1" ID ="stocktable" DATASRC = "#stocks">
   <TR>
Ⓑ  <TD><DIV DATAFLD = "Symbol">Stock Symbol Here</DIV></TD>
   <TD><DIV DATAFLD = "Company">Company Name Here</DIV></TD>
   <TD><DIV DATAFLD = "Quote">Quote Here</DIV></TD>
   <TD><DIV DATAFLD = "Change">Change Here</DIV></TD>
   <TD><DIV DATAFLD = "Volume">Volume Here</DIV></TD>
   </TR>
```

Figure 9-5. Displaying data in a table.

stored within *stocks.txt,* shown in Figure 9-4. This file stores all
the data for your database.

Figure 9-4 shows the format to follow when creating data for
the data binding control. All of the headings for your data are put
on the first line of text. The headings are important because you
will use them (and their names) to access data. As you can see,
each column heading is separated by a comma. Also note that
you need to specify a data type for each heading (unless it's plain
text). For example, the *Quote* column contains numbers (stock
quotes), so after naming the heading, we specify that the data in
the column is all numerical *(:FLOAT)*. Once you've named your
headings, you can add all of your data column by column,
separating columns on each line with commas, and separating
rows with a carriage return.

To display all of this data in your document, you'll need to
add some special attributes to your tags. Figure 9-5 shows how to
display all the stock data contained in *stocks.txt* in a table.

To route all the data from the data binding control named
stocks (which points to *stocks.txt*), add the *DATASRC* attribute to the
table Ⓐ (or form or *DIV* tag, etc.) and set it equal to a pound sign
plus the name of the control (*#stocks*). The *DATASRC* attribute
must be placed within an HTML element that encompasses the
elements where the information will be displayed.

Now you can insert the data from the source file into your
table. To insert the contents of the first column (which is named
"Symbol"), create a *DIV* tag with the *DATAFLD* attribute set to
"Symbol." Ⓑ Do the same thing for the other column headers.
Figure 9-6 shows the results.

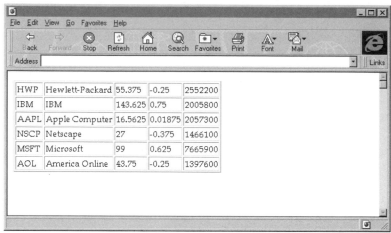

HWP	Hewlett-Packard	55.375	-0.25	2552200
IBM	IBM	143.625	0.75	2005800
AAPL	Apple Computer	16.5625	0.01875	2057300
NSCP	Netscape	27	-0.375	1466100
MSFT	Microsoft	99	0.625	7665900
AOL	America Online	43.75	-0.25	1397600

Figure 9-6. The table generated by the *stocks* data binding control.

```
<A HREF="#"
    onClick="stocks.sortColumn = 'Symbol';
    stocks.reset( )">
Sort stocks
</A>
```
Ⓐ
Ⓑ

Figure 9-7. The column-sorting code in an event handler.

Now it's time to add some JavaScript. Why not create a script that organizes all of the data by stock value or by ticker symbol? You may be cringing at the thought, but actually it's quite easy. To sort all of the ticker symbols in the "Symbol" column alphabetically, all you need is a bit of code, which can be put in an event handler within a button or even with the table's column header. Figure 9-7 shows the code for a link that will sort the data.

First, specify that you want to sort the "Symbol" column by setting the *sortColumn* property Ⓐ of the *stocks* data binding control to "Symbol." Then, run the *reset( )* method Ⓑ to redisplay all of your newly organized data. Figure 9-8 shows the sorted table.

To organize the numerical stock quotes in the "Quote" column, all you need to do is change the reference from "Symbol" to "Quote." The rest of the code can remain the same because the data binding control differentiates between

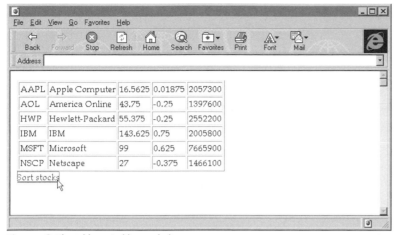

Figure 9-8. The table sorted by symbol.

numerical and alphabetical values automatically (because when you enter you data, you specify data type, e.g. *FLOAT*).

Pattern: A Dynamic HTML game

So far we've only touched on the power of Dynamic HTML. To give a more complete picture of Dynamic HTML, I wrote a little game called Pattern. It's a lot like the popular Simon game. The program plays a pattern on the screen and the player has to repeat the pattern by pressing the arrow keys on the keyboard. I recommend playing the game before going much further, as it will provide you with a better context for under-standing this section, and you may even end up having fun.

I've used cxamples from Pattern to illustrate many specific aspects of Dynamic HTML that we haven't discussed so far, namely:

- Absolute positioning of content.
- Animating absolutely positioned content.
- Creating content "on the fly."
- Expanding and collapsing menus (with new event model).
- Catching keystrokes (with the new event model).
- Multichannel audio with the mixer control.

Each example will be explained in full; you will also learn how each example ties into Pattern and what it adds to the experience.

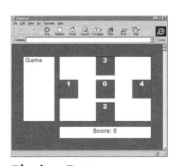

Playing Pattern
To play Pattern, run Internet Explorer 4 and open the file *pattern.htm*.

Absolute positioning

Absolute positioning lets you place blocks of content anywhere you wish, with exact *x, y* (left and top) coordinates. It also gives you the ability to stack those blocks of content above or below each other, with what is called a *z* coordinate. With JavaScript, those blocks of content can be hidden, moved, rotated, and animated in response to various events.

Positioning objects at exact coordinates on the page requires only style sheets, but to hide, show, or move those elements to different coordinates on the page you will need to incorporate Dynamic HTML's ability to control style sheets. Pattern uses a plethora of absolutely positioned elements, often hiding and showing them at timed intervals and even sliding them about the screen.

Figure 9-9. Text elements for the opening screen of the game are absolutely positioned.

Style sheets and absolute positioning in IE4

The first step in Pattern is to use style sheets to absolutely position objects with style sheets. The code in Figure 9-10 creates the Pattern logo that you see upon entering the game. Figure 9-9 shows the game's opening screen. A special style sheet class, *logo,* Ⓐ is defined for the Pattern logo. Set the *logo* style's position property Ⓑ to *absolute,* as opposed to *relative.* This tells the page to place the logo exactly where we specify; the placement will not be affected by any other content on the page.

Next, the coordinates of the logo are defined with the *left* and *top* properties. The *top* property Ⓒ determines the location of the logo's top side relative to the top of the page, and the *left* property Ⓓ determines the location of the logo's left side relative to the left side of the page. (*Top* and *left* are equivalent to *x* and *y,* respectively.) The Pattern logo is positioned in roughly the middle of the page: 38% from the top of the page and 44% from the left of the page. These values take into account the size of the

```
    <STYLE>
Ⓐ  .logo              {
Ⓑ  position:          absolute;
Ⓒ  top:               38%;
Ⓓ  left:              44%;
Ⓔ  height:            40px;
Ⓕ  width:             200px;
Ⓖ  visibility:        visible;

Ⓗ  font-size:         32;
Ⓘ  font-weight:       bold;
Ⓙ  font-family:       arial;
    }

    </STYLE>
    <BODY>
Ⓚ  <DIV CLASS = "logo" ID = "patternlogo">Pattern</DIV>
    </BODY>
```

Figure 9-10. The *logo* style sheet class for the Pattern logo.

font. The *left* and *top* values can be in either percent values or
pixel units; pixel units are indicated by *px* and percent values
with a percent sign.

The *height* Ⓔ and *width* Ⓕ properties, which are not
required, are used to "force" the height and width of the logo. The
logo is defined as visible by setting the *visibility* property Ⓖ to
visible, as opposed to *hidden.* (We don't actually have to define the
style as visible; all elements are visible by default.) Finally, the
look of the logo's text is defined as 32-point Arial bold with the
font-size, Ⓗ *font-weight,* Ⓘ and *font-family* Ⓙ properties.

After defining the *logo* style, we apply it by placing the
"Pattern" text within a *DIV* tag Ⓚ with the *CLASS* attribute; the
text is also named *patternlogo* with its *ID* attribute. Because
style sheet classes can be applied to multiple HTML elements,
the *logo* class can be used to position any other content in the
game. We'd only want to do this, of course, with content that has
similar characteristics.

Here's an example: the game has a warning message that signals the game is about to begin. This warning message uses the logo *class* as well:

```
<DIV CLASS = "logo" ID = "beginlogo" STYLE = "visibility: hidden;"> Begin </DIV>
```

Since this will be displayed in the same position as the Pattern logo, we set its *visibility* property to *hidden* for later use (otherwise the two would overlap).

Style sheets and absolute positioning in Navigator 4

Navigator 4.0 supports absolute positioning with style sheets like IE, but there's a catch. While the two browsers support nearly identical style sheet syntax, the document object models, through which you access those styles in JavaScript, are different. Let's use the Pattern logo code to illustrate these differences.

Look at Figure 9-10 again. What we have is an HTML element called *patternlogo* and a special style sheet class called *logo*. As you already know, to access the *left* property of this HTML element, *patternlogo*, in IE, you have to specify *document,* then *all* (referring to all the elements in the document), then *patternlogo,* then *style* (for the associated sytles sheet) and finally *left:*

```
document.all.patternlogo.style.left;
```

In Navigator 4.0x, however, the syntax is different (and shorter):

```
document.patternlogo.left;
```

With Netscape, we simply access *document,* then *patternlogo,* and then the *left* property. The important lesson here: When accessing properties of styles through JavaScript in Navigator 4.0x (relative to IE), omit both the *all* object and the *style* object. Other than that, absolute positioning of content through Navigator 4.0 and IE is very similar; most of what you read in this section applies to Navigator as well as IE.

Cross-browser positioning

Because absolute positioning in Navigator and IE is so similar, there's a simple workaround for creating absolutely positioned pages that work in both browsers. First, determine which browser is being used:

Designing with JavaScript

```
var isNS = (navigator.appName == 'Netscape' &&
parseInt(navigator.appVersion) >= 4)
```

Here we create a variable, *isNS*, that tells us if the browser is Navigator 4 or IE 4. Actually, this code only looks for Navigator, but we can assume that if it's not one 4.0 browser, it's the other.

After we've determined which browser is being used, we can use something called a *conditional* to assign the HTML elements on the page, like the Pattern logo, to shortcut variables which will be accesible to both browsers. A conditional, which is like a mini *if* statement, looks like this:

```
(if this condition is true) ? then do this : otherwise do this
```

Here's how we can apply the conditional:

```
var patlogo = (isNS) ? document.patternlogo :
document.all.patternlogo.style;
```

This conditional does a lot of things in just one line of code. First, it creates a variable name *patlogo*. Then it determines which browser is being used, by comparing *isNS*, and says: if it's Navigator, then use the Navigator syntax *(document.patternlogo;)* if it's not, use the IE syntax, *(document.all.patternlogo.style)*.

After giving our HTML element to a shortcut variable in an *if*-like fashion, we can then control the element through the variable in both Navigator and IE. For example, to change the *left* property of the Pattern logo now, we can use this code:

```
patlogo.left = 100;
```

or, we could change the *visibility* property to hide the logo:

```
patlogo.visibility = 'hidden';
```

Now you see it, now you don't

When Pattern starts, the logo disappears and you are warned that the game is about to begin. This small feat is accomplished by changing the visbility of the logo through JavaScript. To change the visibility of the Pattern logo (named *patternlogo*), we have to access the element's style property and from there the *visibility* property. Similarly, we make the Begin logo (named *beginlogo*) visible by accessing the same property. Figure 9-11 shows the code that hides the Pattern logo Ⓐ and turns on the Begin logo. Ⓑ Figure 9-12 shows the results.

Figure 9-11. Code for changing the visibility of elements.

This utilitarian technique of hiding and showing HTML elements can be used for more than simple eye-candy; throughout Pattern, it's used to manage a page that's full of content. You'll find that as you create larger applications, managing content — controlling what should be seen when — becomes increasingly important.

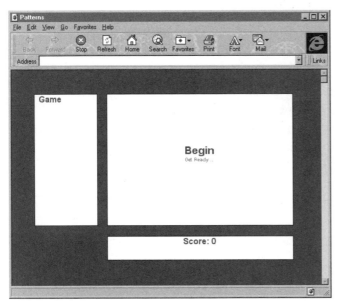

Figure 9-12. When the game starts, the word "Pattern" is replaced with the word "Begin."

Sliding into the finish

When you complete a game of Pattern you'll notice that the word "Finished" slides down to the middle of the page. This effect, simulated in Figure 9-13, is accomplished with a function that moves the content incrementaly until it has reached the middle of the page.

To create this effect, you need to change the *left* and *top* properties of the HTML element in question. In Pattern, the word "Finished" is within an HTML element named *finishedlogo*.

```
document.all.finishedlogo.style.left = 44%;
document.all.finishedlogo.style.top = 38%;
```

In this example, the words are positioned 44% from the left of the page and 38% from the top of the page. Essentially, this code centers the text. To create a fluid effect however, you need to change these values just slightly each time, as in an animation. This is accomplished with the *slide* function, shown in Figure 9-14, which creates the sliding entrance of the word "Finished" when the game is completed.

The HTML element in question, *finishedlogo*, is initially at the very top of the page and 44% from the left. The initial position is

Designing with JavaScript

defined by a style sheet class. This function moves *finishedlogo* down the page 2% at a time, until it reaches the 38% mark.

It works like this: the function is initially passed values of 0 and 38 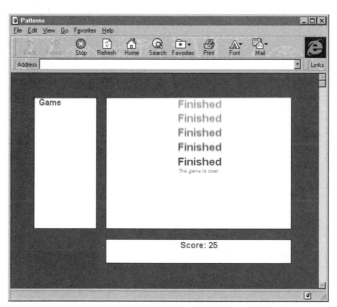 as arguments *currentPos* and *finalPos* Ⓐ (*currentPos* is the current top position of the HTML element and *finalPos* is the final top position). An *if* statement Ⓑ determines if *currentPos* is less than *finalPos*. If it is, the function increases the value of *currentPos* by 2 Ⓒ and gives that number to the HTML element's *top* property Ⓓ (plus a percent sign, so it will be a percent value), thereby moving the object down the page 2% at a time. The *setTimeout( )* method Ⓔ is used to repeat the function in 25 milliseconds, continuing the process until the HTML element is placed 38% from the top of the page.

This type of function can serve you in many ways: For example, to make a function that slides an HTML element named *whoosh* across the page from 0 to 800 pixels, you can use the variation shown in Figure 9-15.

Notice that in this example, *currentPos* is increased by 10 pixels Ⓐ every time the function runs, which increases the speed of the movement across the page. We're now effecting the *left* property Ⓑ instead of *top*, and we've changed the unit from percent values to pixels. We've also increased the lull time Ⓒ to 100 and changed the value of *finalPos* Ⓓ to 800.

Figure 9-13. The word "Finished" slides down the screen.

Around and around

One of the most compelling effects in Pattern is the circular rotation that ensues after achieving a perfect score. Let's take a practical approach at understanding and implementing this, without getting into the math that controls the effect. Figure 9-16 shows the script for the rotation effect.

First, define a radius Ⓐ for the circle of the content that you want to rotate, and *x* Ⓑ and *y* Ⓒ offsets for the placement of the center of the circle on the page.

```
A  function slide(currentPos, finalPos) {
B      if (currentPos < finalPos) {
C      currentPos += 2;
D      document.all.finishedlogo.style.top = currentPos + '%';
E      setTimeout('slide(' + currentPos + ',' + finalPos + ')', 25);
       }
   }
F  slide(0, 38);      // run slide initially, pass it current and final positions
```

Figure 9-14. The *slide( )* function.

Next, determine by how much you want the circle to rotate during each cycle (each time the rotation function is run). Here, a rotation of 4 degrees is used for each cycle; to get a smoother spin you can try 2 degrees by replacing the 45 with a 90. **D**

Next, create an array **F** for each of the objects that will rotate. In Pattern, four HTML elements are rotated in the circular path. We've added these four HTML elements, named *fly1*, *fly2*, *fly3*, and *fly4*, to the *objects* array. If you have more objects, just add them to the array.

After you've defined your objects, the script automatically creates an array of positions **G** for each of them (saving you a great deal of trouble). These arrays are placed in a function called *initObjects( )* **E** which is run when the document loads **I**

Finally, the script finishes with a function to animate the menagerie. **H** Explaining exactly how this works would require a crash course in basic trigonometry, so trust me … this will rotate the objects you've specified in a circular path.

If this sets your head "spinning," don't worry: a few minutes of experimentation and this will quickly come into focus.

Creating content on the fly

To display the current score, Pattern uses Dynamic HTML's ability to dynamically replace the content of an HTML element. First, a piece of text is sectioned off with a *DIV* tag: this is where the score, 0 to 100, will be displayed.

Score: <DIV ID = "score">0</DIV>

```
    function slide(currentPos, finalPos) {
        if (currentPos < finalPos) {
A       currentPos += 10;
B       document.all.finishedlogo.style.left = currentPos + 'px';
C       setTimeout('slide(' + currentPos + ',' + finalPos + ')', 100);
        }
    }
D   slide(0, 800);      // run slide initially, notice that you pass it 0, 800
```

Figure 9-15. This function slides an element across the page from left to right.

The next step is to determine the score: for the sake of brevity, let's say the score is contained within a variable *currentScore*. To display the current score in the *score* HTML element, use Dynamic HTML's *innerText* property.

In Pattern, we want to display the current score, so pass the variable where the score is contained: *currentScore*.

```
    score.innerText = currentScore
```

IE4's event model

Dynamic HTML provides scripting languages with a more powerful *event model* (the event model is the way in which a scripting language handles events such as *onClick*). Every event, whether it be the clicking of a mouse or the pressing of a key (yes, Dynamic HTML can capture keystrokes), is put into a special object — *event*. The *event* object, though it may not sound exciting, is quite useful because it provides information about where an event came from (which object on the page), where the mouse was located at the time, or which key was pressed.

Pattern takes advantage of this event model in two ways: first, with an expanding and collapsing menu system; and second, by allowing patterns to be replicated through the keyboard's arrow keys. Table 9-2 shows some of the event object properties.

Expanding and collapsing menus

The menu system in Pattern uses style sheets and the Dynamic HTML event model to dynamically expand and collapse text. The menu consists of a supermenu item, "Game," which has

```
<HTML>
<HEAD>
<SCRIPT LANGUAGE = "JavaScript">
Ⓐ var r = 160;                  // radius
Ⓑ var xoff = 180;               // x offset
Ⓒ var yoff = 170;               // y offset
  var pi = Math.PI;             // get pi
Ⓓ var inc = pi / 45;            // degrees per rotation cycle
  var objects;                  // objects to be rotated
  var pos;                      // position for objects

Ⓔ function initObjects( ) {
Ⓕ   objects = new Array( );     // define your objects
    objects[0] = document.all.fly1.style;
    objects[1] = document.all.fly2.style;
    objects[2] = document.all.fly3.style;
    objects[3] = document.all.fly4.style;

Ⓖ   pos = new Array( );
    pos[0] = 0;
    for (i = 1; i < objects.length; i++) {
    pos[i] = parseFloat(pos[i - 1] + ((2 * pi) / objects.length));
    }
    rotateObjects( );
    }

Ⓗ function rotateObjects( ) {
    for (i = 0; i < pos.length; i++) {
    pos[i] += inc; objects[i].visibility = "visible";
    objects[i].left = (r * Math.cos(pos[i])) + xoff
    objects[i].top = (r * Math.sin(pos[i])) + yoff;
    }
    setTimeout ("rotateObjects( )", 75);
    }
</SCRIPT>
</HEAD>
Ⓘ <BODY onLoad = "initObjects( )">
<DIV ID = "fly1" STYLE = "position: absolute;">
Fly 1
</DIV>
<DIV ID = "fly2" STYLE = "position: absolute;">
Fly 2
</DIV>
<DIV ID = "fly3" STYLE = "position: absolute;">
Fly 3
</DIV>
<DIV ID = "fly4" STYLE = "position: absolute;">
Fly 4
</DIV>
</BODY>
</HTML>
```

Figure 9-16. Script for rotating four objects in a circle.

Various event object properties

Event property	What it returns
keyCode	the numeric ASCII keycode of the key that was pressed
srcElement	the HTML element from which the event came
x	the horizontal position, in pixels, of the mouse relative to the window
y	the vertical position, in pixels, of the mouse relative to the window

Table 9-2.

submenu items, "Start" and "Rules." These submenus have their own submenus as well, which let you start a game or read the rules, as shown in Figure 9-17.

To expand and collapse the menus, use the style sheet *display* property. If an object's *display* property is set to *none*, the object becomes invisible and the space that it occupied is "released" (the *visibility* property, by contrast, simply makes the object visible or invisible but doesn't free up the space). If an object's display property is set to nothing (empty quotes), the object will be visible on the page. If you combine these two traits and put them in a hierarchical structure, you will get menus that expand and collapse. The code in Figure 9-18 is an example of this. Initially, this code displays the word "Super." When the user clicks on "Super," the text "Sub appears below. Here's how it works:

First take look at the "Sub" text surrounded by *DIV* tags. **B** The *STYLE* attribute in this line is an inline style sheet; it applies specified styles to the object in the tag where it resides. In this case, the inline style sheet sets the *display* property to *none.* This means the "Sub" text is invisible.

Now take a look at the "Super" link. **A** Inside the *A* tag is an *onClick* event handler with code that changes the *display* property of the *sub* object to nothing. When you change the *display*

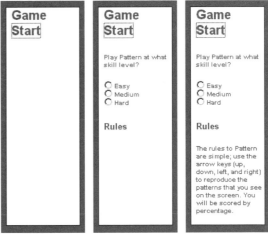

Figure 9-17. Pattern has a series of expanding menus, which reveal options for starting the game and reading the rules.

```
Ⓐ  <A HREF = "#" onClick = "document.all.sub.style.display = '';">Super</A>
Ⓑ  <DIV ID = "sub" STYLE = "display: none;">Sub</DIV>
```

Figure 9-18. Code for expanding a menu when the user clicks.

property to nothing, the object is displayed on the page. So when the user clicks on "Super," the "Sub" text is displayed. If we add more supers and subs, we'll have that menu system we were talking about.

If we are working with a complex system of menus, however, we'll want a uniform method of expanding and collapsing text. This can be done by using the event model's ability to determine where an event originated (which allows us to create one function for all of the menus). Before we get into this, let's create a setup to which we can apply this method.

Figure 9-19 shows the code for a menu made of a series of nested *DIV* tags (which I've structured and commented in an attempt to make things clearer). Notice that the outermost *DIV* tag Ⓐ calls function *controlExpand( )*. This function will control

```
Ⓐ  <DIV onClick = "controlExpand( )">
       <! -- Game Super Menu -->
Ⓑ      <DIV ID = "game">Game</DIV>
       <! -- Game Sub Menu -->
Ⓒ      <DIV ID = "gameSub" STYLE = "display: none;">
         <! -- Start Super Menu -->
Ⓓ        <DIV ID = "start">Start</DIV>
         <! -- Start Sub Menu -->
Ⓔ        <DIV ID = "startSub" STYLE = "display: none;">Start Menu Contents</DIV>
         <! -- Rules Super Menu -->
Ⓕ        <DIV ID = "rules">Rules</DIV>
         <! -- Rules Sub Menu -->
Ⓖ        <DIV ID = "rulesSub" STYLE = "display: none;">Rules Menu Contents</DIV>
       </DIV>
     </DIV>
```

Figure 9-19. Setup for the Game menus area.

```
    function controlExpand( ) {
 A      var sup = event.srcElement.id;               // ID of super menu that was clicked
 B      if (sup != '') {
 C          var sub = document.all[(sup + "Sub")]     // ID plus "Sub//"
 D          if (sub != null) {                        // if sub menu exists, toggle display
 E              if (sub.style.display == 'none') sub.style.display = '';
 F              else sub.style.display = 'none';
            }
        }
    }
```

Figure 9-20. The *controlExpand( )* function.

the expanding and collapsing menus (this *onClick* event handler
will handle all of the click events for the *DIV* tags that are nested
within this *DIV* tag).

If you look at the ID attributes of all of these *DIV* tags, you'll
notice a pattern. First there's *game,* ❸ then, *gameSub.* ❸ Within
gameSub, we have *start,* ❶ *startSub,* ❸ *rules,* ❶ and *rulesSub.* ❸.
Each of the *DIV* tags with IDs ending with "Sub" are submenus of
their similarly named counterparts. For example, *gameSub* is
game's submenu. Note that each of the submenus have inline
style sheets with *display* properties set to *none*; this means they
will be invisible (collapsed) by default. When a submenu's
supermenu is clicked, the *controlExpand( )* function decides
whether or not to display (i.e., expand or collapse) that submenu.
For instance, clicking on the *start* HTML element expands or
collapses the *startSub* element.

The *controlExpand( )* function, shown in Figure 9-20, makes
use of the *event* object, which holds the properties of the most
recently fired event. When one of the supermenus is clicked, the
onClick event handler in the outermost *DIV* tag is executed, and it
runs this function, which then uses Dynamic HTML's powerful
event model to determine the ID of supermenu that was clicked.
❶ (In this line, *event* is the *event* object, *srcElement* is the object
that fired the event, and *id* is the ID property of that object.) It
gives this value to the variable *sup.*

Dynamic HTML   157

```
        <SCRIPT LANGUAGE = "JavaScript">
 Ⓐ    function showKey( ) {
 Ⓑ    var key = event.keyCode;
 Ⓒ    alert("You pressed: " + key + ".");
      }

      </SCRIPT>
 Ⓓ    <BODY onKeyPress = "showKey( )">
      </BODY>
```

Figure 9-21. Script to report which key was pressed.

The next line Ⓑ determines if *sup* has a value, which it would only if the mouse were clicked on a supermenu. If *sup* does have a value, the function finds the name of the related submenu Ⓒ by adding "Sub" to the contents of *sup*. If that sub menu exists Ⓓ the function toggles the *display* property to expand a collapsed submenu Ⓔ or collapse an expanded submenu. Ⓕ

The great thing about this method of expanding and collapsing menus is that you don't need to add more code if you add more menus, the *controlExpand( )* function does all of that for you.

Catching keystrokes

The object of Pattern is to repeat the rapidly changing patterns that the game displays. With the mouse this is a slow and clumsy process; fortunately, Dynamic HTML provides a way to capture keystrokes from the user through the event model (and more specifically through the *event* object).

Figure 9-21 illustrates how this can be done. If you load this document into a browser, every time you press a key, it will shoot back a dialog box with a number in it: this number is the ASCII equivalent of the key (for example, "a" equals 109).

There are a couple of methods for capturing keystrokes, all similar in form and function. Here, we have an *onKeyPress* event handler in the *BODY* tag, Ⓓ which runs a function, *showKey( )*, to handle the keystroke. This function **Ⓐ** extracts the key code property, *event.keyCode*, from the *event* object **Ⓑ** and gives it to variable *key*. The keystroke can now be dealt with like any other variable. In this example, an alert box is generated. **Ⓒ** In Pattern, the key code is used to determine if you've matched the patterns correctly.

This *if* statement, for example, handles the pressing of the Up arrow key in Pattern:

```
if ((point == 0 && event.keyCode == 38)) {
showPoint(point, currentPattern + 1);
                        //display properly matched pattern
match.play( );          // bing of approval
realScore++;            // increase score
}
```

If point 0 (the top point) is the next pattern point and the Up arrow key is pressed (key code 38), a match occurs. The code within the *if* statement that handles this condition displays the properly matched pattern point, sounds a "bing" of approval, and increases the score by 1. As illustrated in this snippet of code, adding keystrokes to your list of catchable events isn't a big deal, programming-wise, but for the user, the benefit of being able to use the keyboard certainly is.

The mixer control

Sound, as any person will tell you, is an essential part of any interactive experience. Pattern uses the mixer control, a built-in multiplatform ActiveX control that plays multichannel audio, to signal different points in the game. For example, whenever you match a pattern, the game gives you a "bink" of approval. When you mismatch a pattern, you'll receive a sterner "bunk" sound.

You can begin using the mixer control by embedding its control in your document with the *OBJECT* tag:

```
<OBJECT ID = "mixer" CLASSID="CLSID:9A7D63C1-5391-
11D0-8BB6-0000F803A803">
</OBJECT>
```

You can place the control anywhere on the page, as it is invisible and won't affect your layout. After embedding the control, make

Design tip

Add left margins to the submenus so that the menu system's structure will be more visible. You can do this by adding the *margin-left* property to the inline styles of the submenus, or you can create your own class for submenus. Either way, a margin of *10* should be enough.

```
Ⓐ soundA = mixer.newSound("URLwav");        // create new sound object
Ⓑ channelA = mixer.newChannel( );           // create new channel object
Ⓒ soundA.loadMedia("miss.wav", 1, 1000);    // load file into sound object
Ⓓ channelA.input = soundA;                   // set sound object as channel object's input
```

Figure 9-26. Script to play sounds through the mixer control.

sure that the user has a working sound system; this can be done using the mixer control's *SoundCardAvailable* property, which returns *true* if the user has a working sound system.

```
if (mixer.SoundCardAvailable) {
```

Then, if the sound system is in working order, you can begin to load your sounds and assign them channels. Figure 9-26 illustrates how to set up a sound and a single audio channel for that sound.

Although this may seem elaborate for one little sound file, its actually quite pragmatic. The first line Ⓐ creates a new sound object of type *URLwav* named *soundA*. Next we create a new channel object Ⓑ named *channelA* (the sound is actually played through this object). The following line Ⓒ loads a sound file into the sound object (in this case, "miss.wav") using the *loadMedia( )* method. The final line Ⓓ sets that sound object as the channel object's input. To play this sound, run the *play( )* method of the channel object. Add an event handler, and you get sound that responds to events:

```
<DIV onClick = "if (soundA.isAvailable) channelA.play( )">
Honk!</DIV>
```

Notice the *if* statement: it makes sure the sound file in the sound object, *soundA*, is ready for playing (meaning it's loaded) by testing its *isAvailable* property. This is always a good idea, as you will get an error if you try to play the sound when the sound file isn't ready.

If you wish to play more than one sound using the mixer control, use the above model, but be sure to use different names for your respective channel and sound objects.

Designing with JavaScript

Figure 9-22. Clicking on the button displays the name of the button.

Netscape 4's event model

Patttern was cool. But it was in IE 4 only, right? Wrong. You already know how to do absolute positioning in Navigator 4. Add to that the new event model, and the sky, certainly not Pattern, is the limit. That's why I've decided to include this section. Navigator 4 enhances the power and flexibility of its event model many-fold over 3.0. It incorporates many of the same features that IE 4's improved event model does, allowing a game like Pattern to be created just as easily and effectively in Navigator as IE. The new event model allows events to be captured and handled without assigning event handlers in the HTML, it adds more events than you can shake a stick at (if that's your idea of a good time), and it gives the event model the ability to catch events "higher up," saving you from placing event handlers all over the page for every little form input and link.

Navigator 4 has a very powerful event model. As in IE, the new event model brings along with it a new object, the *event* object. But the *event* object is not like any other object you've seen before in this book. Figure 9-22 shows a page with a button labelled "What's my name?" Clicking on the button displays an

```
<SCRIPT LANGUAGE = "JavaScript">
(A) function handle(e) {
(B) alert(e.target.name)
    }
</SCRIPT>
<BODY>
<FORM NAME = "myform">
<INPUT TYPE = "BUTTON" VALUE = "What's my name?"
(C)    NAME = "mybutton" onClick = "handle(event)">
</FORM>
</BODY>
```

Figure 9-23. Using the event object to pass the button's name to an alert box.

alert box with the name of the button. Let's look
at how Netscape 4's event model makes this possible.

As Figure 9-23 shows, when the button is pressed, it runs the
handle( ) function. (C) If you look at the *onClick* event handler,
you'll see that it passes this function the word *event*. This word is
actually the *event* object; the *event* object exists only when it's a
parameter in the event handler. (See Table 9-3 for a list of the
event object's properties.)

When the *event* object arrives at the *handle( )* function, it
becomes variable *e* (A) (but it's still the event object). Once there,
you can treat it like any other object. In this example, the
function accesses the *event* object's *target* property, (B) which
contains the HTML element that originated the event (the
button), and then accesses the *name* property, which returns the
name of the button, *mybutton*. That name is given to *alert*, and an
alert box with the name of the button is displayed.

There's much more to the new event model. Event handlers
can now be directly assigned through a script, meaning that you
no longer need to put event handlers directly in the HTML.
Figure 9-24 shows how we'd create our last example using this
method of assigning event handlers.

We've removed the *onClick* event handler from the form
button and added a script below it. Take a close look at this
script. It appears to access the form button using the classic

Designing with JavaScript

```
<FORM NAME = "myform">
<INPUT TYPE = "BUTTON" VALUE = "Hi There"
   NAME = "mybutton">
</FORM>
<SCRIPT LANGUAGE = "JavaScript">

document.myform.mybutton.onClick = handle;

</SCRIPT>
</BODY>
```

Figure 9-24. Assigning a function to an event handler.

JavaScript nomenclature, but then things take a strange turn. We assign what looks like the button's *onClick* property to *handle*. Event handlers, when assigned directly through a script, are treated like properties of the element for which they are handling events.

We've assigned the *onClick* event handler to execute function *handle( )*. The *onClick* event handler belongs to *mybutton*, so when *mybutton* is clicked, function *handle( )* will be run (when assigning functions to event handlers like this, leave out the function's double parentheses). When assigning event handlers in this manner, the *event* object is automatically passed to any functions that the event handler runs.

There's one more aspect of the new event model to understand: the ability to capture events "higher up" in the event model. Essentially, this means that you can create one function to handle all events and do away with event handlers for every little button, text input, link, etc.

Figure 9-25, which uses this new capability, is a real-time forms validation script. This means that as you type into the form elements, every keystroke is validated. If you're typing in the name field, for example, any numbers you type will be filtered out, and conversely, if you're typing in the phone number field, any letters you type will be filtered out.

Let's first talk about how all the event handling and capturing is done. In Figure 9-25 we've instructed the window to capture all *KeyPress* events using the *captureEvents( )* method. ⓓ This means every time a key is pressed, regardless of where the cursor is, the

```
<SCRIPT LANGUAGE = "JavaScript">
function checkForms(e) {
   if (e.target.name == "myname") {
      if (e.which >= 48 && e.which <= 57) {
      alert("Your name doesn't have any numbers.");
      return false;
      }
   }
   if (e.target.name == "myphone") {
      if ((e.which < 48 || e.which > 57)
         && e.which != 32 && e.which != 45 && e.which != 8) {
      alert("Your phone number doesn\'t have any letters.");
      return false;
      }
   }
   return true;
   }
window.captureEvents(Event.KEYPRESS);
window.onKeyPress = checkForms;
</SCRIPT>
<BODY>
<FORM NAME = "myform">
<INPUT TYPE = "TEXT" NAME = "myname"><BR>
<INPUT TYPE = "TEXT" NAME = "myphone"><BR>
<INPUT TYPE = "SUBMIT" VALUE = "Send Info">
</FORM>
</BODY>
```

Figure 9-25. Real-time forms validation script.

window's event handler (which we have yet to specify) will handle that event. Note that when you instruct the object to capture an event, you must type the event's name in all caps, thus *KeyPress* becomes *KEYPRESS*, and *Click* becomes *CLICK*. To capture more than one event, separate the event names with the | (pipe) character.

After instructing the window to capture all *KeyPress* events, we can assign an event handler for that event. We've made a function, *checkForms( )*, to handle the *KeyPress* event. ⑤ (Again, notice that we did not use double parentheses with the function name.)

When *checkForms( )* is run, ⓐ which is whenever a key is pressed, the *event* object is used to determine where you were typing and what you typed. The first *if* statement in the function **B** determines whether or not you were typing in the name element, *myname*. If you were, it determines if you tried to type any numbers by testing the *which* property of the *event* object; *which* returns the ASCII keycode for the key that you pressed.

Since keycodes 48 through 57 are the number keys, the *if* statement determines if the *which* property is between those values; if it is, that means you typed a number. In that case, the code within the *if* statement points out that your name can't have numbers and returns *false*, just like in forms validation, so the keystroke never reaches the name element. **C** Similarly, the second *if* statement determines if you tried to type letters on the phone number field.

At first take, this may seem like a more difficult way of handling events, but the reality is that they are very powerful. With the event object's *which* property, for instance, we can now determine which keys a user has pressed, and respond to those keys in our scripts. The *event* object also allows us to determine the position of the mouse in relation to the document. When you combine this with the new *onMouseDown* and *onMouseUp* event handlers, anything is possible. Keep in mind, however, that you can still, and in many cases should still, create event handlers in the old-fashioned inline method (within the HTML tags). To see how all this applied to Pattern, look at *pattns4.htm* on the CD.

10

Getting Acquainted with Layers

Why layers?

When Netscape released the first public beta of Navigator 4.0, they trumpeted a new feature called layers, which enabled JavaScript to position, hide, show and dynamically write content. With the advent of layer controls in cascading style sheets, layers represent unnecessary complexity for page developers; cascading style sheets and JavaScript are all you need, as explained in Chapter 9, *Dynamic HTML*. Netscape maintains support for layers in the final release of Navigator 4, for backwards compatibility reasons; for similar reasons, we include this chapter on layers, originally published in *Web Review* in March 1997.

Like all things in HTML, layers have their own tag: *LAYER*. This tag is chock full of properties, so instead of talking about each of them separately, here's a list that explains what each does and how it affects a layer.

- *name:* the layer's name.
- *left:* the location (in pixels) of the layer in relation to the left side of the window.
- *top:* the location (in pixels) of the layer in relation to the top of the window.
- *width:* the desired width (in pixels or percent) of the layer.
- *z-index:* determines which layers the layer will be "above" and which layers it will be below. For example, if one layer has a z-index of 5, and another has a z-index of 3, the layer with the higher value, 5, will appear "on top" of the other.
- *visibility:* determines how the layer will be displayed on the screen. The values for this property, "show" and "hide," are self-explanatory.
- *clip:* the visible region (a rectangle) of the layer in pixels. Defined as *x1, y1, x2, y2* coordinates.
- *bgcolor and background:* the background color and background image of a layer.

Once you know all of these properties, creating a layer is a cinch:

```
<LAYER VISIBILITY = "SHOW" BGCOLOR = "#FF0000"
TOP = 100 LEFT = 100>
This is my first layer.
</LAYER>
```

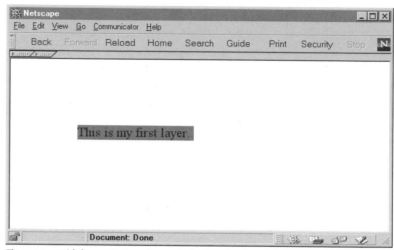

Figure 10-1. With layers, text can be precisely placed and assigned a background color.

On the CD

This chapter shows how to use layers and JavaScript to create a complex animation effect. To see it in action, open the file *index.html* in Netscape 4 and click on the *Layers Demo* link. As the demo opens, a motion-blurred image races down from the top of the window as another races from the bottom. The two converge to create a brightly colored splash screen. After the splash screen wipes away, the phrase "They run circles around traditional HTML," is displayed and centered while four geometric objects rotate around it.

As shown in Figure 10-1, the above layer is inset 100 pixels from the top and left of the window and has a red background color.

There are a few characteristics of layers that you need to understand to work with them. By default, all layers are transparent, meaning anything behind them will show through. Even with transparent GIFs, transparency prevails. However, the layer becomes opaque the moment you add a background color.

When you put something (preferably HTML) inside a layer, it acts similarly to a table cell. For example, if you place a 300×200 image in a layer, the layer will expand to that size.

After you've played around with layers for a while, you may start to get bored and wonder: "What do I do now?" The answer to that question is JavaScript.

All of the properties of a layer are accessible through JavaScript. If you create a layer and give it a name, you can control it through JavaScript.

```
<LAYER NAME = "control" VISIBILITY = SHOW
TOP = 0 LEFT = 0>
Control me through JavaScript.
</LAYER>
```

To get access to this layer in JavaScript, refer to it by name, like so:

```
controlLayer = document.layers["control"];
```

This creates a variable, *controlLayer,* and "gives" it the layer on the page named *control.* This variable serves as a shortcut. Instead of saying *document.layers["control"]* every time you want to access the layer, you can simply say *controlLayer.* Now that you have access to the layer through JavaScript, you can control its properties. For example, to hide the layer, change its *visibility* property to *hide.*

```
controlLayer.visibility = "hide";
```

Two of the more interesting properties to play around with are *left* and *top.* When you change these, the physical location of the layer (on the page) is changed too, resulting in movement. Instead of working with these two properties, though, there are a couple of methods that you can use to save typing: *moveTo( ),* and *moveBy( ).* The *moveTo( )* method moves a layer to an exact left/top coordinate.

```
controlLayer.moveTo(100, 25);
```

This would move the layer 100 pixels to the left of the window and 25 from the top. The *moveBy()* method performs a similar

Layers glossary

For a more detailed list of layers properties, zip on over to Netscape's layers documentation at *http://home.netscape.com/ comprod/products/communicator/ layers/layers_glossary.html*

```
    <HTML>
    <HEAD>
    <TITLE>Layers</TITLE>
    </HEAD>
    <BODY>
Ⓐ  <LAYER NAME = "control" VISIBILITY = SHOW
        TOP = 0 LEFT = 0>
    Howdy!
    </LAYER>
    <SCRIPT LANGUAGE = "JavaScript">
    <! --

Ⓑ  controlLayer = document.layers["control"];
Ⓒ  controlLayer.moveTo(100, 25);

    // -->
    </SCRIPT>
    </BODY>
    </HTML>
```

Figure 10-2. HTML for changing the position of a layer.

Figure 10-3. Sliding the image in from top and bottom.

Figure 10-4. The completed image.

function, but instead of moving the layer to the exact position, it offsets the layer by the given values.

```
controlLayer.offset(25, 10);
```

If the layer were located 100 pixels from the left and 100 pixels from the top of the window, this would move it 25 pixels over and 10 down from that position. Both of these methods make moving layers a friendlier task (rather than dealing with *left* and *top* every time).

Before I go any further into the intricacies of controlling layers with JavaScript, let's build anHTML document that demonstrates what you've learned so far. This document, shown in Figure 10-2, should give you a better understanding of how it fits together.

First, the layer is created and given a name: *control*. Ⓐ Next, a script gives the layer to variable *controlLayer*. Ⓑ Finally, the *moveTo( )* command Ⓒ is used to change the location of the layer to 100 pixels from the left and 25 pixels from the top. This is how most of your layer/script pages will be set up: create the layer, access it in JavaScript, and then do something to it.

To move layers, clip layers (crop), and do other exciting things with layers, you need to create functions. For example, the code for the sliding entrance of the demo is similar to the code shown here:

Designing with JavaScript

Figure 10-5. Clipping over time creates the wiping effect.

```
function slideSplash( ) {
splashLayer.offset(0, 10);
if (splashLayer.top < 140) setTimeout('slideSplash( )', 50);
}
```

Figure 10-3 shows how the two parts of the opening image slide in from the top and bottom. Figure 10-4 shows the completed image.

The layer in question, *splashLayer,* begins at coordinates 0, 0, and is moved down the page in 10-pixel increments until it's 140 pixels from the top. Each time this function is run, it moves the layer down by 10 pixels using the *moveBy()* method. Next, it determines if the layer is 140 pixels down the page using an *if* statement.

```
if (splashLayer.top < 140) setTimeout('slideSplash( )', 50);
```

If it's less than 140 pixels from the top of the page, the function runs itself again (after waiting 50 milliseconds) using *setTimeout( )*. The result is a layer that slides down the page 140 pixels, then stops.

You may have noticed that when the splash screen disappeared it didn't suddenly go away, but was gradually wiped away using clipping. Gradual clipping like this can be done in a couple of ways, but first you have to understand how to control clipping. Let's do this by using a few examples. To clip (hide) 10 pixels off the left side of a layer, try this:

```
splashLayer.clip.left = 10;
```

```
<HTML>
<HEAD>
<TITLE>Demo</TITLE>
</HEAD>
<BODY BGCOLOR = "#FFFFFF">
<LAYER VISIBILITY = HIDE NAME = "splash">A Little Text</LAYER>
<SCRIPT LANGUAGE = "JavaScript">
<! --
function slideSplash( ) {
splashLayer.offset(0, 10);
if (splashLayer.top < 140) setTimeout('slideSplash( )', 50);
else wipeSplash( );                                  // when layer has reached
}                                                    // 140 pixels, run wipe
function wipeSplash( ) {
splashLayer.clip.left += 10;
if (splashLayer.clip.left < 200) setTimeout('wipeSplash( )', 50);
}
splashLayer = document.layers["splash"];             // create variable for layer
splashLayer.visibility = "show";                     // show layer
slideSplash( );                                      // run sliding function
// -->
</SCRIPT>
</BODY>
</HTML>
```

Figure 10-6. HTML for the introductory part of the demo.

or to clip 25 pixels off the top, try this:

```
splashLayer.clip.top = 25;
```

There are two other properties than you can clip with as well: *right* and *bottom*. These do the inverse of *left* and *top*, and their values must reflect that. If you increase the clipping value over a period of time using a function, you will get the wiping effect, as shown in Figure 10-5.

The function below increases the left clipping of the layer by 10 pixels every time it is run. The function repeats every 50 milliseconds using *setTimeout( )* as long as the clipping is less than 200 pixels; otherwise the clipping is halted.

```
function wipeSplash( ) {
splashLayer.clip.left += 10;
if (splashLayer.clip.left < 200) setTimeout('wipeSplash( )', 50);
}
```

When these functions are combined, you can create multiple, consecutive effects that take place when and where you want.

```
<HTML>
<HEAD>
<TITLE>Pages That Make You Dizzy</TITLE>
</HEAD>
<BODY BGCOLOR = "#FFFFFF">

<LAYER VISIBILITY = HIDE NAME = "n1">
<IMG HEIGHT = 72 WIDTH = 65 SRC = "1.gif">
</LAYER>
<LAYER VISIBILITY = HIDE NAME = "n2">
<IMG HEIGHT = 80 WIDTH = 71 SRC = "2.gif">
</LAYER>
<LAYER VISIBILITY = HIDE NAME = "n3">
<IMG HEIGHT = 72 WIDTH = 77 SRC = "3.gif">
</LAYER>
<LAYER VISIBILITY = HIDE NAME = "n4">
<IMG HEIGHT = 69 WIDTH = 80 SRC = "4.gif">
</LAYER>
<SCRIPT LANGUAGE = "JavaScript">
<! --

r = 160;                              // radius
xoff = 180;                           // x offset
yoff = 170;                           // y offset
pi = Math.PI;                         // get pi
inc = pi / 45;                        // degrees per rotation cycle

lyr = new Array( );                   // define your layers
lyr[0] = document.layers["n1"];
lyr[1] = document.layers["n2"];
lyr[2] = document.layers["n3"];
lyr[3] = document.layers["n4"];

var pos = new Array( );
pos[0] = 0;
for (i = 1; i < lyr.length; i++) {
pos[i] = parseFloat(pos[i - 1] + ((2 * pi) / lyr.length));
}

function rotateThings( ) {
for (i = 0; i < pos.length; i++) {
pos[i] += inc; lyr[i].visibility = "show";
lyr[i].moveTo((r * Math.cos(pos[i])) + xoff, (r * Math.sin(pos[i]))
+ yoff);
}
setTimeout ("rotateThings( )", 75);
}

rotateThings( )                       // run the function to start rotation!
// -->
</SCRIPT>
</BODY>
</HTML>
```

Figure 10-7. Full source for the layers demo.

Figure 10-7. Rotating numbers illustrate the phrase, "They run circles around traditional HTML."

Using just these two functions, you can create an intro similar to the demo, as shown in Figure 10-6. As each effect finishes, the next is run; for full explanations see the source in Figure 10-7.

The next part of the demo involves rotating four numbers in a circle, as shown in Figure 10-8. How was this done? Let's take a practical approach without getting into the math. First, define a radius for the circle, and x, y offsets for the placement of the center of the circle.

```
r = 160;        // radius
xoff = 180;     // x offset
yoff = 170;     // y offset
```

Next, determine by how much you want the circle to rotate during each cycle (each time the rotation function is run). Here, a rotation of 4 degrees is used for each cycle. However, to get a smoother spin you can try 2 degrees by replacing the 45 with a 90.

```
pi = Math.PI;   // get pi
inc = pi / 45;  // degrees per rotation cycle
```

Create an array for each of the layers that you want to be part of the rotating circle.

```
lyr = new Array( );
lyr[0] = document.layers["n1"];
lyr[1] = document.layers["n2"];
lyr[2] = document.layers["n3"];
lyr[3] = document.layers["n4"];
```

In the demo, four layers (the number/shape graphics) are rotated in the circular path. These four layers, named *n1, n2, n3,* and *n4,*

are all put in the *lyr* array: from element 0 to element 3. If you
have five or six layers that you want included in the rotation, just
add them to the array.

```
var pos = new Array( );
pos[0] = 0;
for (var i = 1; i < lyr.length; i++) {
pos[i] = parseFloat(pos[i - 1] + ((2 * pi) / lyr.length));
}
```

After you've defined your layers, the script automatically creates
an array of positions for each of them (saving you a great deal of
trouble).

```
function rotateThings( ) {
for (var i = 0; i < pos.length; i++) {
pos[i] += inc;
lyr[i].moveTo((r * Math.cos(pos[i])) + xoff, (r *
Math.sin(pos[i])) + yoff);
}
setTimeout ("rotateThings( )", 75);
}
```

Finally, the script finishes by supplying you with a function to
animate the menagerie. Explaining exactly how this works would
require a crash course in basic trigonometry, so take for granted
the fact that it will rotate the layers you've specified in a circular
path. When it's all put together, your rotating page should look
something like Figure 10-7. If this sets your head "spinning,"
don't worry: a few minutes of experimentation and this will
quickly come into focus.

11

The Show: Dynamic HTML Applied

WebCoder article

This article appeared in *Web Review* on May 30, 1997. The URL is *http://webreview.com /97/05/30/coder/*

In October 1996, I created a game called The Show. I did it for two reasons: one, because I wanted to show off the then-new features of Netscape 3.0, and two, because I thought it would be an enjoyable experience for my visitors.

However, times have changed since October and so has the Web, so I decided to rewrite my game to capitalize on the powers of Dynamic HTML. With all of this said, I present to you The Show 2.0. To view it you'll need the latest preview release of Netscape Navigator 4.0 (PR 4 or greater), a sound card (the MIDI music sounds terrible unless you have a real MIDI card), and a few IQ points to spare. If you meet all of these requirements, let the game begin.

Once you've played the game, you'll most likely want to know how it was created, so I'm going to tell you, step by step. The following points will be covered in this article:

- how Dynamic HTML is incorporated
- how to create the scrolling background effect
- how the logo bounces
- how the questions and answers are displayed
- how the sound and music are played on cue

Incorporating Dynamic HTML

One thing is for sure: all of the effects in The Show can be created with both Microsoft's and Netscape's implementations of Dynamic HTML. However, the reason that I chose the "Netscape-only way" is simple: As of this writing, there are probably more people using Navigator 4.0 than there are Internet Explorer 4.0.

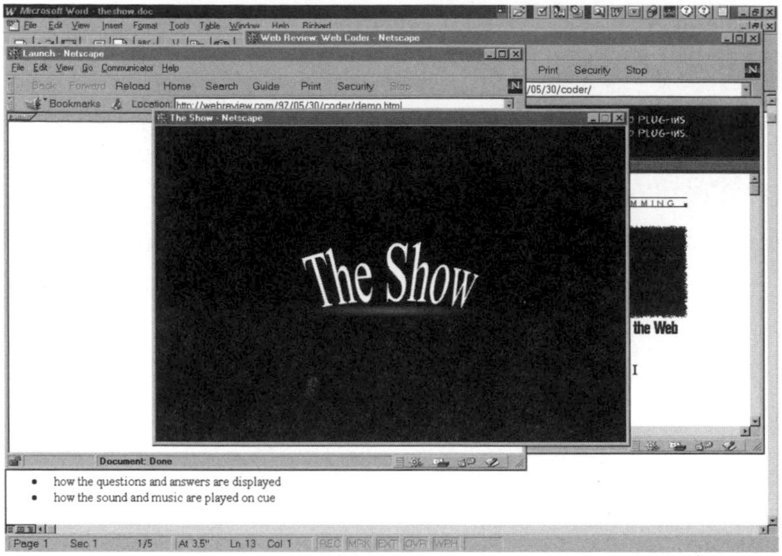

Figure 11-1. The Show's window is automatically centered on the user's screen.

Why layers?

I used layers because, at the time I wrote The Show, Netscape Navigator 4 didn't properly support absolute positioning with cascading style sheets. Now that Netscape 4 and IE 4 both support layers as part of cascading style sheets, *that* is the preferred technology.

Running The Show

To run The Show open *index.htm* in Netscape 4.0b4 or later and click on *Play The Show.*

Most of the effects that you see in The Show are achieved using a combination of layers and JavaScript. All of the layout and animation — sliding of the spotlights, bouncing of the logo, etc. — are done with layers. If you're not familiar with layers, I suggest you read Chapter 10, *Getting Acquainted with Layers.*

Also important, but not totally related to Dynamic HTML, is the ability to determine screen height and width, and window height and width. For instance, notice that the game window is positioned in the center of the screen, as shown in Figure 11-1.

To do this, I used the new screen object's height and width properties.

```
var winX = screen.width;
var winY = screen.height;
window.open("index2.html", "game",
"outerWidth=635,outerHeight=450,left=" +
(winX - 635) / 2 + ",top=" + ((winY - 440) / 2) - 5) +
",resize=0");
```

I took the width and height of the screen, subtracted the height and width of my game window, and divided by 2 in each case (so much for randomly positioned windows).

Designing with JavaScript

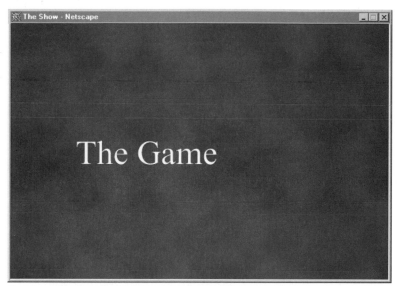

Figure 11-2. The introduction features two layers of independently moving images: the words "The Game" and a tiled background image.

Second-place winner
The Show took second place in the Netscape/WebMonkey Dynamic HTML contest, held in conjunction with the 1997 Netscape Developers' Conference.

To find the inner height and width of the current window, I used the window's newly introduced *innerHeight* and *innerWidth* properties. What's great about these properties is that they actually tell you the width of your document (not just the outer widths of the window).

In The Show, the spotlights are positioned just out of view using these properties by setting the *left* property of the layer equal to the width of the window:

```
spotRightLayer.left = window.innerWidth;
```

Without these properties, exact positioning like this would be almost impossible.

When it comes right down to it, those are the only two aspects of Dynamic HTML (or at least new JavaScript features) that I needed. Therein, however, lies the code.

The scrolling background effect

During the introduction to the game, the phrases "The Game" and "Is Here" scroll across an already moving background, as shown in Figure 11-2, creating an almost three-dimensional effect that does an effective job of catching the eye.

To put together a scrolling background like this, you'll need two things: a layer and a repeated image. Take your repeated image and set it as the background for a layer:

```
<LAYER NAME = "floatBg" HEIGHT = "460"
WIDTH = "924" BACKGROUND = "lights.gif">  </LAYER>
```

The height and width of this layer are important, because the layer must continually cover the page. Make the height of the layer a little more than the height of the window. To determine the width of the layer, calculate the total width, in pixels, of the number of images it takes to span the entire window, and add the width of one more image.

For example, my background image is 308-pixels wide. Because my window is 610-pixels wide, I determined it would take a total of two images, a combined 616 pixels in width, to cover the entire window. I added the width of one more image, 308 pixels, to that value, for a total of 924 pixels, which I set as the width of my layer. This ensures that the background images are always covering the window, with no empty space at any time.

After creating the background layer and giving it proper a width and height, you need to create a function that will move the layer across the page.

```
function floatBg(difX) {
if ((difX < 0 && floatBgLayer. left > -308) ||
(difX > 0 && floatBgLayer. left < 308)) {
    floatBgLayer.left += difX;
    }
else floatBgLayer.left = 0;
var bgTimer = setTimeout(floatBg, 25, difX);
}
```

The layer, which I've given to shortcut variable *floatBgLayer*, is moved a given number of pixels each time this function is run. An *if* statement in the function determines if the layer has moved one whole image by checking its *left* property's value. In this example, if the layer has moved 308 pixels (the width of one of my background images) the layer is reset. The function automatically runs itself every 25 milliseconds using *setTimeout( )*.

Designing with JavaScript

To start this function, pass it the number of pixels, either positive or negative, that you want the background layer to move during each cycle.

```
floatBg(4);
```

The bouncing logo

I thought it would be interesting to have a bouncing logo. This function is complex at first glance, so I'm going to walk you through the whole thing.

```
function dropShowLogo(difY, down, dist) {
    var recursive = true;
```

When the function first runs, it takes three arguments: *difY, down,* and *dist.* The first of these variables, *difY,* determines by how many pixels the layer (in this case, the logo) will move each time the function is run; this is essentially the speed of the layer's movement. The second variable, *down,* determines which direction the layer is headed. If the layer is "falling down," then the value is true; if the layer is bouncing back up, then the value is falsc. The last argument, *dist,* is the relative distance that the layer is falling. This is used to determine the amount of bounce.

```
if (down && dist > 0) {
    if (showLogoLayer.layer.top + difY <= 145)
      showLogoLayer.layer.top += difY;  }
    else {
    showLogoLayer.layer.top +=
    Math.abs(showLogoLayer.layer.top - 145); down = false;
    }
}
```

This *if* statement handles all cases in which the layer is moving down: if the distance, *dist,* is greater than 0 and if *down* is true. If this is the case, another *if* statement determines if the layer has reached "the floor." In this case, the floor is reached when the *top* property of the layer is equal to 145 (i.e., when the layer is 145 pixels from the top of the page). If it has not yet reached its floor, then it is moved down by adding to the *top* property. If it has reached its floor, then it's time to bounce, so the value of *down* is set to *false.* This means the next time the function it run, it will send the layer up instead of down. That's what the second half of the function handles:

```
else if (!down && dist > 0) {
    var bounce = Math.floor(dist / 4);
    if (showLogoLayer.layer.top - difY >= Math.abs(145 -
    bounce)) {
        showLogoLayer.layer.top -= difY;
    }
    else {
    showLogoLayer.layer.top -= Math.abs
    (showLogoLayer.layer.top - (145 - bounce));
    down = true;
    dist = bounce;
    }
}
else {
    recursive = false;
}
fgTimer = (recursive) ? setTimeout(dropShowLogo, 25, difY,
    down, dist) : null;
}
```

This *if* statement handles all cases when *down* is false and the distance, *dist*, is greater than zero (i.e., when the layer is bouncing up.) The first thing the code within this *if* statement does is determine how high the layer should bounce. I've used an effective but unscientific method to do this: I just divided the falling distance, *dist*, by four. The only difference between the rest of this code and the previous code is that the *top* property of the layer is decreased (moving the layer up) and the distance the layer travels is one-fourth that of which it traveled down.

This entire process is repeated over and over until the distance that the layer "drops" is no longer significant: when it's less than one pixel. To begin the dropping and bouncing, run the function and pass it the desired movement in pixels per cycle, the initial direction (*true* for *down*), and the dropping distance.

```
dropShowLogo(20, true, 145);
```

I have some simple tips for modifying this:

- Replace all references to *showLogoLayer.layer* with your layer's name;
- Replace all references to 145 with the value (relative to the top of the page in pixels) that you want the layer to drop to.

Displaying the questions and answers

Each layer on the page has its own document object. You can even think of each layer as a separate document, as with frames.

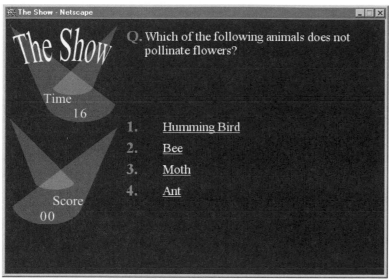

Figure 11-3. A question and four possible answers.

To write a question from the "question database" (a bunch of arrays) to the question layer on the page, I used the familiar *document.write( )* method.

```
questBodyLayer.layer.document.write('What\'s the point of
it all?'); questBodyLayer.layer.document.close( );
```

I used the *document.close( )* method when I was finished writing to the layer, which closes the "stream" to the layer, thereby displaying the content. The four possible answers to each question are displayed this way too. Figure 11-3 shows one of the questions and possible answers.

This brings us to another point: How are the answers submitted to the game? Each answer is actually a link, as you probably guessed. An *onClick* event handler inside the link calls a function that submits the answer to the game. The links look like this, where the number that's passed to the function is 0 through 3 (answers 1 through 4):

```
<A HREF = "#" onClick = "submitAnswer(0);
return false;">
```

HTML similar to this is written along with the actual text each time an answer is dynamically generated. When the link is

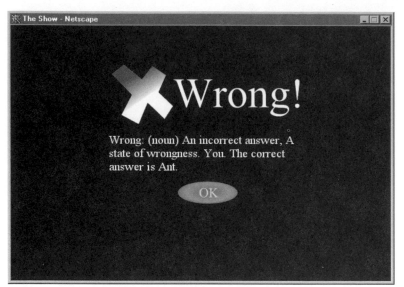

Figure 11-4. One of the game's "wrong" answer messages.

clicked, the answer is submitted, the clock is stopped, and the game determines if the question was answered correctly and acts accordingly. Figure 11-4 shows the game's response to a wrong answer.

Playing the sound and music on cue

The Show uses an old-fashioned but tried-and-true method to play the sound and music on demand. Think of it this way: when you put one of those *EMBED* tags in your document and set the *AUTOSTART* attribute to *true*, the sound is played as soon as it loads. If you create this embed (which launches Netscape's LiveAudio) dynamically, you have a simple, guaranteed-to-work method of playing sound. First, create an empty and invisible layer; this is where the LiveAudio embed is created:

```
<LAYER NAME = "sound" VISIBILITY = "HIDE">
</LAYER>
```

Then create a function to play the sound on demand. This function will create the HTML for the *EMBED* tag, insert the name of the file, and then write the combination to the layer.

```
function playAudio(target, file, loop) {
    target.document.open('text/html');
    target.document.write('<EMBED SRC = "' + file + '"
    HIDDEN = "TRUE" LOOP = "' + ((loop) ? 'TRUE' :
    'FALSE') + '" AUTOSTART = "TRUE">');
    target.document.close( );
}
```

To use the function, pass it the target layer, sound, the name of
the sound file you want to hear, and a Boolean value (true or
false) which determines if the sound will be looped.

```
playAudio(document.layers['sound'], 'sweep.au', false);
```

Naturally, this discussion hasn't covered everything in The Show.
For a more in-depth view, take a look around. The full source
code for The Show is on the CD as *theshow.html*.

12

Advanced Applications

T his chapter deals with the concepts of scripting that many of us want to avoid, but cannot if we wish to grow as programmers. Here you'll read a primer on *object-oriented* scripting (more accurately, *object-based* scripting), which is followed by some hard-hitting examples of object-oriented thinking and organization in action.

In this chapter, I've chosen to explain the code (and how to implement it) in very different ways. In the Quiz, we go through the script on a line-by-line basis, so you can go on to create your own object-based scripts.

In the Tour Guide, I show you how object-based scripting can be made quite powerful when combined with other scripting techniques (such as control of frames, dynamic creation of text, and audio). Instead of explaining the code line by line, I discuss the techniques the script uses and how to use them in your own creations. The final example, the Relational Menu, also offers a conceptual description of the script.

Creating your own objects

You deal with objects all the time in JavaScript: the *document* object, the *window* object, the *navigator* object, and many others. The next step is to create your own objects, refered to as *user-defined objects*. Why? Because a good object-oriented script is easier to understand, more adaptable, and more efficient than a script that is not. Up to this point, our creations have been relatively small, so they didn't need to be object-oriented. This is not to say that object-oriented means large — object-oriented means easier to manage. Some of these concepts may be a little hard to swallow at first, so if you don't master it the first time around, don't get worried.

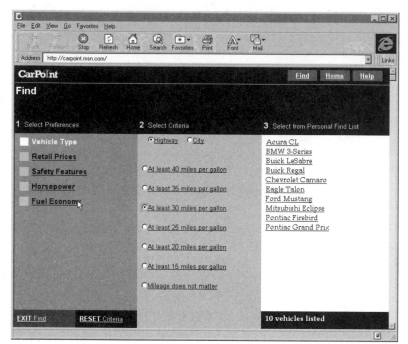

CarPoint
http://carpoint.msn.com/

Figure 12-1. CarPoint's "Find" interface.

Who needs user-defined objects?

With JavaScript's built-in objects (such as the *document* object and the *navigator* object) the properties and methods are defined for you. With user-defined objects, you define the objects' properties and methods. User-defined objects can make scripts more efficient and easier to work with. Here's a scenario that illustrates this. The engineers at CarPoint, part of the Microsoft Network, were told to design a system to quickly and efficiently find a vehicle based on a number of specifications: brand, horsepower, and price being just a few of them. Figure 12-1 shows the site's interface to this system.

We are going to simplify CarPoint's application, however, to explain why the object way is often a better way to program. Imagine you are a CarPoint engineer. You are instructed to create an application that will recommend a car — from a list of some 250 entries — based on four properties: color, brand, horsepower, and price. The user specifies a range for each of these properties

Designing with JavaScript

```
color[0] = "Red";          // first car
color[1] = "Pink";         // second car
brand[0] = "Ford";         // first car
brand[1] = "Cadilliac";    // second car
horsepower[0] = 160;       // first car
horsepower[1] = 300;       // second car
price[0] = 15000;          // first car
price[1] = 40000;          // second car
```

Figure 12-2. In the non-object method, the properties for each car are pulled from four different arays.

and then receives a list of cars that fit those specifications. For example, a user might ask for a blue Ford with at least 180 hp and priced between $17,000 and $20,000.

The non-object way

There are two ways to do this task: the object way and the non-object way. We'll begin with the latter. Since there are 250 cars in the list, it makes sense to put them in an array. Because there are four properties, however, you will need four arrays, one for each property. The first element in the color array, *color[0]*, contains the color of the first car. The first element in the brand array, *brand[0]*, contains the brand name of the first car. A car, in this sense, is made up of specific elements from each of the arrays. If you were to create a car in these terms, here's how you could organize it:

First Car
{
```
color[0] = "Red";
brand[0] = "Ford";
horsepower[0] = 160;
price[0] = 15000;
```

Second Car
{
```
color[1] = "Pink";
brand[1] = "Cadillac";
horsepower[1] = 300;
price[1] = 40000;
```

As you can see, the first car's properties are all in the first element of each array, the second car's properties are all in the second element of each array, etc. Though it makes sense conceptually, especially when you organize it like this, were

```
// first car
car[0].color = "Red";
car[0].brand = "Ford";
car[0].horsepower = 160;
car[0].price = 15000;
// second car
car[1].color = "Pink";
car[1].brand = "Cadilliac";
car[1].horsepower = 300;
car[1].price = 40000;
```

Figure 12-3. In the object method, each car is an element in a single array.

you to actually code it, it would not be quite as clear, as shown in Figure 12-2.

The object way

Now let's analyze the task in the object-oriented way: instead of having four different arrays for each property, why not have one array that contains all four properties within it?

Essentially, each element of the array constitutes one whole car (object). In Figure 12-3, we see the objects built out of an array called *cars*. The first car is the first element in the array, *cars[0],* and *color, brand, horsepower,* and *price* are properties of that element.

Creating user-defined objects

As you see from this example, the object-oriented way simply makes more sense, and this is the way CarPoint created their car finder script. To do this, however, you have to know how to create your own object frameworks, called *constructor*

```
function Car( ) {
this.color;
this.brand;
this.horsepower;
this.price;
}
```

Figure 12-4. The *Car( )* constructor function.

Designing with JavaScript

```
function Car(color, brand, horsepower, price) {      // the four arguments
    this.color = color;                   // set the color property equal to color
    this.brand = brand;                   // set the brand property equal to brand
    this.horsepower = horsepower;         // set the horsepower property equal to horsepower
    this.price = price;                   // set the price property equal to price
```

Figure 12-5. The *Car( )* object with arguments for each property.

functions. These constructor functions define an object's properties and methods. Figure 12-4 shows the constructor function for the car object.

The syntax of the constructor function may seem odd at first glance, but you'll quickly get used to it. This constructor function creates four properties: *color, brand, horsepower,* and *price*. To create a car object using this function, use the new operator followcd by thc namc of thc function:

```
mycar = new Car( );
```

This creates a new car object named *mycar* with the four properties, *color, brand, horsepower,* and *price*. Let's take a closer look at *Car( ):* it's clearly not a conventional function.

The *Car( )* function uses a special word, *this,* to define the car object's *(mycar)* properties. When the *Car( )* function says *this.color*, it is actually saying *mycar.color*. What's the significance of that? By saying *this.color,* the function defines a new property, *color,* for *mycar*. You can access the newly created *color* property like this:

```
mycar.color = "Red";
document.write(mycar.color);
```

Since *Car( )* is a function, you can assign the car object's properties all at once by adding arguments for each of the properties, as shown in Figure 12-5.

In this scenario, *Car( )* takes four arguments: *color, brand, horsepower,* and *price.* The values of each of these arguments are then given to *this.color, this.brand, this.horsepower,* and *this.price,* respectively. Thus, as the properties of the new car object are created, they are given values as well. (Note that the argument names here are the same as the property names, but

```
function showBrand( ) {
document.write(this.brand);
}
```

Figure 12-6. Function to display the brand of the car.

they don't have to be; it just makes more sense.) Here is the object for a car whose color is red, brand is Ford, horsepower is 160, and price is $15,000.

```
mycar = new Car("Red", "Ford", 160, 15000);
```

When you create a new car object in this way, keep in mind the order of the arguments. You must pass properties in the order defined in the function — *color, brand, horsepower,* and *price.*

You can also create new car objects and assign them to elements of an array. This is especially useful when you have a large number of objects (as CarPoint did). Here is an array with the first two elements.

```
cars = new Array( );
cars[0] = new Car("Red", 'Ford", 160, 15000);
cars[1] = new Car("Pink", "Cadilliac", 300, 40000);
```

User-defined objects can have methods as well as properties. For instance, with the car object, you can easily add a method to display the brand name of the car. First, create a separate function to display the brand using *document.write( ).* In Figure 12-6, we've created a function called *showBrand( ).*

Notice the use of *this.brand:* since this function is (going to be) a method of the car object, it must refer to it as *this,* just as the properties do. To turn this function into a method of the car

```
function Car(color, brand, horsepower, price) {
this.color = color;
this.brand = brand;
this.horsepower = horsepower;
this.price = price;
this.showBrand = showBrand;
```

Figure 12-7. Car object with *showBrand( )* as a method of the object.

```
HTML>
<HEAD><TITLE>"Fun" with Objects</TITLE>
<SCRIPT LANGUAGE = "JavaScript">

// The Car Object Constructor
function Car(color, brand, horsepower, price) {
this.color = color;
this.brand = brand;
this.horsepower = horsepower;
this.price = price;
this.showBrand = showBrand;
}

// The showBrand( ) Method of the Car Object
function showBrand( ) {
document.write(this.brand);
}
</SCRIPT>
</HEAD>
<BODY BGCOLOR = "#FFFFFF">
A Car Object: <P>
<SCRIPT LANGUAGE = "JavaScript">

mycar = new Car("Red", "Ford", 160, 15000);          // create new car object
mycar.showBrand( );                                   // run its showBrand method

</SCRIPT>
</BODY>
</HTML>
```

Figure 12-8. HTML document for showing the brand of a car object.

object, you need to modify the object constructor function, as shown in Figure 12-7.

Despite the fact that all five lines in this function look similar, they are quite different. While the first four lines assign properties to variables, the last line links the function, *showBrand( )*, to the object, thereby creating a method. (Notice that there are no double parentheses when you refer to *showBrand( )* in the object constructor.)

After modifying the object constructor and creating the *showBrand( )* function, you can create a new car object and run its *showBrand( )* method like this:

```
var mycar = new Car("Red", "Ford", 160, 15000);
mycar.showBrand( );
```

This simply displays the word "Ford," the car object's brand. Figure 12-8 shows all the functions and objects we've discussed in this example.

I hope this has given you a better understanding of how to create and work with user-defined objects. Although most of this is stereotypical programmer talk, you will find that these next two examples, which lean heavily on user-defined objects, are more practical and applicable to your site.

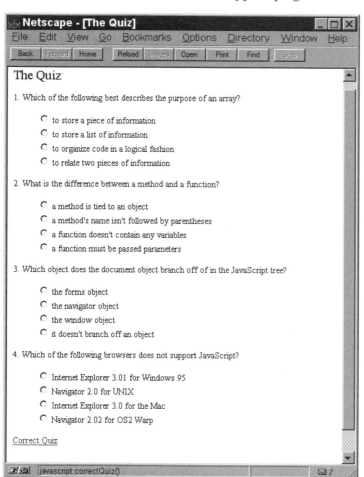

Figure 12-9. The quiz consists of four multiple-choice questions. After answering the questions, users can click on "Correct Quiz" link to see how they did.

The Quiz: Testing your readers

Looking for a way to get your users to interact more with your content? Why not use the old teachers' trick and pop a quiz? Besides providing you with some interesting feedback, it's often entertaining for your visitors. This script creates a simple multiple-choice quiz using form radio buttons, as shown in Figure 12-9. But unlike school, when you had to wait a day or two to receive your graded quiz, the Quiz script gives instant feedback. Figure 12-10 shows the correction message, which appears in a separate window.

Understanding the question object

Since we're learning how to create user-defined objects, we are going to create this quiz in an object-oriented way. We'll create one question object for each question in the quiz.

Figure 12-11 shows the object constructor function for creating each of the questions. Although it looks daunting at first, you'll soon see that it's not.

Let's begin by describing the properties of the question object:

- The *question* property 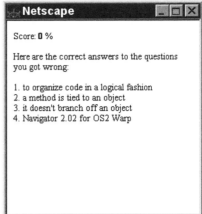 contains the actual content of the question.

- The *correctAnswer* property ⑩ contains the number of the correct answer.

- The *userAnswer* property ⑪ contains the number the user picks as the answer. If *userAnswer* matches up with *correctAnswer*, then the question has been answered correctly.

- The *userChoices* property ⑫ is an array. That's right, properties can be arrays. The *userChoices* array contains several possible answers to the question (the number of possible answers is infinite), one of which is correct.

Figure 12-10. The correction box reports the user's score.

In addition to these properties, there are two methods — *isCorrect( )* ⑬ and *showForm( )* ⑭ — to this object.

The *isCorrect( )* method determines if the question is answered correctly. Figure 12-12 shows the *isCorrect( )* function.

The method simply determines if the user's answer choice, *userAnswer*, is the same as the correct answer choice, *correctAnswer*. If they match up, the question was answered correctly and the method returns *true.* Otherwise, it returns *false.*

```
Ⓐ function makeQuestion(question, correctAnswer) {
Ⓑ   var args = makeQuestion.arguments;
Ⓒ   this.question = question;
Ⓓ   this.correctAnswer = correctAnswer;
Ⓔ   this.userAnswer = null;
Ⓕ   this.isCorrect = isCorrect;
Ⓖ   this.showForm = showForm;
Ⓗ   this.userChoices = new makeArray(args.length - 2);
Ⓘ   for (var i = 0; i < args.length - 2; i++) {
Ⓙ     this.userChoices[i] = args[i + 2];
   }
}
```

Figure 12-11. The *makeQuestion( )* function.

```
function isCorrect( ) {
if (this.correctAnswer == this.userAnswer) return true;
else return false;
}
```

Figure 12-12. The *isCorrect( )* function.

The second method, *showForm( ),* displays the number of the question, the content of the question, and the possible answer choices. It also creates a radio button for each of the choices. Figure 12-13 shows the function for this method.

Let's take a closer look at the *showForm( )* method to get a better understanding of how it works. It begins by displaying the number of the question (argument *n*) followed by the question's text, *this.question.* Ⓐ A *BLOCKQUOTE* tag is used to set off the answer choices, and a form is started. Each element in the *userChoices* array contains one of the answer choices.

For example, *userChoices[0]* contains the first answer choice. A *for* loop is used to cycle through the array. Ⓑ Inside the *for* loop, code is run once for each of the answer choices. This code creates a radio button followed by the answer choice's text. Ⓒ If you look closely, you will see that located inside the radio button is the *onClick* event handler. When the radio button is clicked, *onClick* sets the *userAnswer* property equal to the number of the choice. Finally, the form and the blockquote are closed off, ending the question. Ⓔ

```
   function showForm(n) {
Ⓐ  document.write((n + 1) + '. ' + this.question + '<BLOCKQUOTE><FORM>');
Ⓑ  for (var i = 0; i < this.userChoices.length; i++) {
Ⓒ  document.write('<INPUT TYPE = "RADIO" NAME = "q' + n + '"
       onClick = "quiz[' + n + '].userAnswer = ' + i + '">');
Ⓓ  document.write(this.userChoices[i] + '<BR>');
   }
Ⓔ  document.write('</FORM></BLOCKQUOTE>');
   }
```

Figure 12-13. The *showForm( )* function.

Designing with JavaScript

Making a question object

Here's how to create a question object using the *makeQuestion( )* object constructor function (Figure 12-11).

```
whyArray = new makeQuestion("Which of the following
best describes the purpose of an array?",
    2,
    "to store a piece of information",
    "to store a list of information",
    "to organize code in a logical fashion",
    "to relate two pieces of information");
```

The first parameter is the content of the question. This value is given to the *question* property of the *whyArray* question object.

The second argument is the number of the correct answer. Here the correct answer is 2, which corresponds to "to store a list of information." (Note that the first choice is referred to as 0, the second as 1, etc.) This number is given to the *correctAnswer* property of the question object. (Refer back to Figure 12-11 if you're unclear about the properties that the *makeQuestion( )* object takes.)

The remaining arguments are the answer choices. You must have two possible answers, but there is no limit to the number of possible answers. All of these choices are given to the *userChoices* property of the *makeQuestion( )* object. Remember that the *userChoices* property is an array, so choice 0 will be given to *userChoices[0],* choice 1 will be given the *userChoices[1],* and so on.

After creating the question object, you can display and correct it easily using its two methods. For example, to display *whyArray* question object on the page, run its *showForm( )* method:

```
whyArray.showForm(0);
```

Creating the quiz

Now that you know how to make a question object, you need a way to tie together multiple question objects into a fully functioning quiz. First, create an array, *quiz,* to hold all of the question objects. Initialize the length of the array to the total number of questions in the quiz. If your quiz has four question objects, initialize the *quiz* array to a length of four.

```
quiz = new makeArray(4);
```

Next, create your question objects. If you have four questions, use elements 0 through 3 of the *quiz* array, making each element a question object. Remember the order in which you pass the contents of each question object to *makeQuestion( )*: question, correct answer, answer choices. The *quiz* array is shown in Figure 12-14.

Now we have four question objects, each stored in elements of the *quiz* array. To display the contents of the first question object, *quiz[0],* run its *showForm( )* method.

```
quiz[0].showForm(0);
```

Instead of doing this "manually" for each question object, let's create a *for* loop to automatically go through each question object and run its *showForm( )* method.

```
quiz[0] = new makeQuestion(
"Which of the following best decribes the purpose of an array?",
    2
    " to store a piece information ",
    " to store a list of information ",
    " to organize code in a logical fashion",
    " to relate two pieces of information ");

quiz[1] = new makeQuestion(
"What is the difference between a method and a function?",
    0,
    " a method is tied to an object ",
    " a method's name isn't followed by parentheses"
    " a function doesn't contain any variables",
    " a function must be passed parameters");

quiz[2] = new makeQuestion(
"Which object does the document object branch off of in the JavaScript tree?",
    3,
    " the forms object ",
    " the navigator object"
    " the window object"
    " it doesn't branch off an object");

quiz[3] = new makeQuestion(
"Which of the following browsers does not support JavaScript?",
    3,
    " Internet Explorer 3.01 for Windows 95",
    " Navigator 2.0 for UNIX",
    " Internet Explorer 3.0 for the Mac",
    " Navigator 2.02 for OS2 Warp");
```

Figure 12-14. The *quiz* array.

```
for (var i = 0; i < quiz.length; i++) {
quiz[i].showForm(i);
}
```

This loop goes through each element of the *quiz* array (each question object) and runs its *showForm( )* method. Essentially, this displays the entire quiz on the page.

Correcting the quiz

At this point, you've created the questions, displayed them on the page, but you have not corrected them. That's what the next function is for: it goes through all the questions, corrects them, opens a new window, displays the percent correctly answered, and the answers to any questions that were done incorrectly (shown in Figure 12-10). Figure 12-15 shows the *correctQuiz( )* function.

There are two variables that go along with *correctQuiz( )*; they define which comments will be added to the corrections.

```
ifAced = "<P>Well done, you aced it.<P>";
ifWrong = "<P>Here are the correct answers to the
    questions you got wrong:<P>";
```

```
function correctQuiz( ) {
var correct = 0;
correctPage = '<HTML><TITLE>Corrections</TITLE><BODY BGCOLOR = "#FFFFFF">';
   for (var i = 0; i < quiz.length; i++) {
   if (quiz[i].isCorrect( )) correct++;
   }
var score = Math.round((correct / quiz.length) * 100);
correctPage += 'Score: <STRONG>' + score + '</STRONG> %';
   if (correct < quiz.length) {
   correctPage += ifWrong;
      for (var i = 0; i < quiz.length; i++) {
         if (!quiz[i].isCorrect( )) {
         correctPage += (i + 1) + '. ' +
         quiz[i].userChoices[quiz[i].correctAnswer] + '<BR>';
         }
      }
   }
   else correctPage += ifAced;
correctPage += '</BODY></HTML>';
correctwin = window.open ('', '', 'height=300,width=300,scrollbars=yes');
   if (correctwin.opener == null) correctwin.opener = window;
correctwin.location = 'javascript:opener.correctPage';
}
```

Figure 12-15. The *correctQuiz( )* function.

The variable *ifAced* contains the message to display if all of the questions are answered correctly. The variable *ifWrong* contains the message to display if any questions are answered wrong.

The last thing that your quiz needs is a button to run the *correctQuiz( )* function after the quiz has been finished. You can do this a couple of ways. With a form button:

```
<FORM><INPUT TYPE = "BUTTON" VALUE = "Correct"
onClick = "correctPage( )">
```

Inside *correctPage( )*

The process that *correctPage( )* goes through to correct the quiz is rather elaborate, but if you follow closely and examine the code, it should come into focus.

```
var correct = 0;
correctPage = '<HTML><HEAD><TITLE>Corrections</TITLE></HEAD>
<BODY BGCOLOR = "#FFFFFF">';
```

First, the function assigns correct an initial value of 0 and *correctPage* is given *HEAD* and *BODY* tags to begin an HTML document (where the corrections will be displayed). Since we are building an HTML document for the corrections, you can customize it to fit your needs. Just change the attributes in the *BODY* tag; it won't mess up the code. If you want a background image, or a picture of a graduation hat, just add the HTML. (Note: Use absolute URLs for any images.)

```
for (var i = 0; i < quiz.length; i++) {
    if (quiz[i].isCorrect()) correct++;
}
```

A *for* loop cycles through all of the question objects in the *quiz* array and runs their *isCorrect( )* methods. In our example, the quiz array has 4 elements, and therefore has a length of 4. That means the *for* loop starts at *quiz[0]* and ends at *quiz[3]*. Each time *isCorrect( )* returns *true,* meaning the answer is right, the correct is increased by 1. If a question is answered wrong, *correct* is not increased, and therefore no credit is given.

```
var score = Math.round((correct / quiz.length) * 100);
correctPage += 'Score: <STRONG>' + score + '</STRONG> %';
```

After the total number of correct answers is determined, that value, *correct,* is divided by the total number of questions, *quiz.length.* The result is rounded to a whole number and given or with a standard link, using the JavaScript pseudo-protocol:

```
<A HREF = "javascript:correctQuiz( )">
<IMG BORDER = 0 HEIGHT = 28 WIDTH = 98
SRC = "correct.gif"></A>
```

To understand how all of this works together, take a look at what a finished quiz might look like. On the CD, open *index.htm* and click on the link for the Quiz code. With a bit of tweaking, you'll have your own quiz up and running in no time.

to variable *score*. Next, *score*, along with some accompanying text, is added to *correctPage*. (The accompanying text, which you can modify, says, "Score: [percent here] %".)

```
if (correct < quiz.length) {
correctPage += ifWrong;
```

An *if* statement determines if all of the questions are answered correctly. If not, *ifWrong* is added to *correctPage*. Usually, *ifWrong* contains something to the effect of, "Here are the correct answers to the questions you got wrong." If all of the answers are correctly answered, the function jumps to the end and displays a message of congratulations.

```
for (var i = 0; i < quiz.length; i++) {
    if (!quiz[i].isCorrect()) {
    correctPage += (i + 1) + '. ' +
    quiz[i].userChoices[quiz[i].correctAnswer] + '<BR>';
    }
}
```

Once again, a *for* loop is used to cycle through the questions in the *quiz* array. This time, though, an *if* statement uses the *isCorrect()* method to determine if an answer is *not* correct, using *!* (the *false* conditional). If a question is answered incorrectly, then the number of the question and its correct answer are added to *correctPage*.

```
correctPage += '</BODY></HTML>';
correctwin = window.open ('', '', 'height=300,width=300,scrollbars=yes');
    if (correctwin.opener == null) correctwin.opener = window;
correctwin.location = 'javascript:opener.correctPage';
```

Finally, closing *BODY* and *HTML* tags are added to *correctPage*, and the function writes all of the information about the corrected quiz to the window using the JavaScript pseudo-protocol. (We could have used *document.write( )* to write all of the information, as well. Use the method you prefer.)

The tour guide

When someone comes to your site for the first time, wouldn't it be nice to show them around — you know — give them "The Grand Tour?" Perhaps you could bring them to the major areas of the site to tell them what each area is about and show them how to get around. To do this for each visitor, you need the Web's equivalent of a tour guide. That's what this script is all about.

The tour guide is actually a small window that floats atop the main browser window like a remote, as shown in Figure 12-16. It consists of two borderless frames and two hidden frames. All the "talking" is done in the larger top frame; any comments, explanations, or annotations will be displayed in this "talk frame." All of the tour guide's controls are located in the lower frame (the "control frame"). The controls consist of a forward button, a back button, and a play/pause button. The forward and back buttons allow you to skip forward or backward a stop in the tour.

The way the tour works is simple: the main browser window goes to a page of your site for a speficied amount of time, the "talk" frame in the tour guide window gives an explanation of the page, and any sounds (au, MIDI, or even RealAudio) are played.

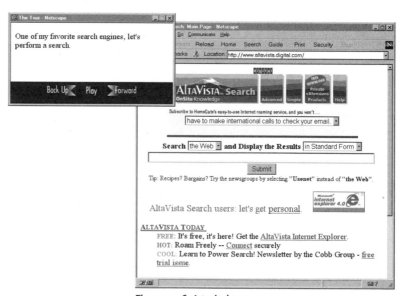

Figure 12-16. A typical tour.

```
function makeTour( ) {
tour = window.open("","tour","width=400,height=200");
tour.location.href = "http://www.domain.com/tour.html";
   if (tour.opener == null) tour.opener = window;
tour.opener.name = "opener";
}
```

Figure 12-17. The tour launching function.

The tour will progress automatically, unless of course the visitor presses one of the forward or back buttons (this will put the tour in manual; to put it back in automatic just press the play button).

You can probably surmise that this is going to be a complex script, but it's designed to be as intuitive as possible (using objects), and is easily customizable. For example, everything in this script revolves around the idea of the "stop." Just like there are stops in a tour of the zoo, there are stops in your tour. The difference is that instead of stopping at the alligator pit and talking about the animals, your tour stops at a page of your site and talks about that.

Let's begin by putting together a tour using the tour script, and later we'll discuss the scripting techniques used in the tour.

Setting up your tour window

Before you do anything, you have to create a window for the tour guide. To do this, we will use a slight variation on the remote launcher. (See the "Remote control" section of Chapter 2, *Doing Windows*). Put this code, shown in Figure 12-17 on the page that launches the tour.

This function creates a new window and loads an HTML document named *tour.html*. This is the document where the tour script is located. All of the sound and image files that go with the tour should be in the same directory as this file. To launch the tour, create a link to run the *makeTour( )* function.

```
<A HREF = "javascript:makeTour( )">Start Tour</A>
```

Figure 12-18 shows the article in *Web Review* with a button to launch the tour.

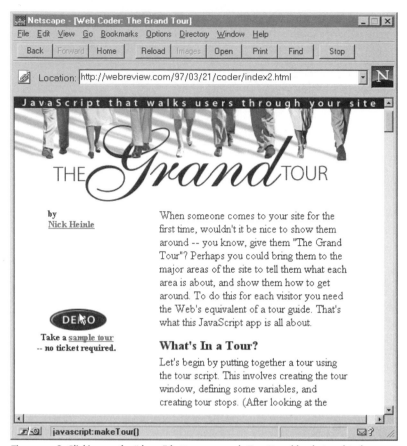

Figure 12-18. Clicking on the "demo" button runs *makeTour( )* and loads *tour.html*.

Assembling your tour

Let's begin the tour script by defining some important variables, shown in Figure 12-19. Here's a rundown of each of the variables:

- *baseHREF* is the directory where *tour.html* is located. All files that you specify in the tour are relative to this location.

- *soundBg* contains the name of any background music (MIDI) that you want to play during the tour. Remember, all of the sound and image files in the tour script are relative to the location of *tour.html* (the value that you give *baseHREF*.) To make life easier, put all of these files in the same directory as *tour.html*.

```
var baseHREF =
   'http://webreview.com/97/03/21/coder/';
var soundBg = 'chill.mid';
var talkDefault = 'tourwait.html'; tour loads
var controlBgColor = '#000000';
var controlFgColor = '#FFFFFF';
var controlPlay = ' Play ';
var controlPause = ' Pause ';
var controlForward = ' Forward ';
var controlBack = ' Back ';
```

Figure 12-19. Variables used by the Tour script.

- *talkDefault* contains the URL of the HTML document to be displayed while the sound and music for the tour is loading. A helpful message, perhaps one that instructs the visitor how to use the tour's controls, is most appropriate.
- *controlBgColor* defines the background color of the control frame.
- *controlFgColor* defines the foreground color of the control frame.
- *controlPlay, controlPause, controlForward,* and *controlBack* are the links, either textual or graphical (with the *IMG* tag), for the play, pause, forward, and back buttons in the control frame.

The reason for all of these variables is to allow plenty of flexibility in the look and feel of the tour. Creating your own images for the controls, using your own color scheme, and adding your own sounds will make the tour all that much better. Customization is the name of the game.

The next step it to create the tour itself. This is done by creating *stop* objects for each stop of the tour. The stop object has four properties: *talk, url, wait,* and *sound.* Here's what each of these variables do:

- The *talk* property contains the URL of the HTML document to be displayed in the talk frame during that tour stop. This page, which should be designed to fit the small space of the tour window, does the work of walking your visitors through the site.

- The *url* property contains the URL of the document to be displayed in the main window (the one that you will talk about).
- The *wait* property is the number of milliseconds to wait at the stop. Since most pages take at least 15 seconds to fully load, a wait of 15 to 20 seconds per stop is preferable.
- The *sound* property contains the name of any sound that you want to be played in sync with the stop. The sound can be an au file, a MIDI file (if you have no background music), or, if your server supports it, a streaming format such as RealAudio. With the exception of streaming audio, all of the sounds are preloaded, so keep them small!

Creating a stop object is easy, especially with the stop object constructor (which we'll get to shortly). First, however, you need to know the order in which to pass the object constructor its properties:

```
newStop(talk, url, wait, sound);
```

Here's an example:

```
newStop('tour1.html', 'http://altavista.digital.com',
20000, 'click.au');
```

This stop displays the HTML document *tour1.html* in the talk frame of the tour window, brings the main window to *http://altavista.digital.com,* plays a sound named *click.au,* and rests at the stop for 20 seconds. If you don't want a sound, or don't want to change the URL, pass the object constructor a null value for each of those properties.

```
newStop('tour2.html', null, 15000, null);
```

In the above example, there would be no sound and the main window's location would not change. This is useful if you want to talk about the same area of your site for more than one stop; the only thing that changes is the HTML document in the tour window.

Before creating your own tour, make sure you have a reason for it. Don't simply show your visitors five pages of your site and call it a tour. Why not use the opportunity to teach them what your site is really about? Until now, all of your visitors had to discover the site on their own: now you can do it with them, and in your own way.

```
function showControls( ) {
controlFrame = controlTop + '<A HREF =
   javascript:parent.toggleTour(false);
   parent.moveTour(-1)">' + controlBack + '</A>';
if (tourEnabled)
   controlFrame += '<A HREF =
   "javascript:parent.toggleTour(false)">' +
   controlPause + '</A>';
else controlFrame += '<A HREF =
   "javascript:parent.toggleTour(true)">' +
   controlPlay + '</A>';
controlFrame += '<A HREF =
   "javascript:parent.toggleTour(false);
   parent.moveTour(1)">' + controlForward + '</A>' +
   controlBot;
parent.control.document.write(controlFrame);
parent.control.document.close( );
}
```

Figure 12-20. *If* statement to toggle play and pause buttons.

How the tour works

Instead of going through the tour script line by line (which would be futile), let's discuss the techniques that were used to create the tour so you can apply them to your own creations. I'm going to focus on how the control frame alternates between pause and play buttons and how the sounds are preloaded and played on demand.

Alternating between pause and play buttons. You'll notice that if the tour is in automatic mode, the control frame displays a pause button. But, when the tour is in manual, the control frame displays a play button. This is done with a simple *if* statement combined with the *document.write( )* method. When the tour's automatic mode is enabled, a variable named *tourEnabled* has a value of *true*. By using an *if* statement to determine if *tourEnabled* is true, we can decide whether or not to display the play button (or, alternatively the pause button) in the control frame. This is shown in Figure 12-20. Note that the variable *controlFrame* contains the HTML for the tour's control frame.

Preloading and playing the sounds. The tour uses the "hidden frame method" to play its sound and music. In addition to the

```
<HTML>
<SCRIPT LANGUAGE = "JavaScript">

(A)  function playSound(mySound) {
(B)    soundFrame = '<HTML><HEAD></HEAD><BODY>';
(C)    if (navigator.appName == 'Netscape') {
(D)      soundFrame += '<EMBED SRC = "' + this.sound +
           '" AUTOSTART = TRUE HIDDEN = TRUE>';
       }
(E)    else if (navigator.appName == 'Microsoft
         Internet Explorer') {
         soundFrame += '<BGSOUND SRC = "' +
           this.sound + '">';
       }
(F)    soundFrame += '</BODY></HTML>';
(G)    parent.hidden.document.write(soundFrame);
(H)    parent.hidden.document.close( );
       }

(I)  var blankFrame = '<HTML></HTML>';

   </SCRIPT>
   <FRAMESET ROWS = "100%, *" FRAMEBORDER = 0
     FRAMESPACING = 0 BORDER = 0>');
   <FRAME NAME = "visible" SRC = "somepage.html">
   <FRAME NAME = "hidden" SRC =
     "javascript:parent.blankFrame" SCROLLING = NO>
   </FRAMESET>
   </HTML>
```

Figure 12-21. Writing sounds to a hidden frame.

two visible frames *(control* and *talk)* in the tour window, there are
two hidden frames: *fgsound* and *bgsound.* Initially, these two
frames are blank, but when the tour begins, the tour "puts" the
sound files in the frames. For example, say you specified a sound
file with the name *flip.au* for one of the tour stops. When that
stop is reached, the tour script creates a small HTML document
in "memory" (with *flip.au* embedded inside it), and prints that
HTML in one of the hidden frames, which plays the sound.

Figure 12-21 shows a simplified setup, in which you can play
a sound in the hidden frame, *hidden,* by running the *playSound( )*
function (A) and passing it the name of the desired sound file.

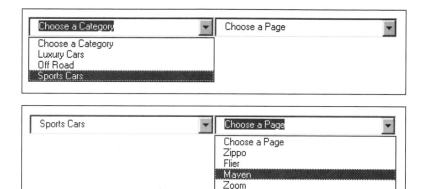

Figure 12-22. With relational menus, making a selection in one menu brings up a related list in the accompanying menu.

The *playSound( )* function begins an HTML document **B** and gives it to variable *soundFrame*. Next, it determines if the browser is Netscape **C** and if it is, creates an *EMBED* tag for the sound file. **D** If the browser is Internet Explorer, the script creates a *BGSOUND* tag instead. **F** Finally, the HTML document in *soundFrame* is given closing *BODY* and *HTML* tags, **G** and the HTML is written to the frame using *document.write()*; thereby playing the sound. **H**

If you have a script located in *somepage.html* (the visible frame), you can play a sound at any time using this format:

```
parent.playSound('http://www.domain.com/directory/flip.au');
```

For example, to play a sound when a link is clicked:

```
<A HREF = "someotherpage.html"
onClick "parent.playSound('http://www.domain.com/
flip.au');"> Home </A>
```

The truth is, this a relatively old-fashioned method of playing sounds, but the advantage is that all versions of Netscape and IE support it, so compatibility is not an issue.

Relational menus

Nowhere in the world is it tougher to find your way from point A to point B than on the World Wide Web. The name Web says it all, "I am a semi-organized interconnected group of documents."

```
newCat('Luxury Cars');                              // new category
newItem('Euro', 'euro.html');                       // pages in category
newItem('Alvan', 'alvan.html');
newItem('Gates', 'gates.html');

newCat('Off Road');                                 // new category
newItem('Mountaineer', 'mountaineer.html');         // pages in category
newItem('Buck', 'buck.html');

newCat('Sports Cars');                              // new category
newItem('Zippo', 'zippo.html');                     // pages in category
newItem('Flier', 'flier.html');
newItem('Maven', 'maven.html');
newItem('Zoom', 'zoom.html');
```

Figure 12-23. Code to create categories and corresponding pages.

This is good and bad. Good if you're just browsing whimsically, bad if you're rushed and looking for specific information. There are, however, many ways to make the Web, and more specifically, a Web site, more orderly and efficient. One of these ways is the relational menu, a device which organizes all of your site's information in a compact and easy-to-navigate manner.

A relational menu consists of two related menus filled with information from which to choose (Figure 12-22). These two menus, which I like to call the category menu (the left-most menu) and the pages menu (the right-most menu), work in tandem. When you select an item from the a category menu, a related list of items, most likely Web pages, is displayed in the pages menu. In Figure 12-22, for example, it has been used to organize a large list of cars into smaller more specialized categories. At first the pages menu is blank. When the user chooses a category, here "Sports Cars," the contents of that category are displayed in the pages menu. The relational menu works in both Netscape and Internet Explorer.

Creating your menus

You can start creating your relational menus by defining the headings that you want to appear at the top of each of the two menus. The following variables do this:

```
var catHeading = 'Choose A Category';
var itemHeading = 'Choose A Page';
var betweenHeading = ' then ';
```

variable *catHeading* defines the heading for the category menu
(on the left). The variable *itemHeading* defines the heading for
the pages menu (on the right). You can modifiy these variables
to create more specific headings. A less ambigious heading for
our category menu heading could be "Choose A Vehicle Type"
and for our pages heading, "Choose A Model." Also note that
you can define text to be placed between the two menus in
betweenHeading. This in-between word shows the relationship
between the two menus. If you read across the relational menus
in this example, they spell out "Choose A Category ... then ...
Choose A Page."

The next step in creating your relational menus is to add
som raw content. You need to define the categories for the
category menu and the pages (in this case, car models) for the
pages menu. For the pages menu, you will be defining both the
names (page descriptions) to appear in the menu and the URLs
that correspond to those names.

As shown in Figure 12-23, to create a new category for the
category menu, just run the *newCat( )* function and pass it a
name for the category. To create pages that will fall into that
category, run the *newItem( )* function and pass it the page's name
and URL (and do this directly under the corresponding category).

How relational menus work

The relational menus are both easy and hard to understand on a
code level. The easy part to understand is how the menus are
related to each other (i.e., how the *pages* menu changes when
you make a selection from the *category* menu). Understanding
the object-based structure where the information for the menus
is kept is more difficult (it's not the idea that is tough, but
JavaScript's odd user-defined object syntax).

Let's begin by looking at the categories and pages as they are
arranged in the code. All of the categories and their respective
pages are kept in an array named *cats*. The first element of that
array, *cats[0]*, contains a user-defined object for the first category
in the relational menu. So in our demo, *cats[0]*, contains all of the

items that fall under the Luxury Cars category. To get the name of the category stored in *cats[0]*, use its *name* property:

```
cats[0].name;
```

This would supply you with the category's name, "Luxury Cars." Here's the fun part: within this array, there is yet another array (this is referred to as a two-dimensional array). Within that array is a user-defined object for the pages in that category. This user-defined object has two properties: *name* and *url*. The *name* property contains the name (or description) of the page and the *url* property contains the URL of that page. So to access the name and URL of the first page in the "Luxury Cars" category, you would say this:

```
cats[0][0].name;
cats[0][0].url;
```

Knowing this, how would you access the name of the second page in the third category ("Sports Cars")? First you'd ask for the third element of the *cats* array, *cats[2]*, then you'd ask for the second element of the array contained within that array, *cats[2][1]*, and finally you'd ask for the *name* property, ending up with this:

```
cats[2][1].name;
```

The purpose of all this "object-oriented-ness" is to make the relational menu's contents easier to create and easier to manipulate. When you put together the categories and pages for your

```
function relateItems(cat) {
    if (cat > 0) {
    catsIndex = cat - 1;
    with (document.m.m2) {
        for (var i = options.length; i > 1; i—) options[i] = null;
        for (var i = 0; i < cats[catsIndex].length; i++) {
            options[i + 1] = new
            Option(cats[catsIndex][i].name);
            }
        }
    }
    itemsIndex = 0;
}
```

Figure 12-24. The *relateItems( )* function.

menu, for example, you probably noticed that the format was very intuitive and easy to work with. Similarly, the core relational menu code is very brief (though it balloons in size when you make it compatible with IE). The Netscape-only version of the function that relates the menus, *relateItems( )*, is relatively short, as shown in Figure 12-24.

When an item is selected from the category menu, the index of that item (the index is the number of the item in the menu) is sent to this function as variable *cat*. The remaining code essentially plugs *cat*, which tells us which category has been selected, into the *cats* array, thereby giving us the proper category and all of its pages (these pages are added to the menu with a *for* loop).

The code that you may find the most helpful to understand and modify is probably the simplest. This is the code that changes the location of the window based on the item selected from the *pages* menu. This code is contained in the *gotoPage( )* function:

```
if (url != null) window.location.href = url;
```

This may be of interest to you because if you wish to target the relational menu to another window or frame, this is the code you must change. To target the relational menu to a frame named main, for example, your code would be changed to this:

```
if (url != null) parent.main.location.href = url;
```

Epilogue

Now that you've read the entire book, it seems appropriate to offer some closing words. First, I'll admit something that we all know but often wish to repress: scripting languages, and the Web, are evolving all the time. We will never be up to date. Never. A published book, especially of this nature, follows that rule as well. This is why I point you to the Web for the future. And, more specifically, *webcoder.com* (I bet you thought I was going to point you to some big public domain index of scripting language content, didn't you? But no, I took the self-promotional propaganda route.) *webcoder.com* hosts the support site for this book, and it's where I spend my time writing about scripting languages and client-side technology in general.

Now it's time to talk about you. If you've read this book from beginning to end, you know JavaScript pretty darn well. And, you've read about and applied (I hope) quite a few scripts. Because of this, you now have the power to learn efficiently and effectively by example: a power that will serve you well throughout your life as a scripter and creator of Web content. From here on in, you will look at the *View Source* command in your browser as a gateway to knowledge, which will allow you to create a better Web experience (and also a great way to borrow ideas).

So what's next? What's next is to launch your browser and peruse the Web to see the impact that client-side scripting has had on the Web. Then look back to your site and see how it matches up, and say, "Hmm ... that guy could really use a lesson or two in scripting."

A The Document Object Model

The JavaScript tree, also known as the document object model, is quite complex, so I've organized it into a large refererence section in an object-by-object manner. Though this covers many of the JavaScript 1.1 (Netscape 3 and Internet Explorer 4) and 1.2 (Netscape 4) objects, it is intended as a quick reference only, not a definitive listing. Each object featured below will be detailed in this reference section with its most important and commonly used methods and properties. I've discussed many of these objects in this book — but there are many that I haven't touched on.

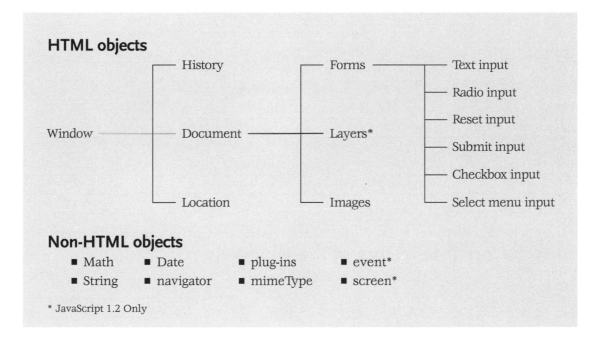

HTML objects

Window — History

Document — Forms — Text input
— Radio input
— Reset input
— Layers* — Submit input
— Checkbox input
— Images — Select menu input

— Location

Non-HTML objects

- Math
- String
- Date
- navigator
- plug-ins
- mimeType
- event*
- screen*

* JavaScript 1.2 Only

window (browser window)

Properties

.name	the window's name
.parent	if window is within frame, the parent window
.top	the uppermost browser window
.self	synonym for the current window
.opener	the creator of current window
.status	the window's status bar
.defaultStatus	the status bar's default message
.frames[ ]	array of all frames contained within window
.innerHeight*	the vertical dimension, in pixels, of the window's content area
.innerWidth*	the horizontal dimension, in pixels, of the window's content area
.outerHeight*	the vertical dimension, in pixels, of the window's outside boundary
.outerWidth*	the horizontal dimension, in pixels, of the window's outside boundary

Methods

.open("url", "name", "atrb")	opens a new window with specified attributes
.close( )	closes a window
.focus( )	focuses a window; places it front of all other windows
.blur( )	blurs a window; places it behind all other windows
.find("text")*	finds the specified text in the window
.scrollTo(x, y)*	scrolls the window to the specified pixel coordinates
.scrollBy(x, y)*	scrolls the window by the specified pixel amount
.moveTo(x, y)*	moves the window to the specified pixel coordinates
.moveBy(x, y)*	moves the window by the specified pixels
.resizeTo(x, y)*	resizes the window to the specified pixel coordinates
.resizeBy(x, y)*	resizes the window by the specified pixel amount
.forward( )*	brings the window one level forward in page history
.back( )*	brings the window one level back in page history
.stop( )*	stops any downloading in the window
.home( )*	brings the window to the "home" site
.print( )*	displays the print dialog box

window.history (the history of the window)

Properties

.length	the number of pages in the history

Methods

.go(value)	travel forward/back a number of pages in history (if you pass this a value of 0, the current page will reload)
.back( )	travel one level back in the page history
.forward( )	travel one level forward in the page history

window.location (the location of the window)

Properties

.host	gives you the domain of the current location
.href	the "full" URL of the current location

Methods

.replace("url")	replaces the currently displayed page (useful because it does not affect the window's history)
.reload( )	performs a "soft" reload on the current window

window.document (the document dispayed in the window)

Properties

.title	title of the document
.cookie	your domain's cookies
.referrer	the URL that brought you to the current document; for example, if *a.html* links to *b.html,* then *b.html's* referrer is *a.html*
.bgColor	background color
.fgColor	foreground color
.alinkColor	active link color
.vlinkColor	visited link color
.linkColor	link color

Methods

.write( )	writes text to the current document
.close( )	closes the text "stream" to a document (when you write to a document after it has been initially created, the *write( )* method should be followed by this method)

window.document.forms [ ] (the forms in a document)

Example of a form object:

```
<FORM NAME = "myName" ACTION = "/cgi-bin/one.cgi" METHOD = "GET">
Form Elements
</FORM>
```

Accessing the form object through JavaScript:

```
document.forms ["myName"] or document.myName
```

Properties

.action	the action of a form
.method	the method of a form: *get* or *post*
.name	the name of a form
.target	the target window where the form's output will be displayed

Methods

.reset( )	resets a form
.submit( )	submits a form, but, for security reasons, only when inside an *onClick* event handler

window.document.layers [ ] (the layers in a document)

Example of a layer object:

```
<LAYER NAME = "myName" LEFT = "100" TOP = "50">
Layer Content
</LAYER>
```

Layer object through JavaScript:

```
document.layers["myName"] or document.myName
```

Properties

.name	the name given to the layer through the *NAME* attribute in the *LAYER* tag
.left	horizontal position of the layer's left edge in pixels, relative to the origin of its parent layer
.top	vertical position of the layer's top edge, in pixels, relative to the origin of its parent layer
.pageX	horizontal position of the layer, in pixels, relative to the page
.pageY	vertical position of the layer, in pixels, relative to the page
.zIndex	the relative *z*-order of this layer with respect to other layers in the page; layers of higher *z*-orders are displayed in front of those with lower *z*-orders
.visibility	whether or not the layer is visible

.clip	the clip properties define the clipping rectangle, which specifies the
.clip.top	part of the layer that is visible. Any part of a layer that is outside the
.clip.left	clipping rectangle is not displayed.
.clip.right	
.clip.bottom	
.clip.width	
.clip.height	
.background	the background image of a layer
.bgColor	the background color of a layer
.parentLayer	the layer object that contains this layer, or the enclosing window
.src	the source of the content for the layer, specified by URL

Methods

.scrollTo(x, y)*	scrolls the layer to the specified pixel coordinates
.scrollBy(x, y)*	scrolls the layer by the specified pixel amount
.moveTo(x, y)*	moves the layer to the specified pixel coordinates
.moveBy(x, y)*	moves the layer by the specified pixels
.resizeTo(x, y)*	resizes the layer to the specified pixel coordinates
.resizeBy(x, y)*	resizes the layer by the specified pixel amount
.moveToAbsolute(x, y)	moves the layer to the specified pixel coordinates, but relative to the entire page, not just the parent layer (if one exists)
.moveAbove(layer)	stacks this layer above the specified layer
.moveBelow(layer)	stacks this layer below the specified layer
.load(src, width)	changes the source of a layer to the contents of the file indicated by src, and simultaneously changes the width at which the layer's contents will be wrapped

window.document.images [ ] (the images in a document)

Example of an image object:

```
<IMG NAME = "myName" SRC = "myImageFile.gif">
```

Image object through JavaScript:

```
document.images ["myName"] or document.myName
```

Properties

.src	the source file, or image file, of the image
.name	the name of the image

Math (the *Math* object)

Properties

.PI	The value of pi (3.14259...)

Methods

.abs(value)	calculate absolute value of a number
.sin(value)	calculate sin of a number
.cos(value)	calculate cosine of a number
.tan(value)	calculate tangent of a number
.log(value)	calculate log of a number
.ceil(value)	round a decimal up to nearest integer
.floor(value)	round a decimal down to nearest integer
.round(value)	round a decimal to nearest integer
.random( )	retrieve a random value from 0 to 1
.sqrt(value)	calculate the square root of a value

string (object for any string of text)

Example of a string object:

```
var myString = "This is a string."
```

Properties

.length	length of the string in characters

Methods

.charAt(value)	retrieves character at the location, counted by character, of a string of text
.indexOf("value")	determines the placement, by character, of a string of text within a string of text, e.g. *myString.indexOf("is")* gives us 2.
.substring(begin, end)	retrieves the text between beginning and end values
.toLowerCase( )	makes all characters in a string of text lowercase
.toUpperCase( )	makes all characters in a string of text uppercase

Date (the date and time)

Example of a *Date* object:

```
var myDate = new Date( );
```

Methods

.setDate( )/.getDate( )	sets/gets the day of month

.setDay( )/.getDay( )	sets/gets the day of week, where 0 is Sunday, 6 is Monday
.setHours( )/.getHours( )	sets/gets the hour of the day, from 0 to 23
.setMinutes( )/.getMinutes( )	sets/gets the minute of the hour, from 0 to 59
.setMonth( )/.getMonth( )	sets/gets the month, where 0 is January and 11 is December
.setSeconds( )/.getSeconds( )	sets/gets the time in seconds, from 0 to 59
.setTime( )/.getTime( )	sets/gets the time in milliseconds
.setYear( )/.getYear( )	sets/gets the year
.toGMTString( )	gets time in relation to Greenwich Mean Time
.toLocaleString( )	gets local time as date and time
.toString( )	gets time as date, zone, and time

navigator (information about the browser)

Properties

.appCodeName	browser's code name
.appName	browser's name
.appVersion	browser's version information
.userAgent	browser's user-agent header

Methods

| .javaEnabled( ) | is the browser Java enabled? |

navigator.plugins (information about plug-ins)

Example of a *plugins* object:

```
navigator.plugins["LiveAudio"]
```

If this *plugin* object is present, it will return a value, if it is not present, it will return nothing.

Properties

.description	a *plugin* object's description
.filename	a *plugin* object's primary file name
.length	the number/length of installed plug-ins
.name	a *plugin* object's name

Methods

| .refresh( ) | refreshes all plug-ins; this is useful if a plug-in has been installed and you don't want to restart the browser |

event object* (information about an event)

Example of an *event* object:

```
function myEvent(e) {
alert("The event object " + e);
}
onload = myEvent;
```

In this example, argument *e* is the *event* object.

Properties

.type	the event type, e.g. *mouseDown, mouseOver, keyPress*
.pageX	the cursor's horizontal position in pixels, relative to the page
.pageY	the cursor's vertical position in pixels relative to the page
.screenX	the cursor's horizontal position in pixels, relative to the screen
.screenY	the cursor's vertical position in pixels, relative to the screen
.which	number specifying either the mouse button that was pressed or the ASCII value of a pressed key
.data	an array of strings containing the URLs of the dropped objects (passed with the *dragdrop* event)

screen object* (information about the display)

Properties

.width	the width of the screen in pixels
.height	height of the screen in pixels
.pixelDepth	the number of bits per pixel in the display
.colorDepth	the number of colors possible to display. The number of colors is found using the color palette if one is available, or using the pixel depth.

* JavaScript 1.2 only

B
Event Handlers

E vent handlers allow the page to interact with the user. Here is a full listing of the JavaScript 1.1 and 1.2 event handlers:

Event Handler	It Occurs When
onAbort	a download is aborted
onBlur	a window or frame is blurred; when it's not the active window
onClick	an element is clicked with the mouse
onChange	a form element is changed or modified
onDragDrop*	the user drops an object into the browser window
onError	an error occurs; e.g. a script syntax error
onFocus	a window or frame is focused; when it becomes the active window
onKeyDown*	a key is depressed
onKeyPress*	a key is pressed
onKeyUp*	a key is released
onMouseDown*	the mouse button is depressed

Event Handler	It Occurs When
onMouseOver	the mouse cursor moves over an element
onMouseOut	the mouse cursor moves out of an element
*onMouseMove**	the mouse moves
*onMouseUp**	the mouse button is released
*onMove**	a window is moved
onLoad	a document has finished loading
onReset	a form is reset
*onResize**	a window is resized
onSubmit	a form is submitted
onSelect	an element is selected
onUnLoad	a document is closed or "unloads"

* JavaScript 1.2 Only

C

Which Browser
Supports What ?

A big problem with learning (and using) JavaScript, especially for beginners, is the difference from one browser to the next. Navigator 3 supports dynamic images, IE 3 does not. Both IE 3 and Navigator 3 support JavaScript-to-Java communication, but Navigator 2 does not. The list goes on ad infinitum. This list is dedicated to explaining those differences.

Array: The *array* object

The array object allows JavaScript to create, access, sort, and join arrays with the full functionality that Java and most other languages enjoy.

Related Material:

Chapter 5, *Getting In Line with Arrays*

The Browser	Is it supported?
Navigator 4	Fully Supported
Navigator 3	Fully Supported
Navigator 2	Not Supported
IE 4	Fully Supported
IE 3	Fully Supported

Cookie: *document.cookie*

With the cookie, JavaScript can save small amounts of data on a user's machine for access at a later time. This is useful for remembering names, passwords, and other bits of information that need to

On *webcoder.com*

Since new versions of Navigator and IE come out every minute or so, a printed list can never be up-to-date. For this reason, a regularly updated online version of the list is available at *http://webcoder.com/*. If you find any discrepancies in this printed list, please report them to the online list. This list only documents features that *do not work* in one or more JavaScript-enabled browsers. All of this information should mean more to you as your knowledge of JavaScript increases. Instead of reading directly through it, you may want to refer to it when questions about compatibility arise.

be saved for more than one browser session. The cookie does not give access to any part of the user's hard drive or local files.

Related Material:

Chapter 8, *Customizing a Site with Cookies*

The Browser	Is it supported?
Navigator 4	Fully Supported
Navigator 3	Fully Supported
Navigator 2	Fully Supported
IE 4	Fully Supported
IE 3	Fully Supported (but does not work locally)

Dynamic images: *document.images*

Dynamic images, introduced in Navigator 3, allow JavaScript to change the source of an image directly on the page. With this capability, JavaScript can create highlighted images, animations, and many other eye-catching creations.

Related Material:

Chapter 7, *Dynamic Images*

The Browser	Is it supported?
Navigator 4	Fully Supported
Navigator 3	Fully Supported
Navigator 2	Not Supported
IE 4	Fully Supported
IE 3	Not Supported (except in version 3.01 for Mac)

External scripts

External scripts, unlike traditional scripts, are stored in totally separate documents that contain the *.js* extension. Though rarely used, this feature can be helpful if you want to use the same functions repeatedly in a large site.

The Browser	Is it supported?
Navigator 4	Fully Supported
Navigator 3	Fully Supported
Navigator 2	Not Supported
IE 4	Fully Supported
IE 3	Not Supported (Supported in 3.01)

Layers: *document.layers*

Layers, introduced in Navigator 4, allow objects, such as text, images, and plug-ins, to be placed on the page with absolute control (*x, y,* and *z* coordinates). In addition, the placement, clipping, and visibility of layers can be controlled through JavaScript, leading to many lively and animated sites. Layers have been outmoded, however, by CSS, a technology supported by both Navigator and IE.

Related Material:

Chapter 10, *Getting Acquainted with Layers*
Chapter 11, *The Show: Dynamic HTML Applied*

The Browser	Is it supported?
Navigator 4	Fully Supported (but CSS is preferable)
Navigator 3	Not Supported
Navigator 2	Not Supported
IE 4	Not Supported (CSS only)
IE 3	Not Supported

Modifiable select menus

Modifiable select menus allow JavaScript to add, delete, and modify the options in select menus right on the page. Useful for devices such as the relational select menu, which can contain gobs of data but take up little space on the page.

Related Material:

Chapter 12, *Advanced Applications*

The Browser	Is it supported?
Navigator 4	Fully Supported
Navigator 3	Fully Supported
Navigator 2	Not Supported
IE 4	Not Supported (ActiveX can be used instead)
IE 3	Not Supported

Plug-In Detection: *document.plugins* and *document.mimeTypes*

Plug-in detection, a very useful feature introduced in Navigator 3, allows JavaScript to determine if a plug-in or file type is supported and then tailor the page accordingly.

Related Material:

Chapter 7, *Too Many Browsers? Not Really*

The Browser	Is it supported?
Navigator 4	Fully Supported
Navigator 3	Fully Supported
Navigator 2	Not Supported
IE 4	Not Supported
IE 3	Not Supported

Random Numbers: *Math.random( )*

Math.random( ) generates a random number, 0 through 1, using the system clock. There are better random number generators on the Web, but this one will do for most purposes.

Related Material:

Chapter 5, *Getting in Line with Arrays*

The Browser	Is it supported?
Navigator 4	Fully Supported
Navigator 3	Fully Supported
Navigator 2	Not Supported
IE 4	Fully Supported
IE 3	Fully Supported

Window: the *window* object

The window object allows JavaScript to create a new browser window and modify its properties (such as location). It also allows an opened window to talk back to its opener window and allows for focusing and blurring of windows.

Related Material:

Chapter 2, *Doing Windows*

The Browser	Is it supported?
Navigator 4	Fully Supported (ads methods to move, resize, etc.)
Navigator 3	Fully Supported
Navigator 2	Partially Supported (no focusing or blurring)
IE 4	Fully Supported
IE 3	Partially Supported (no focusing or blurring, object model slightly different)

D JavaScript Syntax

This appendix gives the syntax for common statements and operators.

Important control flow and syntax examples

Functions

Syntax

```
function function name (parameter1, parameter2, ...) {
statements
}
```

Example

```
function helloFriend(friendName) {
alert("Hello" + friendName);
}
```

if statements

Syntax

```
if (condition) {
statements
}
```

Example

```
if (outerEarPressure < innerEarPressue) {
popEars( );
}
```

while loops

Syntax

```
while (condition) {
statements
}
```

Example
```
while (dinnerIsNotCooked) {
cookDinner( );
}
```

for loops

Syntax
```
for(variable declaration; condition; variable operator) {
statements
}
```

Example
```
for (var rowValue = 0; rowValue < totalRows; rowValue ++) {
document.write(databaseColumn[rowValue]);
}
```

Important operators and conditionals

Testing for conditions

a == b	*a* equal to *b*
a != b	*a* not equal to *b*
a > b	*a* greater than *b*
a < b	*a* less than *b*
a >= b	*a* greater than or equal to *b*
a <= b	*a* less than or equal to *b*
! a	not *a* (testing for false condition)

Testing for multiple conditions

a *&&* b	condition *a* and *b*
a ‖ b	condition *a* or *b*

Operators

a + b	*a* plus *b*
a - b	*a* minus *b*
a * b	*a* multiplied by *b*
a / b	*a* divided by *b*
a % b	*a* modulus (remainder) *b*
a ++	*a* increased by one
a --	*a* decreased by one

Index

fontSize property, 138, 139, 147

fontWeight property, 139, 147

for loop
    for multiple-choice quiz,
    196, 198, 200, 201
    for select menu display, 79-80

form buttons
    adding *onClick* event handler
    to, 18-19
    code for creating, 18

form elements
    focus in, 55-56
    as form properties, 48-49

forms
    changing window locations
    with, 18-19
    creating, 48-49
    defined, 47
    for generating custom view
    of site, 130, 132-33
    MadLibs, 50-54
    multiple choice questions
    on, 75
    as properties of document
    objects, 47-48
    referring to with *this,* 48-49
    remembering input, 126, 129-30
    search, as remote control, 30-32
    select menus in, 75-82
    syntax for, 47-49

forms validation, *See also* email
    form validation
    comment forms, 54-56
    email, 56-65
    Netscape Navigator 4 event
    handlers for, 163-65

forward buttons, for frames, 39-40

frame borders, in single-frame
    method, 90-91

frames, 35-46
    back and forward buttons
    for, 39-40
    changing multiple frames with
    one click, 40-43

controlling links in HTML,
    35-36
controlling links in JavaScript,
    36-37
expanding and collapsing, 38-39
hidden, playing sound and
    music in, 207-8
as navigational devices, 35
nested, code for avoiding, 40, 41
parent, 37
remote control and, 37
rotating content with, 43-46
select menus in, 80-82
single, for browser-specific
    features, 90-92
TARGET tag with, 22
toolbar/main, 35-37, 40-43

FRAMESET tag, 35

FRAME tag, 36

functions
    arguments in, 27-28, 78
    declaring, 26
    defined, 28
    methods vs., 13, 21
    naming, 28
    as objects, 79
    opening new window with,
    23-24
    running, 27
    writing, 27-28

G

Gabby Cabby Web site, 35-37

getChip( ), 134, 135

getCookie( ), 119-21, 123

getDay( ), 9-11

getHours( ), 10

getMinutes( ), 10

getMonth( ), 10

getSeconds( ), 10

getTime( ), 15

getValue( ), 129, 131

getYear( ), 10

go( ), 28-29

goPage( ), 81

gotoPage( ), 213

graphical buttons, launching
    windows with, 24

graphic links, *See also* images
    browser-specific, 88

H

handle( ), 162, 163

height properties, of layers,
    178-79, 180

height property, in *window.open,*
    21, 22, 147

history
    defined, 15
    moving back and forward in,
    38-40

HREF tags
    adding *onClick* event handler
    in, 23
    code for adding status bar text
    to, 3
    for remote control window, 29

HTML
    absolute positioning, 137
    code for creating buttons, 18
    comments, hiding JavaScript
    with, 11
    controlling frame links in, 35-36
    JavaScript tree and, 15
    printing with *document.write( )*,
    7-8

HTML elements
    defined, 138
    dynamically replacing, 152-153
    sliding across page, 150-51, 153
    style properties, 138

I

IBM Web site, 108-9

ID attributes
    for data binding control, 142
    this statement and, 140

if statements
    Booleans and, 60

for bouncing logo effect,
181, 182
for browser detection, 86
defined, 8
for dynamic images, 89
for email forms validation,
57-58, 62-64
for forms validation, 164-65
for image billboards, 112-13
for mixer control, 165
for moving layers, 180
for multiple-choice quiz, 201
in Night and Day script, 8-9
for remote control, 27
for retrieving cookies, 121
syntax of, 8
for tour guide, 207
for translating numeric dates to
days of the week, 9-11
image billboards, 111-15
arrays for, 113, 114
browser detection for, 113
rotator code, 115
rotator function for, 114-15
URLs for, 114
variables for, 112-13, 114
image objects, 99-101
changing with *onMouseOver* and
onMouseOut, 101-2
creating cached image
with, 100-1
multiple, responding to same
action, 108-11
naming, 100, 105
placeholder, 110-11
preloading, 101
script for creating, 105
suffixes for, 106, 107
image rollovers, 102-7
animated GIFs in, 102
browser detection for, 106
multiple, 108-11
naming system for, 105
images, *See also* dynamic images
animated, 102, 112-13

controlling with JavaScript, 100
displaying in Night and Day
script, 9
HTML code for, 99-100
preloading, 100
random, 73
replacement, support for, 85
imgAct( ), 106, 107, 111
imgInact( ), 106, 107, 111,
IMG tag, 99, 101
NAME property, 99-100
SRC property, 99-100
inactive links, styles for, 139
indexOf( )
for email form validation, 60-61
for operating system detection,
97-98
retrieving cookies with, 121
inline style sheets, nested, 155
innerHeight property, 179
innerWidth property, 179
integers
extracting with *parseInt( ),* 86
validation of, 64, 65
Internet Explorer
development of, 83
MIME types, 93
plug-in detection, 94
Internet Explorer 3
appVersion property, 85
cookies in, 122
navigator properties, 84
Internet Explorer 4
browser-specific page for, 90
detecting, 85
Dynamic HTML, 137
event model, 153, 155-58
navigator properties, 84
Pattern game, 146-48
style sheets in, 146-48
isAvailable, property of sound
object, 160
isCorrect( ), 195-96

isEmail( )
for email form validation,
57, 60-61, 62
passing form elements to, 58-60
isFilled( )
for email form validation,
61-62, 65
for form validation, 58
isReady( )
for email form validation,
57, 61, 62
form validation with, 57

J

JavaScript Tip of the Week Web
site, 68-69
JavaScript tree, 14-15
"jumpin jive" script, 75-82
jump lists, 75

K

keyCode event property, 155
KeyPress events, in Netscape
Navigator 4, 163-64
keystroke capture, 158-59, 163-64

L

language option, in *SCRIPT* tag, 6
layers, 167-75
bouncing logo effect, 181-82
characteristics of, 168
clipping, 171-72, 174
controlling, 169-75
creating, 167-68, 169
features, 167
height and *width* properties,
178-79, 180
hiding, 169
moving, 169, 170-75, 180
naming, 170
properties of, 167-69
for question database, 183-84
rotation function for, 174-75
scrolling background effect,
179-81

quotation marks
  double, 4
  single, 4
  for window properties, 22

R

radio buttons, for multiple-choice
  quiz, 194, 196
randomizing script
  creating, 68-69
  for images, 73
  for sounds, 73
random number generator, 71-73
  code, 72
  running, 71
relateItems( ), 212
relational menus, 209-13
  creating, 210-11
  operation of, 211-13
remote control windows, 25-30
  adding search function to, 30-32
  creating, 26-27
  defined, 25
  frames and, 37
  launching, 27
  redirecting links to opener
  window, 31-32
  specifying URL for, 27
  template for, 32
  template for page launching, 32
  tour guide as, 203
reset( ), 144
resizable property, 21
return, simulating variables
  with, 71
rollovers. *See* image rollovers
rotate( ), 44-46
rotation effect, 151-52
  with frames, 43-46
  script, 154
rotation function, for layers,
  174-75
rotator function, for image
  billboards, 114-15

S

screen object, 178
SCRIPT tag, 6
scrollbars, property of
  window.open, 21
scrolling background effect,
  in The Show, 179-81
search function, adding to
  remote control, 30-32
selectedIndex property, 81-82
select menus
  creating, 75-82
  creating arrays for, 75-77
  displaying on page, 78-80
  in frames, 80-82
  jumping to selected page, 80-82
  source code, 81
semicolons, use of, 4
setChip( ), 134, 135
setCookie( ), 118, 123
setTimeout( ), 46, 151
  for image billboards, 113
  for layers, 171, 172
  for moving layers, 180
setValue( ), 129, 130
Shockwave, detecting, 92-96
showForm( ), 125-26, 195-96,
  197, 198
showKey( ), 158
Show, The
  bouncing logo, 181-82
  displaying questions and
  answers, 182-84
  Dynamic HTML in, 177-79
  game, 177-85
  layers in, 178
  scrolling background effect,
  179-81
  sound and music, 184-85
showWelc( ), 125
single-frame method
  for browser-specific features,
  90-92
  frame borders in, 90-91
  HTML for, 91

margin heights and widths
  in, 91
single quotes
  apostrophes inside, 4
  surrounding text to be placed
  in status bar, 4
slide( ), 151-52
sortColumn property, 144
sorting, data files, 143-44
SoundCardAvailable property, 160
sound property, for tour guide, 206
sounds
  mixer control for, 159-60
  playing, 207-9
  preloading, 207
  random, 73
  in The Show, 184-85
  writing to hidden frames, 207-8
srcElement event property, 155
SRC property
  changing, 100-101
  defined, 99-100
status bar, descriptive links in, 2-4
status property, 21
stop objects, for tour guide, 205-6
STYLE attribute, 155
style sheets, 137-40, 146-48
  absolute positioning and, 146-48
  all property, 138
  active link styles, 139, 141
  background property, 139
  CLASS attribute, for HTML tags,
  140, 147
  documentation for, 139,
  inactive link styles, 139
  inline, 155
  in Internet Explorer 4, 13,
  155-58
  left property, 146-47
  logo class, 146
  in Netscape Navigator 4, 148
  properties, 138, 139
  style classes, 140
  top property, 146-47

More Titles from O'Reilly

Web Review Studio Series

GIF Animation Studio

By Richard Koman
1st Edition October 1996
184 pages, Includes CD-ROM
ISBN 1-56592-230-1

GIF animation is bringing the Web to life—without plug-ins, Java programming, or expensive authoring tools. This book details the major GIF animation programs, profiles work by leading designers (including John Hersey, Razorfish, Henrik Drescher, and Erik Josowitz), and documents advanced animation techniques. A CD-ROM includes freeware and shareware authoring programs, demo versions of commercial software, and the actual animation files described in the book. *GIF Animation Studio* is the first release in the new Web Review Studio series.

Shockwave Studio

By Bob Schmitt
1st Edition March 1997
200 pages, Includes CD-ROM
ISBN 1-56592-231-X

This book, the second title in the new Web Review Studio series, shows how to create compelling and functional Shockwave movies for web sites. The author focuses on actual Shockwave movies, showing how the movies were created. The book takes users from creating simple time-based Shockwave animations through writing complex logical operations that take full advantage of Director's power. The CD-ROM includes a demo version of Director and other software sample files.

Designing with JavaScript

By Nick Heinle
1st Edition September 1997
256 pages, Includes CD-ROM
ISBN 1-56592-300-6

Written by the author of the "JavaScript Tip of the Week" web site, this new Web Review Studio book focuses on the most useful and applicable scripts for making truly interactive, engaging web sites. You'll not only have quick access to the scripts you need, you'll finally understand why the scripts work, how to alter the scripts to get the effects you want, and, ultimately, how to write your own groundbreaking scripts from scratch.

Designing Web Graphics with Photoshop

By Mikkel Aaland
1st Edition February 1998 (est.)
264 pages (est.), ISBN 1-56592-350-2

While Adobe Photoshop is the graphics tool of choice for web graphics, its full potential is rarely tapped. Mikkel Aaland has interviewed dozens of top web designers and distilled their best tips and techniques for creating great effects in Photoshop in the smallest possible GIF and JPEG files. Besides sharing techniques from designers at clnet, HotWired, Discovery Channel, Second Story, and others, Aaland explains how to set up Photoshop for web work, how to process photographs, how to work with vector graphics in Photoshop, and how to use Photoshop as a layout tool. While this book is accessible to beginning users, it provides advanced explanations and techniques.

O'REILLY™

TO ORDER: **800-998-9938** • **order@oreilly.com** • **http://www.oreilly.com/**
OUR PRODUCTS ARE AVAILABLE AT A BOOKSTORE OR SOFTWARE STORE NEAR YOU.
FOR INFORMATION: **800-998-9938** • **707-829-0515** • **info@oreilly.com**

Songline Guides

NetActivism: How Citizens Use the Internet

By Ed Schwartz
1st Edition September 1996
224 pages, ISBN 1-56592-160-7

Let a veteran political activist tell you how to use online networks to further your cause. Whether you are a community activist, a politician, a nonprofit staff person, or just someone who cares about your community, you will benefit from the insights this book offers on how to make the fastest-growing medium today work for you.

Net Lessons: Web-based Projects for Your Classroom

By Laura Parker Roerden
1st Edition March 1997
306 pages, ISBN 1-56592-291-3

Net Lessons features 70 K-12 classroom-tested lesson plans that harness the unique potentials of the Web, plus hundreds of extensions and ideas for all subject areas. The book also includes curriculum frameworks for creating your own successful web projects, assessment tools, and the advice of teachers who have used the Web in their classrooms.

NetResearch: Finding Information Online

By Daniel J. Barrett
1st Edition February 1997
200 pages, ISBN 1-56592-245-X

NetResearch teaches you how to locate the information you need in the constantly changing online world. You'll learn effective search techniques that work with any Internet search programs, present or future, and will build intuition on how to succeed when searches fail. Covers America Online, CompuServe, Microsoft Network and Prodigy, as well as direct and dial-up Internet connections.

NetSuccess: How Real Estate Agents Use the Internet

By Scott Kersnar
1st Edition August 1996
214 pages, ISBN 1-56592-213-1

This book shows real estate agents how to harness the communications and marketing tools of the Internet to enhance their careers and make the Internet work for them. Through agents' stories and "A day in the life" scenarios, readers see what changes and what stays the same when you make technology a full partner in your working life.

NetTravel: How Travelers Use the Internet

By Michael Shapiro
1st Edition April 1997
312 pages, Includes CD-ROM
ISBN 1-56592-172-0

NetTravel is a virtual toolbox of advice for those travelers who want to tap into the rich vein of travel resources on the Internet. It is filled with personal accounts by travelers who've used the Net to plan their business trips, vacations, honeymoons, and explorations. The author gives readers all the tools they need to use the Net immediately to find and save money on airline tickets, accommodations, car rentals, and more.

Net Law: How Lawyers Use the Internet

By Paul Jacobsen
1st Edition January 1997
254 pages, Includes CD-ROM
ISBN 1-56592-258-1

From simple email to sophisticated online marketing, *Net Law* shows how the solo practitioner or the large law firm can turn the Net into an effective and efficient tool. Through stories from those who've set up pioneering legal Net sites, attorney Paul Jacobsen explains how lawyers can successfully integrate the Internet into their practices, sharing lessons "early adopters" have learned.

NetLearning: Why Teachers Use the Internet

By Ferdi Serim & Melissa Koch
1st Edition June 1996
304 pages, Includes CD-ROM
ISBN 1-56592-201-8

In this book educators and Internet users who've been exploring its potential for education share stories to help teachers use this medium to its fullest potential in their classrooms. The book offers advice on how to adapt, how to get what you want, and where to go to get help. The goal: To invite educators online with the reassurance there will be people there to greet them.

O'REILLY™

TO ORDER: **800-998-9938** • *order@oreilly.com* • *http://www.oreilly.com/*
OUR PRODUCTS ARE AVAILABLE AT A BOOKSTORE OR SOFTWARE STORE NEAR YOU.
FOR INFORMATION: **800-998-9938** • **707-829-0515** • *info@oreilly.com*